JOHN CASSAVETES

Lifeworks

Tom Charity

OMNIBUS PRESS

Exclusive Distributors
Book Sales Limited,
8/9 Frith Street,
London W1D 3JB, UK.

Music Sales Corporation,
257 Park Avenue South,
New York, NY 10010, USA.

The Five Mile Press,
22 Summit Road,
Noble Park,
Victoria 3174, Australia.

To the Music Trade only:
Music Sales Limited,
8/9 Frith Street,
London W1D 3JB, UK.

Every effort has been made to trace the copyright holders of the photographs in
this book but one or two were unreachable. We would be grateful if the photogra-
phers concerned would contact us.

Printed by Creative Print & Design (Wales), Ebbw Vale, Wales
Typeset by Mac Style, Scarborough, N. Yorkshire
A catalogue record for this book is available from the British Library.

www.omnibuspress.com

Contents

Acknowledgements

There are many people to thank:

Angela Smith, now at emfoundation, whose inspiration it was.

Chris Charlesworth at Omnibus Press, who commissioned this book and waited very patiently for longer than I care to remember.

Geoff Andrew lent me videotapes of hard-to-get movies – in some instances for years. Rod Vardeman sent me videotapes of *I'm Almost Not Crazy* and *To Risk Everything To Express It All* just for the love of Cassavetes. David Thompson lent me a tape of the BBC Arena documentary on Cassavetes (1989) and put me in touch with its director, Debbie Gellar, who helped me with research. Dennis Lim dug out some contacts for me and put me in touch with Joe McGovern, who did a lot of legwork for me for little in return (thanks Joe!). Geoffrey Macnab and Brian Case lent me tapes of their interviews with Gena Rowlands and John Cassavetes respectively, and Brian was a mine of information on Mingus and Bobby Darin, among other things. Trevor Johnston and Tomoko Yabe Johnston advised me on the highbrow music.

I'd also like to thank those film-makers who have selflessly contributed their thoughts on Cassavetes for this book: Olivier Assayas, Pedro Almodóvar, Nicolas Winding Refn, John Sayles, Jim Jarmusch and especially Gary Oldman, who was tremendously supportive and encouraging, and by far the quickest to deliver the goods.

And not forgetting Charles Macdonald and Jonathan Rutter, Emma Pycroft and Andi Engel (Artificial Eye), Chris Holden (Second Sight), Michel Ruben (el deseo), Steve Jenkins (BBC), Nick Johnstone, Nikki Lloyd at Omnibus, Sue Sharpe, who translated the Assayas piece, Hannah, Meg and Joe Charity, Joanne Koch at Lincoln Center, Tony Rayns, Nick Royle and Kate Ryan, and my employers at *Time Out* magazine. My appreciation to Meg McSweeney, then at the American Academy of Dramatic Arts, who was also particularly helpful.

In the course of researching and writing this book I have spoken to many people who knew John Cassavetes as a friend, a collaborator and a mentor.

I have been moved by their generosity towards me, and their devotion to John Cassavetes' memory. Thanks to Al Ruban, Seymour Cassel, Peter

Falk, Peter Tanner, John Hough, Jenny Runacre, Elaine Kagan, Jeremy Kagan, Helen Caldwell, Peter Bogdanovich, Zohra Lampert, Harry Mastrogeorge, Bo Harwood, Joan Almond and Mike Ferris.

Finally those who have worked hardest on my behalf: Fiona Morrow, who put up with the whole damn thing, watched the movies with me, read the roughest drafts, even paid the phone bills, and Rob Stone, who edited this manuscript with patience, sensitivity, imagination and insight.

I would like to dedicate this book to Fiona and Jay.

Open Letter To John Cassavetes

Jim Jarmusch

There's a particular feeling I get when I'm about to see one of your films – an anticipation. It doesn't matter if I've seen the film before or not (by now I think I've seen them all at least several times) I still get that same feeling. I'm expecting something I seem to crave, a kind of cinematic enlightenment. As a film fan or as a filmmaker (there isn't really a clear dividing line for me anymore) I'm anticipating a blast of inspiration. I want formal enlightenment. I need the secret consequences of a jump-cut to be revealed to me. I want to know how the rawness of the camera angles or the grain of the film material figures into the emotional equation. I want to learn about acting from the performances, about atmosphere from the light and the locations. I'm ready, fully prepared to absorb 'truth at twenty-four frames-per-second'.

But the thing is this: as soon as the film begins, introduces its world to me, I'm lost. The expectation of that particular enlightenment evaporates. It leaves me there in the dark, alone. Human beings now inhabit that world inside the screen. They also seem lost, alone. I watch them. I observe every detail of their movements, their expressions, their reactions. I listen carefully to what each one is saying, to the frayed edges of someone's tone of voice, the concealed mischief in the rhythm of another's speech. I'm no longer thinking about acting. I'm oblivious to 'dialogue'. I've forgotten the camera.

The enlightenment I anticipated from you is being replaced by another. This one doesn't invite analysis or dissection, only observation and intuition. Instead of insights into, say, the construction of a scene, I'm becoming enlightened by the sly nuances of human nature.

Your films are about love, about trust and mistrust, about isolation, joy, sadness, ecstasy and stupidity. They're about restlessness, drunkenness, resilience and lust, about humor, stubbornness, miscommunication and fear. But mostly they're about love, and they take one to a far deeper place than any study of 'narrative form'. Yeah, you are a great filmmaker, one of my favorites. But what your films illuminate most poignantly is that celluloid is one thing, and the beauty, strangeness and complexity of human experience is another.

John Cassavetes, my hat is off to you. I'm holding it over my heart.

Jim Jarmusch
9/2000
(Writer/director: *Stranger Than Paradise, Down By Law, Night On Earth, Dead Man, Ghost Dog: Way Of The Samurai*)

Introduction

'The only people for me are the mad ones, the ones who are mad to live, mad to talk, mad to be saved, desirous of everything at the same time, the ones who never yawn or say a commonplace thing, but burn, burn, burn.'

Jack Kerouac, *On The Road*

There ought to be more books about John Cassavetes. Those were the first words I wrote, in a letter to Cassavetes' widow, Gena Rowlands, a couple of years ago as I embarked on this project.

Within the last few years there have been three new weighty biographies on Orson Welles, three on Steven Spielberg, and at least as many on Stanley Kubrick and Quentin Tarantino. Yet Ray Carney's essential *The Films Of John Cassavetes* (Cambridge University Press, 1994) is the only English language text in print on arguably the most important American film-maker of the last 50 years – and Carney's equally invaluable *American Dreaming* (University of California Press, 1985) is its solitary antecedent.

So I wrote to Gena Rowlands and told her some things she knew very well: how vital and relevant John Cassavetes' films seem, now more than ever; how influential he is for film-makers around the world; and how much all of us can learn from his passion, his integrity and determination. And I confessed some of the things I didn't know: little has been recorded about those first 30 years before Cassavetes made *Shadows*; and only scraps thereafter. She replied very graciously but quite adamantly: "I wish I could cooperate with you in talking about John and his work. But he specifically asked me not to as he wanted his work only to speak for him".

Possibly I should have abandoned the book then and there, as others have done confronted with the same limitations. Certainly I thought long and hard about it. But still it seemed to me irrefutable: there really ought to be more books about John Cassavetes.

Because he insisted on his independence, Cassavetes' work has always been marginalised by the mono-money-culture of late twentieth century capitalism. Distribution was always a struggle in his lifetime, and some of his most important films are not currently available on video or DVD either in Britain or the US. Nevertheless, even Hollywood found his films were too potent to ignore, and Cassavetes is one of only a handful of artists to have been nominated for the Academy Award in three different disciplines: as an actor, a writer and a director.

It was as an actor that he proved most adaptable to Hollywood's requirements, and it is John Cassavetes the actor who is best known to the public at large: he is the shifty husband who allowed his wife to be impregnated by the devil in *Rosemary's Baby*, and the loudmouth trouble-maker who steals *The Dirty Dozen* away from under the noses of Lee Marvin, Robert Ryan, Charles Bronson *et al.*

These films are not without interest, and Cassavetes' contribution to each is considerable, but his very worst film as a writer-director tells us more about what it is to be human – to love and to fear and to fail – than either of these big box-office entertainments.

"My life? It's not very exciting," Cassavetes said once. "The excitement is the work. I live through my films. They are my life." On the face of it that may sound like an unpromising foundation for a critical biography, but on the contrary, I think it begins to suggest how inextricably related Cassavetes' life and work really were. Famously – notoriously in some quarters – he made 'personal' films. He cast friends and family, shot them in his own home, sometimes edited them in his garage.

He directed twelve feature films – his own dirty dozen – if we count *Big Trouble*, which he took over at Peter Falk's behest mid-way through the shoot. He wrote (or co-wrote) ten of these. The first, *Shadows* (1959), is a landmark film, a clarion call for American independent film-makers to take to the streets, 16mm cameras in hand, a worthy counterpart to the French new wave's *A Bout De Souffle*, made the very same year. *Faces* (1968) is one of the most searing portraits of the cowed inertia of the middle-classes made anywhere, any time. It put Cassavetes at the forefront of an American counter-cultural cinema movement which would flourish briefly in the late Sixties and early Seventies. Yet *Husbands*, *Minnie And Moskowitz* and *A Woman Under The Influence* clarified the nature of Cassavetes' radicalism: he didn't despise the bourgeoisie, he wasn't interested in class, only in emotional expression:

"In my opinion, these people and these small emotions are the greatest political force there is," he said. "These small emotions, these character disagreements are of vital necessity. I have seen people destroy themselves in the smallest way. I've seen people withdraw, I've seen people hide behind political ideas, behind dope, behind the sexual revolution, behind fascism, behind hypocrisy, and I've myself done all these things. So I can understand them. We have terrible problems, but our problems are human problems."

If acting is the art of empathy, then Cassavetes was an actor first and foremost. It was the duty of the artist to give sincere account of human behaviour. But he was dismayed at the distortions Hollywood foisted upon the actor: "There are two ways to play it," he noted. "The professional way is to make things as credible as possible within the limits you are given. The other way is creative interpretation, which aims – without worrying about career or profit – at rendering one's own life clearer through the expression of feeling and the exercise of intelligence. That goes beyond cinema: to find yourself in the character. Too many actors earn millions of dollars without knowing why. They're no longer artists but businessmen."

'Beyond cinema': Cassavetes loved movies – Frank Capra was his favourite director, James Cagney his favourite actor – but he expected more of them. If they didn't relate to people's actual experience, what good were they, ultimately? "We only have two hours to change people's lives," he complained.

He refused to make things easy for himself – or his audience. More than once, he recut movies after preview screenings because the reception had been too positive. He knew that life was complicated and he believed that cinema should be too. He didn't want to sell stories – his films were 'all middle', as Amy Taubin wrote: "They catch you up, turn you around, bore you a little, startle you, and throw you out upset and confused." Cassavetes loved rupture. He had to challenge preconceptions – his own most of all. "Why should I make a film about something I already know?" he asked.

His films were not inherently more 'realistic' than other film-makers', except as a by-product of their low-budgets, but they troubled themselves with character to the neglect of all else. He once rated the technical aspects of movie-making at "about eight per cent" of a film's total worth. Perhaps this is what one obituarist meant when he concluded that "If Cassavetes had had less integrity, he would have been a better film-maker." He was impatient with technique and developed a non-aesthetic aesthetic structured around the freedom of the actor: his films were shot handheld, in long takes, with the most general lighting; often their images are grainy, or ill-focussed. It was Dogme without the dogma. As one of his cameramen, Mike Ferris told me, "Everything I've ever learned about film-making is to have it so well-prepared that it's nailed down, but John was the exact opposite. He didn't want to know what was going to happen. He wanted to discover it, and be surprised. He didn't believe you could make mistakes. With John, somehow the blurriness communicated emotion."

Spontaneity is the essential attribute in Cassavetes' cinema – and maybe why these films seem as immediate as when they were made – even if that spontaneity was (almost) always scripted and refined in take after take – up to 50 of them, on occasion. It wasn't Kubrick's immaculate perfection he was after – he would have hated the sterility of that – but the revelation of human truths, messy and confused as they come.

Orson Welles said that "a work is good to the degree that it expresses the man who created it". By that criterion Cassavetes made nothing but masterworks. In a sense his films tell us all we need to know about the man:

that he was compassionate, stubborn, honest, contrary, romantic, angry, exuberant. All these qualities reveal themselves in everything he touched, and even the sharpest analysis is hard put to keep up. But biography need not simply be about seeking clues to the artist's personality in his creations. It might also hope to show how the life illuminates the work.

The temptation is to force the facts into a narrative – a trap I've doubtless fallen into more than once. Cassavetes always resisted that simplicity to stress the complication and contradiction of a character. "All people are really private," he said. "As a writer and a director you understand that that's the ground rule: people are private."

He was an unreliable narrator to his own life too. He loved to talk, but was much too curious of life, and too enamoured of debate, to adopt consistent positions. He quickly found he wasn't cut out for stage acting – he couldn't stand the repetition. Sometimes it seemed almost a point of honour that he disagree with whoever he was with. No sooner would he win the point and talk around a friend or a colleague to his way of thinking than he'd switch and argue the opposite case. Al Ruban remembers him going into meetings with the most powerful men in Hollywood, sitting down and swinging his feet onto their desks with an insouciance they could only envy. He could be ruthless too. He fired cast or crew if they didn't match his commitment. A friend once asked him why he yelled so much in business meetings. He winked and said it put people off balance; sometimes that was necessary to get the job done. Advising another friend on dealing with the media, he told him, "Always remember you don't owe them the truth."

There is no doubt that he manipulated people. Yet those who knew him – and I've been lucky enough to talk to a few of them over the past couple of years – vouch for his infinite generosity, his integrity and loyalty. More than ten years since his death, he still commands boundless love: almost to a man (and women), his old collaborators cherish him not only as a filmmaker, but as a continual source of inspiration, someone who profoundly changed the course of their lives, a mentor, a brother, or a father-figure. "The thing about John was, he spun a web and you got caught up in it, and you never wanted to be released," his one-time secretary Elaine Kagan wrote to me. "I look at his pictures all over my office, I feel his presence, hear his laugh, see his hands – so long ago and yesterday – I am still a part of it. I always will be."

A story: during the making of *Minnie And Moskowitz*, Martin Scorsese arrived in Hollywood with no money and no place to stay. His first film, *Who's That Knocking At My Door?* had been influenced by *Shadows*, and Cassavetes had become friendly with the movie-mad Italian-American, so he put Marty on the payroll and told him to sleep on the set at night: they would call him the security man. Scorsese helped out in the editing too. He held John as someone else punched him to get the sound effects for a fight scene. A year later he showed Cassavetes *Boxcar Bertha*, an exploitation movie he had directed for Roger Corman. John watched it, invited him into his office, and told him what he thought: "Marty, you've just spent a whole year of your life making a piece of shit." Scorsese had made a more than capable genre movie, but he was worth more than that. Didn't he have anything he wanted to communicate for himself? And out of this stern rebuke came *Mean Streets*, *Raging Bull* and all the rest.

I suppose this is really by way of answering Gena and John. Cinema – especially American cinema – can't have too many artists of this stature. And artists need other artists to keep them on track: father figures to emulate and supplant, brothers to contend with, families to cherish. Not only artists: we all need these things to find our way through life. And so in all humility I must insist: there ought to be more books about John Cassavetes.

1

John Cassavetes

'Life is the only true school of acting'

Charles Jehlinger

It is October 1948 and a memorable day in the eighteen-year-old life of Harry Mastrogeorge, a Greek-American who is a little over-awed to be enrolling as a student at the American Academy of Dramatic Arts, the oldest and most respected acting school in the country.

The Academy is housed at Carnegie Hall, right in the heart of Manhattan on the corner of Seventh Avenue and West 57th Street. Harry approaches the secretary and introduces himself. She looks up and pulls a face. "You're going to have to change your name," she tells him, very matter-of-fact. "It's too long and it's too hard to say and to spell."

Harry hasn't really thought about it like that, but 'Mastrogeorge' is a relatively long name, he supposes, and anyway this woman obviously knows what she's about. "Well, okay," he says, timidly. "Uhhm – what do you think I should change it to?"

The secretary gives him a quick appraising glance. "Why don't you try Harry Masters?" she says, with just a hint of a smile.

So he says "Okay," and Harry Masters signs up for AADA in the hallowed tradition of Edward G Robinson (Emmanuel Goldenberg), Kirk Douglas (Issur Danielovich Demsky), and Lauren Bacall (Betty Joan Perske) and so many others.

✳ ✳ ✳

Four months later, February 1949, and the junior year is augmented by a new intake of students, 'the winter class.' Harry Masters is hanging around the office looking over the fresh meat. He watches as another first-generation Greek-American registers. He's a short, excitable looking guy – maybe 5'8" – black hair smartly combed and slicked back, piercing grey eyes, and acute eyebrows which give his expression particularly dramatic punctuation. He's wearing an expensive suit, a white shirt and a tie – all the freshmen do – and he looks young, even to Harry. But he doesn't seem at all nervous. Just happy to be here.

The secretary – the same secretary – looks up and asks the new kid his name.

"John Cassavetes," he tells her, prompting the familiar well-rehearsed frown.

"You know you're going to have to change it," she informs him. "It's too long, too hard to spell, too hard to say."

He looks her right in the eye, not unfriendly, but firm, and he tells her how it's going to be: "They'll learn," he says. Simple as that.

"Holy shit!" Harry kicks himself: "Why didn't I think of that?"[1]

Cassavetes had recently turned nineteen years of age, and he had already accumulated a certain amount of experience in higher education – none of it good. In the year and a half since graduating from high school, he had tried and quit (or been asked to quit) three different colleges: Mohawk, Champlain and Colgate. His periods at these institutions were so brief, none of them holds any record of his attendance, but Mohawk confirm that at the time they only offered a course in Business and Retail. At Colgate he studied English Lit, and his career plan didn't stretch much beyond 'sports announcer.' Then he read some plays by Sherwood Anderson and became interested in acting. "College was just a way of getting a diploma. to get a job," Cassavetes remarked years later. "I didn't want to go, but it was important to my family."[2]

He remembered classes of up to 200 students, lecturers shouting into microphones. "I wasn't getting anything out of it, didn't like the feel of it, so I split."[3]

He sounds blasé, but it must have been a difficult time. John's father was a self-made man, a successful businessman who had worked his way up from nothing. An immigrant from Piraeus, Greece, Nicholas John Cassavetes had arrived at Ellis Island with his younger brother when he was just eleven years old. As Cassavetes senior liked to tell the story, his life was like a Frank Capra movie, or Elia Kazan's 'America America' – but then both Capra and Kazan were immigrants themselves, and near contemporaries. A missionary had come through Piraeus with promises of brotherhood and fellowship. He told them: "If you want to work and learn, the American people will open their arms and hearts to you." Nicholas took his brother and sister first to Bulgaria, where relatives took in John's aunt, then to Constantinople, where they worked until they had saved up enough money for their passage.

Arriving at Ellis Island in 1910, he had bluffed about a wealthy relative in Providence, Rhode Island. Asked for proof, he admitted he didn't have any. Their relative only arrived on the previous boat, he explained. Then he repeated the missionary's mantra: "I want to work and I want to learn." It turned out to be good advice, because the immigration officer gave him five dollars bus-fare to get them to Providence.

They didn't know anyone there of course, but having located the Greek immigrant community they were taken in and put to work. Nicholas moved on to a job in an ice-cream parlour outside Boston, Massachusetts, and by the time he was 16 he was fluent in English as well as Greek and French, and he'd gone through the Mount Hermon School near Boston on a six-month scholarship. He went on to win a partial scholarship to Harvard and worked his way through college, always keeping faith with what the missionary had told him about America. In 1919 the Oxford University Press published his thesis, 'The Question of Northern Epirus at the Peace Conference,' a prescient analysis of problems of national identity in the region of Albania, Montenegro and northern Greece.

By the time John was born – 9 December 1929 – Nicholas Cassavetes had a fledgling business in import-export, travel and immigration, a young and striking Greek-American wife, Katherine (born 1913!), and two sons to support (the eldest, Nick, was two years John's senior).

By all accounts his business career fluctuated wildly. As one family friend puts it, "He made a lot of money. Lost a lot of money. Made a lot of money again."[4] According to John, in the early days they moved around more than a dozen New York neighbourhoods: "We didn't have any money, but we never worried about it. We would move every 30 days – landlords were so anxious for tenants that they'd offer a month rent-free for moving in. When the month ran out, so did we."[5]

They also spent some time in Greece. When John first went to school in New York, Greek was his first language, English a distant second.

Within ten years, the Cassavetes' finances were on a surer footing. They had moved out to the splashy Long Island neighbourhoods of Port Washington and Sands Point: trees, lawns, big houses. The mafia capo Frank Costello, one of the heads of the 'five families,' was a neighbour. (John would return to Port Washington to shoot the funeral sequence and Harry's home in *Husbands*, imaginatively retracing his father's daily commute to Manhattan and his 42nd Street office.)

It was a happy childhood, loud and boisterous, with Katherine – eagle-eyed and indomitable as she was – allowing her boys the run of the place. They had a German Shepherd and a duck – until the dog ate the duck. When he was ten or 12, John got his teeth capped after they were chipped in a fight. Embarrassed about it, he lost the habit of smiling, he recollected. It was an expression he had to relearn over the years. John and his brother

3

loved playing cops and robbers, sports of any kind – baseball, basketball, softball, football, volleyball – and going to the movies. James Cagney was John's favourite actor: "the guy most responsible, I suppose, for getting me into films. I loved him. He always portrayed an average guy who could somehow knock down giants. He was almost like a saviour to all the short guys in the world. As a kid, I idolised him just because he was short."

"When I was 14 years old, I think I was just about five feet tall," John recalled. "I had enormous problems getting dates with girls. So you have to compensate for it: you become funnier, more outgoing. Being short is a great character-builder."[6]

A cultured man, and an author in his own right (for years John talked about filming a script his father had written about the trial of Christ, *30 Pieces Of Silver*) Nicholas instilled a passion for classical Greek literature in his boys, especially Plato and Aristophanes. But John didn't enjoy school, only history and sports. He thought he might be a professional basketball player, but it wasn't to be. He used to joke, "I'd have been taller, but my legs were too short."

Nick served in the army, and after the war he went to veteran's school at Mohawk, then followed his father into business.

When John dropped out of college for the third time, he had to talk to his father man-to-man. He had vague romantic notions of hitchhiking across the country. One thing he knew for sure: he didn't want to go into business. His father listened and told him sagely: "For every problem there is an answer." What was it that John hoped to do with his life?

Friends had told him that acting school was a great place to meet girls (so he later claimed). Nervously, he suggested maybe he'd like to be an actor, like Cagney or Bogart.

"Well, at least it's something," his old man said. "You realise the responsibility you're taking on? You're going to embody human beings! That's a heavy responsibility!"[7]

It must be admitted that the rowdy and outspoken student who entered the American Academy of Dramatic Arts that February in 1949 bore the burden of this injunction with all apparent ease. He was passionate about everything and serious about nothing. Harry Mastrogeorge remembers him climbing on to the top of the lockers and jumping down to scare the girls. More creatively, he would walk up to a girl, give her a big hug and a kiss and say "Hey, Mary," then: "Oh, I'm sorry, I thought you were Mary!" And walk along. "They'd just laugh, mostly."

The Junior Year at the Academy comprised both fall and winter intakes; the earlier group would take a long summer break during which time the

February students caught up ground, and assuming they were invited back, everyone resumed in one large Senior class in September 1949 for another six months' study culminating in four examination plays.

As well as Mastrogeorge, John's classmates included Anne Bancroft (real name: Anna Maria Luisa Italiano) and Paul Draper (Fred Draper). Harry and Fred Draper – like Mastrogeorge he would revert to his original name after college – shared a railroad apartment on West 57th and 9th. Because of its proximity to the Academy John used to hang out there all the time, and they became fast friends.

Sometimes they would go up to Sands Point and play cards with John's brother Nick – "he adored his brother; and Nick doted on him." Mastrogeorge says. "His mother was a pain in the neck. She didn't like the idea that he was an actor in those early days. She would say to me, 'Keep an eye on him. Keep him out of trouble.' But when he started to be successful of course it was all her idea."

"She was one tough mom," another friend affirms. "She was a fireball and opinionated and she knew how it was supposed to be – in her presence John had a match."[8]

"His father was a prince," Mastrogeorge says. "We'd go down to 42nd Street and visit him in his office. He'd slip John twenty bucks and say 'Don't tell your mother!'"

John, Harry and Fred would cut up on the subways, climbing through the windows if the doors slammed in their faces, careless of the risk. John was the crazy one. In the middle of Rockefeller Plaza he would start yelling. He'd yell "Fuck!" so loud you couldn't tell what he was saying.

"I remember we were walking across the Plaza once and John started yelling, and there was a very proper, prim kind of guy from the Middle East called Moses Moses – we used to say 'Hello, hello,' 'Goodbye, goodbye' – and Moses hit him in the face with his briefcase to shut him up. John fell on to his knees, screaming 'My eyes! I'm blind!' He was just nuts: a little bit of shock value – I think he carried some of that into his films."

Another time, a group from class was out on the street, rubbernecking at a particularly aristocratic premiere marking the Sadlers Wells Ballet's first performance in the United States. It was a ritzy affair, with a red carpet, fancy limos, and police barricades to hold back the gawpers. The group lost John in the crowd – nothing unusual there, he'd often just vanish, diverted by who knew what. Harry and the rest had pushed their way to the front as a Rolls Royce drove off and checker cab pulled up in its place at the foot of the red carpet. Smartly suited doormen came forward and opened the door, and as Mastrogeorge remembers, "out came John in his messy old T-shirt, jeans and sneakers. He was cackling, and he walked up the red carpet – a wonderful slouching, crouchy walk he had – and all the cameras were taking his picture." He got all the way into the lobby before they threw him out. He gave a wave to the crowd and everybody cheered. "It was a glorious time!" recalls Mastrogeorge.

Addressing a new generation of AADA students twenty years on, Cassavetes was asked if his reputation for being a wild student was true. "Escaping from the conformity of the possibility of entering into a business life makes you so heady," he told them. "You don't want to have to go back into that business world, or have anything to do with that world that you came from – so you just act nuts, you're just nuts!"

"As far as being remembered as rowdy and a rebel at the Academy, that probably was true then, and I've done my best not to lose too much faith in myself in that area. The world is very stiff. There's too much formality."[9]

At the time, Draper was considered the star pupil, the most talented actor of the group. John was a bigger personality, more extrovert, funny and dynamic. Harry was more cautious; the others christened him 'the monk' because of it. John once said to him, "Harry, you're such a pain in the ass, it's going to take you ten years longer to do anything than it would take me."

Harry shook his head. "No, no, you're wrong. It's going to take me 20 years longer than you."

Cassavetes studied acting, and also took classes in direction and stage craft. The guiding light at the Academy was Charles Jehlinger, a permanent fixture since 1918, and by this time in his 80s: a dapper, slim gentleman with an elegant grey moustache and eye-glasses. He was revered for having taught Spencer Tracy back in 1923.

What Jehlinger taught had nothing to do with that nebulous and much misunderstood process, 'the Method.' Jehlinger preached simplicity above all. Over the years he developed a litany of invocations which he reiterated until they became the students' watch-words:

"In tennis you learn the strokes, then forget them. In acting you learn your lines, then forget you learned them."

"Be simple – be natural – be honest. Do it simply, do it easily and stop directing yourself."

"Human beings, human currents, human contacts, human response, these are important – not stage business."

"Mechanics will make you a mechanic, never an artist."

"The whole business of acting is listening."

"Listening is not complicated. It is just listening."

"Stop acting. Be a human being."

6

"Continue and increase thought, theme and mood until something happens to change them. That is the basis of acting."

"A good actor does not act. A good actor creates."[10]

✳ ✳ ✳

For all his rebelliousness and high spirits, it's clear that John Cassavetes was profoundly affected by Jehlinger's teachings – and indeed the two of them seem to have been kindred spirits. According to a letter Gena Rowlands wrote to Eleanor Cody Gould, a director of the Academy in 1957, '[John] was very close to Mr Jehlinger and admired him extravagantly. They had many little jokes and incidents together.'

In the same letter, Rowlands (who attended the Academy in 1950–51) said, "The most important thing [Jehlinger] taught me was the principle of accepting criticism as an actor. Without making excuses or confusing it as personal criticism. He taught it to me by sheer mesmerism. I think I have never felt more complimented than the day he said to me 'Well, you will be an actress – you know how to listen'."

"Charles Jehlinger was the best teacher because he was so simple," Cassavetes said. "He had great taste and application, and I never met anyone who had devoted himself so completely to the philosophy of acting."[11]

Jehlinger believed in naturalism in acting just as much as Lee Strasberg or Stella Adler – and Stanislavsky before them – but he didn't subscribe to the psychological probing that was all the rage at the Actors' Studio ('You have to upset yourself! Unless you do you cannot act!'). Rather, he wanted his students to relax, to become less (not more) self-conscious. "Don't use memory – use your brain!" he'd say. "The minute you are a character you are at ease as an actor." Jehlinger believed that children were the most natural actors in the world, and he wanted his students to rediscover that creative intuition.

Harry Mastrogeorge (who joined the faculty at AADA and became a respected acting teacher himself) gives the Method short shrift: "Total immersion; being in the moment. That's not the Method, that's just good acting," he says. "You can't label realism 'the Method' or say that Stanislavsky invented it. Stanislavsky said 'I don't follow any method. I just do what I have to to get what I need out of the actor'."

The Actors' Studio was a lab for established actors, not usually for beginners; after he graduated Cassavetes auditioned for it and was turned down (they invited him back after he had some success, and he returned the compliment). He did study briefly with Lee Strasberg. According to Mastrogeorge, Cassavetes dropped out after three weeks: "He wanted to test the water but he couldn't take it. It was a whole different mentality. We had the sensibility that it was playing pretend, making believe, and fun. Then

7

you get into all that heavy duty stuff, which is very disconcerting and counterproductive a lot of the time. What Jehlinger taught was absolute pragmatic, practical logic about what you're doing and what you're not doing. John wasn't a Method actor at all, he was very intuitive, very much the individual – as Brando was."

Ben Gazzara – a near contemporary who spent three years at the Actors' Studio, 1951–54, also rejects the appellation 'Method' – for himself as well as Cassavetes: "I always hated that label," he told Thierry Jousse. "The Actors' Studio was a special place which furnished a good many American actors for a time, but that doesn't mean anything, except that good actors came from there. It was a school which allowed actors to free their energy, to find a way of embodying someone, and using parts of yourself to create a character. John worked in another direction: he was looking for surprising behaviour; he loved surprise. He didn't look for the actor to be better than he was – he wanted him to be himself."[12]

Watching Cassavetes' early performances in films like *Edge Of The City* and *Crime In The Streets* (both filmed in 1956), it's easy to understand why it was assumed that he was of the Method school: intense, inarticulate, and conflicted, he specialised in 'troubled youth' roles until into his late twenties. Cassavetes was indisputably part of the Method generation, but that generation's qualities were formed by forces much larger than any one particular school. Acting styles respond to playwrights' demands on them, demands which are themselves shaped by innumerable historical factors. In the early Fifties, Arthur Miller, Tennessee Williams and Paddy Chayefsky were intent on forging a new psychological realism, building on the social realism of pre-war Group Theater and tackling previously taboo subjects with a zeal Hollywood could only envy. As a young actor in New York (and with a relatively comfortable allowance from his father) Cassavetes would have had the opportunity to watch Brando on stage in *A Streetcar Named Desire*, Lee J Cobb as Willy Loman in *Death Of A Salesman*, and James Dean in a Tony-winning adaptation of Andre Gide's *The Immoralist*. (Frustratingly, Harry Mastrogeorge only remembers him raving about the Broadway production of *My Fair Lady*!) He would certainly have seen these actors' movies, and indeed, Cassavetes was one of a group of young New York actors who met with Nick Ray in December 1954 when he was casting *Rebel Without A Cause* (according to Bernard Eisenschitz, Ray deemed him too old for the part.) [13] Nick Ray's son Tony would later join Cassavetes' acting workshop and take a leading role in *Shadows*.

Cassavetes, Draper and Mastrogeorge graduated in the spring of 1950. They took an apartment together uptown, first on 71st Street, then on 90th (they shared with a fourth graduate, Peter Thompson). On the twenty fifth of June that year America went to war in Korea. They were all eligible for military service (indeed by law all 18–year-olds had to have registered for the draft in 1948 – a response to tensions over Berlin). Fortunately Cassavetes got wind of a special services company, an army reserve unit comprising actors and musicians – the 306 Special Services Company. He and Mastrogeorge enlisted in it that fall. They were told they would be trained up in the infantry and could be called up to fight within six months. As it turned out, the call never came. "We reported once a week right opposite the Algonquin Hotel (in fact we'd go in there and have a drink), and in the summertime we would go to training," Mastrogeorge says. "John didn't like the military much. He looked just like he did in *The Dirty Dozen*, with his hair shaved right back. I remember one time we were coming back from Camp Watertown in upstate New York and we started playing craps on the train – John didn't want me to play because we were room-mates, he didn't want to compete with me. So I stayed out on the side, and I remember dozing off as he made his seventh straight pass. He made enough money that day to pay our rent for three months!"

The 306 may not have seen active service, but they did put on the odd production for the troops. Cassavetes directed Mastrogeorge in an orginal musical of his own creation, and Harry directed John in extracts from *Mister Roberts* (Cassavetes played Insigna, with Dan Stafford in the title role – Stafford would go on to play one of the jazz musicians in Cassavetes' *Too Late Blues*). In later life, he looked back on at least some aspects of this time with a degree of nostalgia: "In the army, or on tour with different plays: lonely hotel rooms. The first day in town you look for somebody, and find someone you know you'll never see again and yet you become very close because there's a unity of feeling there: an exchange without any penalty, any responsibility. I always thought that was a beautiful thing in our life."[14]

War or no war, Cassavetes carried on in the same devil-may-care attitude he showed at college, drinking beer (a dime a glass in those days!), chasing girls (they worked out a signal with a thumbtack in the door serving as a discreet Do Not Disturb notice), following the Dodgers, or the Mets or the Giants – any of the local teams – and going to the movies. "Movies all the time," Mastrogeorge affirms. "We saw everything. All the time. And John's great hero was . . . Jerry Lewis! He loved him! He wanted to emulate him, I swear! John would imitate his voice and everything. He was very funny."

Like all the other aspiring actors in New York, they would do the rounds of agencies and production offices. But Cassavetes didn't need a stage to create a scene. Mastrogeorge remembers him chewing out one unhelpful secretary in heavy cod-Russian, making out he'd come over from the Kirov or something. Another time he feigned an appendicitis attack right in the middle of a busy office in the Paramount building: "We were wise to his antics, so we fell right into the act and all panic broke loose. By the time we got him into the hallway we were all in hysterics. John wanted to upset people a little bit."

Mostly the graduates would wind up back at the Academy, in the Green Room situated beneath the Carnegie Hall Pharmacy. There they could compare notes, pool news, and simply shoot the breeze.

It was back at the American Academy that Cassavetes first laid eyes on Gena Rowlands, on stage in a student production of *Dangerous Corner* (according to legend, he turned to a friend and declared "That's the girl I'm going to marry!"). Rowlands was dazzling, "a slender, soft blonde with green eyes and a fine smile," to quote Cassavetes' own description in his production notes to *A Woman Under The Influence*. She came from Welsh stock, out of Cambria, Wisconsin – a small town of 700 or so which was still Welsh-speaking during her grandfather's day. Her mother, Lady, was a beauty and an artist; she made ceramics and painted, acted on stage in nearby Madison, attended readings at the local ladies' Shakespeare Club every Thursday and even wrote some plays. Her father was a state senator who moved the family to Washington when Gena was 14. "My parents were like Myrna Loy and William Powell in *The Thin Man* – they were very sophisticated, elegant people," she told Kristine McKenna in the *LA Times*. "When I was little, I was quite shy and an invalid who suffered a series of mysterious maladies . . . it was traumatic and lonely. I wasn't at all a self-confident child – I was a beige, docile creature and I'm sure my glamorous parents must've looked at me and thought 'oh dear'."[15]

Rowlands' date of birth varies from 1930 to 1936 depending on the vintage of the source, and this chronological elasticity extends to her time at the Academy, usually quoted as 1953, but in fact running from the autumn of 1950 to the spring of 1951. (Charles Jehlinger died in the summer of 1952.) It is true that she began acting very young, winning a scholarship to the Jarvis Repertory Theater at the age of 14. For three years she took on the meatiest roles she could find, even playing Richard in *Richard III*. Bette Davis was her idol – she cites *Now, Voyager* (1942) in particular – and she remembers she went to see Elia Kazan's famous production of *Streetcar* with her parents in 1947. At their insistence she attended the University of Wisconsin – she was dubbed a 'Badger Beauty' in the yearbook – but she hated it; eventually she persuaded them that acting was her vocation and enrolled in the Academy.

Harry Mastrogeorge: "I remember the day I met Gena, it was at the apartment on 90th street. I used to work at night, so I was sleeping in, and John wakes me up and I open my eyes and there's Gena looking down at me; I thought I'd died and gone to heaven."

The Anglo-Saxon Rowlands complimented the Mediterranean Cassavetes in all sorts of ways – you could even say they formed a mirror image of John's parents: where he was mercurial and impetuous, she was calm and considered; he was all or nothing, while she tended to be conciliatory, except where John was concerned at any rate. "I was a woman with a plan," she recollects in the documentary *To Risk Everything To Express It All*. "In those days if you got married you quit whatever you were doing. I thought, 'All right, I want to be an actress badly enough, I will just forgo the comforts of love. And I'll be very careful not to expose myself to it.' I went in at lunch to put my books in the locker, and I got to the doorway and I saw John Cassavetes and I thought Uh-oh. Oh damn. No, no, no, no, no, no, no. This is just exactly what I don't want."[16]

Again, the dates don't fit, but according to one version of the romance they were married within four months; according to the press cuttings the wedding took place in 1954.

Rowlands only attended the Academy for six months, apparently for financial reasons. Although it mysteriously vanished from her resumé in later years, she made her Broadway debut assuming the role of the girl of Tom Ewell's dreams in George Axelrod's *The Seven Year Itch*, which opened at the Fulton theatre in November 1952 and played for over a thousand performances. (Rowlands even shot a screen test with Billy Wilder and a young unknown called Walter Matthau, although her role was already earmarked for Marilyn Monroe and Wilder's choice of Matthau would be over-ruled.)

Cassavetes, on the other hand, wasn't getting anywhere fast. His first break came in the spring of 1951 with an offer to take over a supporting role in an award-winning adaptation of Arthur Koestler's *Darkness At Noon*, which starred Claude Rains and Jack Palance. Cassavetes auditioned successfully, and was duly despatched by the producers to see the play. The next morning he went back to see the producers and they asked if he could reproduce the performance of the young man he was replacing. "Well, no," said John. "Why would I want to do that?"

"Well why would we give you the role then?" they retorted, showing him the door.[17]

To pick up a little money he did some work as a movie extra – he's in Henry Hathaway's *Fourteen Hours* (1951), but blink and you'll miss him. For three years in the early Fifties he did summer and winter stock, performing everything from O'Neill on down. He appeared in Tennessee Williams' *27 Wagons Full Of Cotton* in Westport, Connecticut; both he and Gena Rowlands did a spell at the Provincetown Playhouse, Rhode Island . . . but then things went quiet for a while. To make ends meet, Rowlands wrote crime stories for comic books – an experience which seems to have put her off writing for life.

In 1952 Cassavetes was hired by the émigré Russian actor-director Gregory Ratoff. They hit it off and Ratoff gave him a job on a play he was directing as an assistant stage manager at $85 a week. *The Fifth Season* opened at the Cort theatre in January 1953. It was a Jewish farce starring a veteran star from the Yiddish theatre, Menasha Skulnik. Reviews were poor, but it proved a box-office hit, and played for nearly two years.

In addition to his responsibilities as assistant stage manager Cassavetes understudied the male love interest, Richard Whorf – but if he hoped for his big Broadway break he was disappointed: he went on only once. Nevertheless, *The Fifth Season* changed his life. Backstage one afternoon and bored, Cassavetes started goofing around, reciting Plato from memory – in Greek – performing back flips and somersaults and slapstick schtick he'd picked up from Jerry Lewis and Red Skelton. His antics caught the eye of a visitor, Sam Shaw.

Shaw was a photographer, and a bit of a star in his own right. He did news reportage for *Life* magazine, but was especially prominent in showbiz circles: he did famous publicity shots of Brando in his torn tee-shirt for *Streetcar*, snapped Duke Ellington, Louis Armstrong and Charlie Parker in their prime, Picasso, Marcel Duchamp *et al.* In 1955 it was Shaw who caught the poster image of Marilyn Monroe over a subway vent for the movie version of *The Seven Year Itch.*

"That afternoon I had just come from the Actors' Studio, with Kazan, Tennessee Williams and Eli Wallach, where I was working on a story on 'the actor's freedom'," Shaw recalled. "I went to see Gregory Ratoff about a movie he was preparing, *Taxi*, and I saw this young guy, the second assistant director reciting Shakespeare and Plato . . . it was a real river of ideas. He had all the freedom the Actors' Studio were looking for."[18]

Shaw came over and introduced himself. They became friends immediately: Shaw's enthusiasm was a match even for Cassavetes.' A few years his senior, Shaw had a cosmopolitan *savoir faire* the actor respected. If his father taught John about human dignity and respect, and Charles Jehlinger taught him acting, then Shaw completed his education in art and music and movies. Between the three of them, they convinced John Cassavetes not only that he was an artist, but also that being an artist was an honourable profession – perhaps even the most honourable profession there was. "Being an artist doesn't necessarily mean that you're good, it just means you have chosen something," Cassavetes told a class of acting students many years later. "It's a way. But you have to be that. You can't be a phoney and say 'I'm an artist but I'd also like to be a movie star,' to be commercial. You have to be what you are and if you address yourself to that it's what you'll be."[19]

Listening to him talk, Sam Shaw urged John to write something for himself. "If you write something I'll produce it," he promised him. "I know a great writer living in Duxbury, Massachussetts, Edward McSorley. If you drive up there and see him he'll write it with you!"

In the late winter of 1953 John sketched out an outline for a movie, borrowed a friend's rumble-seat automobile, and drove very nervously through the inclement weather. When he reached Duxbury, McSorley struck him as properly 'writerly': "He was a craggy-faced 55–year-old short prune. Somebody who's lived a lot," he recollected. The novelist told him he hadn't seen Sam Shaw for ten years, but welcomed him in anyway, and indeed they wrote a script together, Cassavetes' first. (Sam Shaw successfully sold the script, but it was never made.)[20]

It's not clear how much more Cassavetes wrote in this period; we do know he collaborated on weekends for more than six months with the actor Burt Lane on a screenplay about the Spanish bullfighter Belmonte, a partnership which ended badly with them tearing up the script after a violent disagreement: "We both felt it would demonstrate that we had the confidence and ability to write again," Cassavetes said.[21]

He also made mention of trying to sell comedy material, without much success, apparently.

In any case he cannot have had much time to sit in front of the typewriter, because in 1953 his acting career finally took off. He made his feature film acting début with a bit part in Gregory Ratoff's *Taxi*, then landed his first TV role, a live historical drama starring Richard Greene in the Lux Video Theater slot. "When it was over I raced from the TV studio to where all my friends had met to watch the show and I said 'Did you see me?' They said they hadn't, even though they'd looked for me. I got indignant: 'You morons,' I shouted. 'I was the guy in the iron mask who ran on and said "Halt!" I was magnificent!'."[22]

The real breakthrough came in 1954 when he won the lead role in a teleplay by Budd Schulberg, the author of *On The Waterfront* and *What Makes Sammy Run*? Like Cassavetes' script with Burt Lane, *Paso Doble* was about a bullfighter, this time of Mexican origin. Daniel Petrie directed it, and stood up for his leading man when the bosses at Omnibus realised this was the same actor they'd fired as an extra just a few weeks earlier for making a nuisance of himself. "I weighed about 128 pounds in those days and really looked a little like a bullfighter: skinny and dark," Cassavetes told Lawrence Linderman. "I'd been around New York long enough to pick up a Mexican accent. The day after the show, 20th Century Fox called my agent and asked 'Who was that Mexican guy? Does he speak English? We may have a part for him.' And a few days later I was on my way up to Hollywood for a screen test."

The movie was *The Egyptian*, directed by Michael Curtiz, and the lead role had become available when Marlon Brando walked off the production. Curtiz decided he wanted an unknown and wound up casting Edmund Purdom.

When Cassavetes entered the American Academy in 1949, the acting course had been in 'Theater & Radio.' In all probability he'd have seen his first TV show a year or two before. Within five years the new medium had become America's favourite source of entertainment (and between 1948 and 1958 cinema audiences in the States halved). While Hollywood studios tried to freeze out this new rival, it was boom time for New York actors, writers and directors. Following the model of radio broadcasting, corporate sponsors bought regular time slots: *The Elgin Hour, US Steel Hour* and so on. Then they needed to fill them with shows people wanted to watch. There had never been such a demand for inexpensively-produced drama. And because no-one thought to record these live, kinoscope transmissions, there was little likelihood of the demand drying up either.

An entire generation of film-makers started in this way, among them Sidney Lumet, John Frankenheimer, Arthur Penn; writers like Paddy Chayefsky, Reginald Rose, Horton Foote and Robert Alan Aurthur; and actors like James Dean, Paul Newman, Rod Steiger, Sidney Poitier and Steve McQueen. John Cassavetes and Gena Rowlands were soon caught up in the whirlwind.

---

1 Author's interview with Harry Mastrogeorge.
2 Lawrence Linderman, '*Playboy* Interview: John Cassavetes,' *Playboy*, (October 1971), pp. 55–70, 210–212.
3 Linderman.
4 Author's interview with Al Ruban.
5 Linderman.
6 Linderman.
7 John Cassavetes quotes his father's advice, "For every problem there is an answer" in 'Love Streams,' and explained it in a piece he wrote for the New York Times; the injunction to take responsibility for embodying human beings is related by Lelia Goldoni in the book *John Cassavetes*, edited by Doug Headline and Dominique Cazenave, Ramsay Poche Cinema, 134 (Paris, 1997).
8 Author's interview with Jeremy Kagan.
9 AADA seminar tapes, November 1970 and November 1974.
10 'Charles Jehlinger in rehearsal,' notes transcribed by Eleanor Cody Gould in 1950–1952, published in a limited edition by AADA, 1968.
11 AADA seminar tapes, 1970 and 1974.
12 Thierry Jousse, *John Cassavetes*, Cahiers du Cinéma, (Paris, 1989), p. 127.
13 Bernard Eisenschitz, *Nicholas Ray*, Faber and Faber, (London 1993), p. 237.
14 Brian Case unpublished interview transcript, 1984.
15 Kristine McKenna, 'Under A Woman's Influence,' *LA Times Calendar Section*, May 3 1992, p 8.
16 *To Risk Everything To Express It All*, documentary film on John Cassavetes.
17 Harry Mastrogeorge.
18 Headline and Cavenaze, p. 39–40.
19 AADA seminar, 1974.
20 Cassavetes related this story to students at Columbia College, Chicago in 1975, published as *A Conversation With John Cassavetes*, edited Anthony Loeb, Columbia College Press, 1982. I have also drawn on Cassavetes' AADA seminar tapes. According to Ray Carney's *The Films of John Cassavetes*, Cambridge University Press, 1994, McSorley's writing is "characterised by extreme tonal oscillations."
21 Linderman.
22 Linderman.

2

Shadows

'It's not a question of understanding. If you feel it, you feel it.'

Ben in *Shadows*

Medieval knights, Mexican bullfighters, Southern hicks, brooding romantic leads and goofy comic stooges: John Cassavetes played them all, turning his hand to soap opera, comedy, melodrama, tragedy, and notching up between 80 and 100 television credits between 1954 and 1959. He even performed in a TV opera, lip-synching his songs to a tenor standing just off-camera.

For all this apparent range, he was most often cast in juvenile delinquent roles for his anger and intensity – qualities programme-makers came to know well on screen and off. Extravagantly generous with fellow actors (Paul Mazursky for one credits him for his first big break), Cassavetes was antagonistic towards executives, directors and even technicians.

"I used to walk around angry all the time," he later admitted. He was jealously protective of Gena Rowlands, frustrated by the quality of the material he was being given, and uncomfortable with the strictures of making moving pictures – and then a rebellious streak played well with the press. "On a film set the only person less important than a director is a talent agent," he told one journalist. "Aside from cameramen, everyone else on a set is the actor's natural enemy, because they don't give a damn about what they're doing. You've got to go to war with people like that."[1]

With Gena Rowlands' help, he worked his way through it: "In my early days I would fight with everyone, and never win. Never won one fight. And Gena said to me 'Why do you do that? I work with the same people you work with and I don't fight with them at all'." I said, "Well they like you and you're pretty. This guy, he grabbed me and moved me over here, you can't do that! And this material!"

"And Gena asked me about the material. I was playing a hillbilly, which was a joke in itself. I remember one of the lines: 'Strong I am, and have helped in the building of houses.' She said 'That's fantastic, I wish I had those lines!' We read the whole part, we did take-offs on it, we found ways of doing it and we made it fun. When I got to the set the next day the director said to me 'John, do you want to cut "Strong I am and have helped in the building of houses"?' I said 'No! You can't do that!'."[2]

Rowlands' career went from strength to strength. Late in 1955 she landed the female lead in Paddy Chayefsky's first stage play, *Middle Of The Night*. It was a May-September romance, starring Edward G Robinson as a 53–year-old widower who falls in love with a girl half his age. Eva Marie Saint had played it in a TV version, but when she was unable to commit, Joshua Logan offered the part to an actress he had spotted on *The Philco Hour*: Gena. The production wasn't without problems – between out-of-town try-outs and its Broadway opening in February 1956 the playwright cut dozens of jokes, much to the annoyance of Robinson, on the verge of his first Broadway appearance for 25 years. But the reviews were mostly very good, especially for the two leads, and the production played for a year and a half. Her performance earned her a co-starring role opposite Jose Ferrer in the movie *The High Cost Of Loving* (1957) and a five-year-contract with MGM. "I never expected to do movies," she said later. "I wasn't interested really – it was John who got interested."[3]

Her husband had won strong reviews in his first significant movie role, as the psychotic ringleader of a criminal gang in Andrew L Stone's hostage drama, *The Night Holds Terror* – a taut, superior B movie variation on *The Desperate Hours*, filmed late in 1954 and released a year later.

Sidney Lumet cast him as a charismatic street punk opposite Mark Rydell in *Crime In The Streets*, roles both actors reprised for Don Siegel in the movie version (1956). Cassavetes' Frankie Dean is the terror of the tenement, a leering, scowling presence who lords it over the neighbourhood from the fire-escape outside his window, but who for all his surly aplomb can't bear to be touched.[4]

He was another troubled youth – this time with more romantic inclinations – in John Frankenheimer's teleplay *Winter Dreams*, from a story by F Scott Fitzgerald.

By August 1956, when he played an Italian-American Raskolnikov in *Crime And Punishment*, Cassavetes could be described as 'one of the most important young actors playing the realistic boards.' Reviewing Buzz Kulik's teleplay in the *New York Journal-American*, Jack O'Brian reckoned "it was one of the best TV hours we have witnessed: perhaps the best," and singled out 'amazing' John Cassavetes for special praise, citing his 'coiled emotional wallop, power and perception and great sympathy.'[5]

But it was the liberal social conscience drama *A Man Is Ten Feet Tall* which meant the most to Cassavetes. He played it twice, first as a live TV play, then in a film version, this time shot on the streets of New York and retitled *Edge Of The City*. Cast as another mixed-up youth in the James Dean mould, Cassavetes is Axel Nordman – an army deserter traumatised

16

by the accidental death of his older brother in a car wreck (Axel was driving), and convinced that his father despises him for it. At the beginning of the film he bums a job as a stevedore on the New York waterfront, where he comes under the thumb of a racist foreman, played by Jack Warden. He is befriended by a coworker, Tommy (Sidney Poitier), who draws this uptight and obviously troubled young man out of his shell, invites him into his home and even finds him a girl.

In a portentous exchange, Tommy tells his young friend that a man has to make a choice: "You go with the man and you are ten foot tall; you go with the lower forms and you are down in the slime." And if you don't go with anybody? "Then you are alone – and that's the worst there is."

Writer Robert Alan Aurthur's fixed moral schema has not dated well. Warmly reviewed at the time, *Edge Of The City* now looks didactic and simplistic. Even if we can accept Tommy's unblemished nobility, you have to balk at how casually he is martyred for Axel's sins. There's a lot of special pleading going on for Cassavetes' rather pathetic youth too, less a rebel than a congenital runaway. That said, these actors' genuine affection for each other comes through the screen – Poitier, especially, musters great warmth and sincerity in the less melodramatic domestic scenes.

The film was a favourite of Cassavetes.' Writing the introduction to the published screenplay of *Faces* ten years later, he said that it was one of only two accomplishments from this period in which he took any pride – the other being *Shadows*. Of course he was sympathetic to the film's multi-racial politics, but Aurthur's more general message caught him at just the right time: he looked at Martin Ritt, an actor directing his first feature film at the age of 36, and he decided he too could shoulder more responsibility. It was time he started to direct.

Cassavetes always claimed that his move behind the camera was little more than a by-product of his study with young actors at the workshop he formed with Burt Lane in 1956. That too had been a spontaneous initiative, he said. According to Cassavetes, he had bumped into Lane at a bus stop, and was outraged to hear that his old writing partner was planning to take a job at an advertising agency. "I was stunned," Cassavetes recalled. "I told him: 'I won't let a friend of mine do that. Why don't you teach? You know more about acting and writing than anybody in the world.' So I got about 19 young actors to form a class and everybody paid two dollars a head, including me. We formed a workshop."[6]

They rented a small loft studio with a stage at the Variety Arts Building on 46th Street, a popular rehearsal space frequented by Frank Sinatra and Bob Fosse at the time. The initial plan was to invite actors to come in and workshop in front of casting directors, producers and agents. It didn't work. No-one came. Because they had rented the studio for a year, they decided to throw open the doors and invite anyone with an interest in acting. Seymour Cassel was one hopeful who read the advertisements in *Showbusiness* and the *New York Times*: "John Cassavetes' Workshop. Free!"

Neither Harry Mastrogeorge nor Seymour Cassel entirely believe Cassavetes' disclaimers. "I don't think there was a masterplan, exactly" Mastrogeorge says. "He didn't have a structured framework to his thinking, but he had such momentum he created framework. He wanted to experiment with stuff, and he knew he needed a working organism for that."[7]

"I think he'd decided to direct on *Edge Of The City*," Cassel says. "John always picked things up very quickly. I think it's why he started the workshop – to work with young actors, probably to direct experimental theatre, and the idea of *Shadows* came out of a class improvisation."[8]

Prickly with authority figures, Cassavetes had been a troublesome student; he didn't so much teach his class as put them to work. Most of his pupils were newcomers, and John relished drawing them out. A compulsive smoker – always bumming cigarettes – he was also a compulsive and demanding interlocutor. Impatient with good manners, he preferred to plunge in, and to hell with the niceties. He was sarcastic and enigmatic. He loved to rile people, to push their buttons, anything to get a response. His workshops were practical enquiries into the nature of acting: how to make an entrance; how to begin a play and connect with an audience; how to get a laugh and build on it. He even directed a workshop production of *Waiting For Lefty*.

It was in exploring improvisation that things got really interesting. "Actors would be on the stage doing an improvisation and it turned out to be very bad," Cassavetes recalled. "I found out that by giving an actor some definite activity to do it would make him better. But it still wasn't very good, so we threw actors who were improvising into the midst of a written scene – what happened was we found the actors couldn't go on with the written material. I found out that my study had to be deeper."[9]

After one class, in January 1957, Cassavetes took a number of students aside and asked them to show up the following Sunday afternoon. They arrived without an inkling of what was in store. Cassavetes told 19-year-old dance hopeful Lelia Goldoni she was to play the sister of Hugh Hurd – a fellow actor John had met on *Edge Of The City* who had been helping him with his classes. Goldoni was white, a New Yorker of Sicilian heritage. Hurd was black. Nevertheless, they began to strike up an affectionate sibling relationship. Then Cassavetes threw in Benito Carruthers as another brother, a beatnik who could also pass as mixed race. The improvisation went on for hours, and grew more complicated. A dramatic thread suggested itself in the character of Anthony Ray (director Nick Ray's son):

he was to seduce Goldoni, but when he met Hurd and realised she was black, he would be unable to disguise his disgust.

Next Cassavetes invited cameraman Erich Kollmar in with his 16mm Arriflex and a basic sound and lighting rig, and they imparted rudimentary film-making technique to some of the students. The students also supplied some furniture and props for an apartment scene, which they dressed in the studio. Director Shirley Clarke, a friend and important early influence on Cassavetes, also lent them some equipment. Initially it was more in the nature of a technical experiment than a 'movie,' but when Cassavetes went on Jean Shepherd's WOR midnight hour radio talk-show, *Jean Shepherd's Night People*, February 13, 1957, the project took on a life of its own.

Now Cassavetes enjoyed the *Night People* show, with Shepherd's non-sensical catch phrases ('Excelsior!'), his spirited renditions of 'When The Saints Go Marching In' on nose-flute and kazoo, and his hip, anarchic sense of humour. Shepherd had plugged *Edge Of The City*, and ostensibly Cassavetes' reason for doing the show was to thank him for it. If he went in with another agenda in mind, he never admitted to it.

Eight years Shepherd's junior, but already revving with confidence, John looked across at Jean, flashed his wolfish grin, leaned into the mike, and gave the 'night people' the inside dope. "*Edge Of The City* only scratches the surface," he told them. He had a project he'd been work-shopping at the actors' class he ran which was the real deal. An improv about young people today, black and white, their problems, their entanglements. Shepherd loved what he heard. "Why aren't there movies like this?" he wanted to know.

"Well, if you've got a hundred thousand dollars?" John said. "If people really want to see a movie about people, they might send in a buck."[10]

It's a critical juncture: the moment when – on the back of his biggest career break to date – Cassavetes announces to the world that he's not willing to play the Hollywood game in return for fame and fortune; that he's more than an actor for hire, he aims to be an artist, a truth-seeker, a film-maker. Perhaps it wasn't spontaneous; perhaps he'd planned it this way. He must have been some kind of a salesman, because over the next week the station received more than $2,000 from listeners, mostly in dollar bills.

"One soldier showed up with five dollars after hitchhiking 300 miles to give it to us," Cassavetes told Lawrence Linderman. "Some really weird girl came in off the street; she had a moustache and hair on her legs and the hair on her head was matted with dirt and she wore a filthy polka dot dress – she was really bad. After walking into the workshop, this girl got down on her knees, grabbed my pants and said, 'You are the Messiah!' I had to look that one up. Anyway, she became our sound editor and soon straightened out her life. In fact, a lot of the people who worked on the film were people who were screwed up – and got straightened out working with the rest of us. From that point on, it didn't matter to me whether or not *Shadows* would be any good; it just became a way of life where you got close to people."[11]

Within a week of the *Night People* broadcast, shooting began in earnest. Dispensing with a screenplay, but having spent some weeks doing in-depth life study work, cast and crew mucked in together, usually shooting at night, often right through to dawn.

It was at this point that Seymour Cassel entered the frame. He hadn't heard the WOR broadcast, but he'd seen ads for Cassavetes' free acting workshop and he liked the sound of that. He was an eager, happy-go-lucky twenty-year-old with a big smile and no inhibitions whatsoever. His mother had worked in burlesque, been a dancer at Minsky's and toured with a troupe of 60 vaudevillians; at the age of four Seymour was performing matinees with the 'baggy pants' comics: "I used to run on stage and pull this clown's pants down and steal his wallet."

He had rediscovered the acting bug after his spell in the service, headed for New York and taken some classes at the American Theatre Wing (Dustin Hoffman and Faye Dunaway were classmates). When he turned up at Variety Arts John Cassavetes asked him to come in and talk. Cassel recognised him from his television work and *Edge Of The City*. "I told him I didn't have much money but that I liked his work and I was interested in joining because it was free. John had a gift for listening and he loved to get to know people. And I began to tell him my life story. We spoke about an hour. He told me he came from New York, Long Island, and that during his military service he'd been in an army theatre for two years. Then he said that he'd suspended his lessons four weeks ago because he was doing a movie, and he suggested I could study with Burt Lane. Then he told me he had to go – they were shooting this film. I asked if I might help out on the set and he said 'Sure'."[12]

Seymour was to become one of Cassavetes' closest friends.

The only professionals involved were Cassavetes himself and the German cameraman, Kollmar; but Cassavetes didn't subscribe to received notions of 'professionalism.' Filming *Shadows* was "from beginning to end a creative accident," he admitted. (He admitted too, that the first week of shooting was "just about useless. We were all getting used to each other and the equipment"[13]). As Goldoni remembered it, the shoot "seemed like chaos. Everyone was doing everything. No-one knew what was going on."[14]

The night Cassel showed up he found "one camera, a few lights, a

Perfectone for the sound: that was *Shadows*. I began by watching, and when I saw they were having a problem, I'd go help. This went on all night, from eight until the small hours. They improvised the scenes and began again without a break. We had breakfast and talked. I asked John if I could come back the next night, and with his agreement, I came back every night 'til the end. I learned a lot like that. One day John asked me to take the camera and I said yes straight away. It was the first time I'd done any filming, but I'd been watching for a fortnight. I'd understood. I was quite happy, I felt like a natural cameraman. After the rushes I asked him if it was okay and he said yes, and asked me to do it again. We had a camera-man, Erich Kollmar, but John loved that each member of the team felt responsible and had the chance to progress and do better."[15]

The funds dried up repeatedly, but another $1,000 was raised from sympathetic figures in Broadway and the movies, including columnist Hedda Hopper – a surprising early champion of John's – directors William Wyler, Joshua Logan (who was keeping Gena Rowlands busy with *Middle Of The Night*), Robert Rossen (who had wanted to cast John as Alexander the Great in his 1955 film but had been overruled by the studio and gone with Richard Burton instead), José Quintero, and agent Charlie Feldman. It was enough to keep them going, after a fashion. The shoot stuttered along for four months, and when it was over post-production took more than a year: Cassavetes had merrily shouted "Print it" after his preferred takes, but having neglected to elect a script girl, no-one noted his choices, with the result that all the exposed footage (about 30 hours of it) was printed. Worse, with the team's rudimentary grasp of sound recording and logging, and no screenplay to consult, synching up sound and picture proved a nightmare. Cassavetes even brought in lip-readers to help out.

Yet there had been some method to all this madness. The film was an experiment and a learning process for everyone involved. "On *Shadows* you could learn everything you wanted to," Cassel recalls. "We all did a bit of everything, apart from Erich, the cameraman. You would move the lights or the boom, talk to the guy doing the mixing and recording and learn that. John held it together. No one could get more excited than he could, and his enthusiasm was like a waterfall, it washed over everyone."

As for Cassavetes himself, he explained, "I had worked in a lot of films and I couldn't adjust to the medium, I found that I wasn't as free as I could be on the stage or in a live television show. So for me it was mainly to find out why I didn't particularly like to work in films."[16]

One lesson learned on *Shadows* would govern the production aesthetic of all his films: "In Hollywood . . . everyone is frightened to to do anything that's not traditional . . . there are certain rules and regulations that I think are sct specifically to destroy the actor and make him feel uncomfortable.

[For instance] in a motion picture you have marks to hit, and the lighting cameraman always lights for you at a certain mark. The actor is expected to go through a dramatic scene, staying within a certain region where the lights are. If he gets out of the light just half an inch, then they'll cut the take and do it over again. So then the actor begins to think about the light rather than about [the scene]. With *Shadows* we tried something completely different in that we not only improvised in terms of the words, but we improvised in terms of motions. So the cameraman also improvised, he had to follow the actors and light generally, so that the actor could move when and wherever he pleased."[17]

Cassavetes' films are often misleadingly described as 'improvised,' so it's worth picking up on this distinction between improvised words and improvised motion. Save for *Shadows*, a few scenes in *Husbands*, and a few moments elsewhere, all Cassavetes' films were scripted, even if those scripts were sometimes arrived at through close collaboration with the actors. However, they all involved improvised motion. Where Spielberg, Hitchcock or Scorsese will storyboard each frame in advance of shooting, Cassavetes' cameraman would never arrive at work with a preconceived notion of angles or blocking. In other words, Spielberg prioritises the camera to illustrate a scenario, and Cassavetes – true to his stage training – prioritises the actor to explore the emotions within a scene. Although it took a while to become clear even to Cassavetes himself, his working practice would prove entirely antithetical to the Hollywood industrial model, aesthetically, politically, even morally.

Ironically, Cassavetes was to renounce the first version of *Shadows* on the grounds that it was mere "cinematic virtuosity. With angles and fancy cutting. The one thing that came at all alive [was] now and then the actors survived all my tricks."[18]

This sixty-minute version of *Shadows* showed three times at free midnight screenings at the Paris Theatre in New York late in 1958. There are conflicting reports of its reception. The director remembered it as "absolutely disastrous. There was only one person in the theatre who liked the picture and it wasn't me – it was my father, who thought it was 'pure.' Not necessarily good, but pure. All our really close friends had shown up, people who had helped us, who had contributed to the film in dozens of ways and who really wanted *Shadows* to be good. But no-one tried to phony up their reaction to it; one friend of mine patted me on the shoulder and said 'That's okay, John, you're still a good actor.' I could see the flaws in *Shadows* myself: it was a totally intellectual film – and therefore less than human. I had fallen in love with the camera, with technique, with beautiful shots, with experimentation for its own sake."[19]

Among the guests invited to the Paris Theatre was Al Ruban, a one-time professional baseball player who had fallen in with Seymour and the guys earlier in 1957. John, Seymour and Mo McEndree played baseball every week against a local Puerto Rican team. "They would lose every week. I went to play and they didn't lose quite so often," Ruban says.[20]

Ruban was a no-nonsense New Yorker who was putting himself through a course in journalism by working nights in a garage. "My first impressions of John? I think I saw him how he wanted to be seen: as a regular guy, energetic, one of the boys. Could have been off a street corner, or the playground, or on the ballfield. Kind of a macho guy, or at least gave that image. Very energetic. Loved playing pick-up basketball, even though he was quite short, he was a terror on the court. Much better at basketball than any other sport. Here was a guy you'd like to go to a game with, or have a beer with. No matter what you talked about, he knew something about it. Full of energy. Would argue all the time, which is a very New York attitude. And when I got to meet him he was already established as an actor, which was exciting."

Remembering that first screening, Ruban says simply, "I was both impressed and not particularly impressed. Because it was unlike the kind of movies I was used to seeing. A lot of people left, and a lot of people thought it wasn't particularly good. I told John it was okay in a naive kind of way and he said he thought so too."

It wasn't quite true, though, that John Cassavetes' father was the only person who admired *Shadows* on its midnight premiere. The New York film critic Jonas Mekas admired it greatly, and even arranged with Gideon Bachmann for it to be shown at the Young Men's Hebrew Association on 92nd Street, where it screened to half-a-dozen packed audiences. A Lithuanian emigre just a few years older than Cassavetes, Mekas was an influential figure in avant-garde film, the founder of *Film Culture* magazine, and a contributor to *Village Voice* (in 1961, he became an underground film-maker himself with *Guns Of The Trees*, followed by a series of diary films, notably *Walden* and *Lost, Lost, Lost*).

In January 1959, Mekas and *Film Culture* awarded *Shadows* their first 'Independent Film Award,' because "it presents contemporary reality in a fresh and unconventional manner. Cassavetes was able to break out of conventional moulds and traps and retain original freshness. The improvisation, spontaneity, and free inspiration that are almost entirely lost in most films from an excess of professionalism are fully used in this film."[21]

Improvisation was the driving force across much of what was most exciting in American arts in the late Forties and Fifties, and New York was its focal point. Here, on 52nd Street, Charlie Parker invented bebop – a freeform, experimental, spontaneous jazz. At the Actors' Studio, Lee Strasberg reinvented the Stanislavsky 'Method,' stressing sense memory, technique at the service of empathy (and not the other way around), being 'in the moment.' In Times Square, Jack Kerouac met Herbert Huncke, a hustler peddling stories, who introduced him to the slang word, "Beat"; "the root, the soul of Beatific," Kerouac rhapsodised in *On The Road* (1957). According to Allen Ginsberg, "The entire Beat literary movement was based, to some extent, on Kerouac's estimate of be-bop as an improvised form."

In film, the avant-garde to which Mekas aligned himself shared the Beats' exultation in emotional presence; in the abstract short films of Kenneth Anger, Harry Smith, Stan Brakhage and Jack Smith, there's a visual correlative to Kerouac's enraptured, transcendent lyricism. "The young American film-maker, like the young painter, musician, actor, resists his society," Mekas wrote in *Film Culture*. "He knows that everything he has learned from his society about life and death is false. [. . .] His spontaneity, his anarchy, even his passivity are his acts of freedom." Later in 1959, Mekas wrote a piece for *Sight And Sound*, grouping *Shadows* with the short films of Stan Brakhage, and Robert Frank and Alfred Leslie's *Pull My Daisy* – a semi-improvised film featuring Jack Kerouac, Allen Ginsberg and Gregory Corso – citing their "open ear and open eye. Their disrespect for plots and written scripts." He concluded: "Since their most passionate obsession is to capture life in its more free and spontaneous flight these films could be described as a spontaneous cinema."[22]

Even without the first version, it's easy to understand how Mekas mistook *Shadows* for a breakthrough "Beat" film. As in Beat music, poetry and prose, the film focusses on the bohemian marginalia; it eschews conventional narrative form for something more raw, ragged and spontaneous. By using the actors' real names, for example, it breaks down barriers between art and life; and its treatment of sex and race must have seemed daring, even subversive at the time.

Bebop, Kerouac's "spontaneous prose," Beat poetry, Abstract Expressionism and Jackson Pollock's "action painting" – all these were in the air, and certainly influenced Cassavetes' thinking at the time: after all, *Shadows* is set among the jazz, hipster set. After contemplating using Miles Davis, Cassavetes enlisted Charles Mingus to improvise a soundtrack to the film (in the event, the Julliard-trained Mingus insisted on writing a score, and so slowly that there's less than five minutes of it in the finished film, notably a 12-bar blues which became one of his standards, 'Nostalgia In Times Square.' When he could wait no longer, the director turned to saxophonist Shafi Hadi, who happily blew along with the movie).

In 1959 there wasn't a great independent tradition to refer to. Within the

United States, you could point to a handful of one-offs: King Vidor made his New Deal drama *Our Daily Bread* outside of the studio system in 1933, even mortgaging his own home; in 1952 Orson Welles financed his own *Othello* in exile; the American Mineworkers Union funded the blacklisted production *Salt Of The Earth* in 1953; the same year the prodigious Stanley Kubrick shot *Fear And Desire* for $53,500; *Killer's Kiss* followed in 1955, for $75,000, though in later life Kubrick tended to dismiss both as 'amateur' efforts.

For most people, the costs were prohibitive, and artists drawn to film as a means of personal expression either stuck to short films or animation. The situation was improving though. The advent of lightweight 16mm cameras that could be held in the hand, together with portable sound recording equipment, encouraged some experimentalists to venture out of their garrets, and fed the nascent American neo-realist movement of the late 1950s (in the States, for example: Lionel Rogosin's *On The Bowery*, 1956, and Morris Engel's *Lovers And Lollipops*, 1955). On *Shadows*, Cassavetes and his rotating camera-crew used a 16mm Arriflex, sufficiently portable to allow them to shoot from the backs of trucks, from subway entrances, and even from dustbins – and anyway, they couldn't afford a dolly.

If Cassavetes wasn't necessarily a Beat film-maker in the way that Mekas assumed, to all intents and purposes he was banging the same drum. In April 1959 he even contributed a manifesto to *Film Culture* entitled 'What's Wrong With Hollywood.' It is worth quoting at length:

✶ ✶ ✶

"Hollywood is not failing. It has failed," he wrote. "The probability of a resurrection of the industry through individual expression is slim, for the men of new ideas will not compromise themselves to Hollywood's departmental heads. These artists have come to realise that to compromise an idea is to soften it, to make an excuse for it, to betray it. In Hollywood the producer intimidates the artist's new thought with great sums of money and with his own ego that clings to past references of box office triumphs and valueless experience. The average artist therefore is forced to compromise. And the cost of compromise is the betrayal of his basic beliefs. And so the artist is thrown out of motion pictures and the businessman makes his entrance."

"However, in no other activity can a man express himself as fully as in art. And, in all times, the artist has been honoured and paid for revealing his opinion of life. The artist is an irreplaceable figure in our society too. A man who can speak his own mind, who can reveal and educate, who can stimulate or appease, and in every sense communicate with fellow human beings. To have this privilege of world-wide communication in a world so incapable of understanding and ignore its possibilities and accept a compromise – most certainly will and should lead the artist and his films to oblivion."

"Without individual creative expression, we are left with a medium of irrelevant fantasies that can add nothing but slim diversion to an already diversified world. The answer cannot be left in the hands of the money men [. . .] The answer must come from the artist himself. He must become aware that the fault is his own: that art and the respect due his vocation as an artist is his own responsibility. He must, therefore, make the producer realise, by whatever means at his disposal, that only by allowing the artist full and free creative expression will the art and the business of motion pictures survive."[23]

Shadows in the first version no longer exists. Stung by the criticism of his friends, and urged on by Maurice McEndree and Seymour Cassel, Cassavetes decided that with another ten shooting days, he might salvage the project. The reshoots would double the budget, to approximately $40,000, but with an hour of edited footage to show, another $1,500 was promised by three further sources (two subsequently dropped out, saddling the director with debts, but a fellow Greek, Nikos Papatakis, came through with his share). According to the research of Cassavetes scholar Ray Carney (a virtual one-man Cassavetes Appreciation Society, who has done more than anyone to champion and clarify these films in a number of books and countless articles), two-thirds of the extant, 87 minute *Shadows*, derives from the 1959 reshoots, including those scenes pertaining to Hugh's Philadelphia trip, the MOMA sculpture garden scene, the ending, and the bulk of Lelia and Tony's romance.[24]

As a matter of practicality the reshoots were scripted, effectively forfeiting 'improvisation' as an abstract ideal in itself; Mekas' 'spontaneous cinema' had no sooner been recognised than it was reconsidered.

According to Goldoni, Cassavetes knew that they'd all been through many new experiences in the gap between shooting the two versions: she for instance, had married and divorced Ben Carruthers. "There was no way we could get back the spirit of youthful innocence, the naivete we'd had before. We weren't using the same language any more. So for that reason, he wrote the dialogue for all the additional scenes – although he had such a good ear almost no-one can tell which scenes come from which version."[25] (In a letter he wrote to *Village Voice*, 30 December 1959, Carruthers claimed the actors participated in the reshoots "in the hope that a sale of the film would result in exposure for us.")

It was at this point that Cassavetes invited Al Ruban to join the crew. "There were holes in the story, and he wanted to go out for another couple of weeks to fill those gaps," Ruban says. "I told John I didn't know anything about film-making, and he said nor did he, but everyone was just getting together. It sounded exciting." He became "assistant camera operator" – "really what I did was carry equipment." He learned on the job, like everyone else.

If the reshoots were necessarily more organised than the filming two years previously, it was still a makeshift and haphazard affair. "I remember one day we couldn't shoot on the streets because the police had been following us around kicking us off the streets – we didn't have any permits," notes Ruban. "I suggested we could do this scene with the taxi cab in the garage where I work if we turn out all the lights. And that's what we did. It created within me the same kind of feeling I had when I played ball: the same kind of excitement, instant gratification and instant sorrow."

✳ ✳ ✳

Shadows begins at a bohemian NY party in full flow. As the opening titles roll ('Presented by Jean Shepherd's Night People'), we watch Ben make his way through the packed, noisy apartment. Jazzers jamming. Drinks. Smokes. Broads. Ben looks the part – going through a repertoire of 'cool' beat poses – but he's not interacting directly with anyone.

Scene two: it's early evening, and Ben is slouching towards Times Square, past the movie theatres on 42nd street. This is his turf, so much so that he bumps into first Seymour Cassel (in an unbilled cameo), then his pals Dennis (Dennis Sallas) and Tom (Tom Allen). Boisterous and excited, they dump Seymour and head off to make the most of $20. Spilling into a bar, they chat up a trio of likely girls. Clumsy, *sotto voce* flirtations, and fade to black.

Benny back on the street, head down, hands in jacket pockets: a model for De Niro in *Taxi Driver*. The movie awnings offer ironic counterpoint to the film we're watching, as Ben passes in front of a board proclaiming 'Dean Martin in A Thousand Bedrooms.' He enters a dance rehearsal studio, where Jack Ackermann is putting a chorus line through their paces ('A Real Mad Chick'), and Ben's brother Hugh is in unhappy negotiation over his next gig. It's not enough that he has to work in a crummy Philadelphia strip club, now they want him to introduce the girls. "You're an artist, if you decide to do something you can do it," his manager Rupert (Rupert Crosse) tells him, soothingly. "Ten years ago I was an artist," Hugh complains. Now he has bills to pay. And here's Ben, hand out for another $20 – so of course Hugh swallows his pride and takes the job for $35 a night. It's a beautifully choreographed sequence, one of the most intricate in the film, and the first time we appreciate that this will be more than just Ben's movie. In fact, he's sidelined here, a pest buzzing in Hugh's ear as he comes to terms with this latest humiliation.

Cassavetes uses the space, fore-grounding the closing of the deal between Rupert and Ackermann, for example, while in the background Hugh quietly slips some bills into his brother's pocket. And all the while the chorus girls keep up their routine.

Scene Four: Hugh at the bus station, packed off by his sister Lelia, whose skin is as white as his is black. Lelia is young and flighty – another real mad chick – but responsible enough to have got Hugh there (just) in time for his bus. He cautions her against walking home, but she kisses off his pater-nalistic concern: "Nothing will happen to me – nothing ever does." Later, on the way home past those same 42nd street cinemas, Lelia pauses in front of posters for a Brigitte Bardot movie, obviously intrigued. She's hassled by a strange man for her trouble (though another stranger – an unbilled Cassavetes – valiantly sees him off).

We're ten minutes into the movie, but it already feels like we're in the thick of it, caught up in lives unfolding apace. The three siblings so dex-terously introduced here represent not just shades of skin colour, but shades of maturity: Hugh, just approaching 30 but already a father figure to the others, a provider and a protector, but also someone who is frus-trated in his art, in part because of his family responsibilities, a trier, more than an achiever; Ben, in his early twenties, but still an adolescent at play on the streets of New York, hanging loose, doing nothing with his life, as one character observes, but identifying himself with the beat generation through his shades, his leather jackets, and his studious cool; and then Lelia, the youngest, 'baby sister' to Hugh, but at 20, old and headstrong enough to do her own thing, curious about the world and open to it.

Each of them is self-dramatising: Ben, most obviously, in his Beat 'costume' and his posturing, but Hugh, too, in his assumption of the father's role, and Lelia, constantly, in the airs and graces she tries on through three flirtations in the course of the film. It's a given in *Shadows*, as in Cassavetes' subsequent work, that we're all acting out roles, consciously or not. This film by young New York actors, with its pseudo-parodic rhetoric about 'realism,' 'art' and 'existentialism,' is very much about young New Yorkers simply trying to be real.

Much of what is youthful and liberating in the movie stems from Lelia's vivacity and innocence, inseparable from the exuberance and naivete of Goldoni's performance. She is the embodiment of spontaneity in the film.

Because of her youth, her sex and her skin colour, Lelia is free to move between roles (and between men) often within the same scene. She is still, as Tony observes, "in a cocoon," an unformed chrysalis. See, for instance, how the cultured young intellectual reverts into the kid sister, poking her tongue out in the cafe scene with the writer David (David Pokitillow), Ben and his friends; or how abruptly she drops the rather stuffy David for the less cerebral attractions of Tony.

The men in the film all take a proprietorial interest in her: "Who do you belong to?" Tony demands, typically. But she insists on her independence and freedom: "I belong to me," she declares.

Her falling out with David concerns a story she's written, which he deems "unrealistic" (and which clearly prefigures her own, as if Cassavetes were critiquing his own film, or at least the earlier version of it). It's the story of a girl "who has no control over herself," who goes up and kisses a stranger in the park. Lelia assures him she'd do it if she wanted to, and proves the point delightfully by kissing Tony right there and then. There's also a hint that the relationship in the story goes badly: "She's deeply hurt, yet she goes on as if nothing's happened – it just doesn't make sense," David complains. Lelia explains: "Well, the point is, if you're yourself, you won't get hurt."

She is hurt, though, first as a woman, then as a black woman passing for white. Lelia assumes she is free to express herself sexually, too, so when Tony asks her up for a drink, she accepts; it's not just the prospect of miscegenation which must have shocked audiences in the Fifties, but the alacrity with which this relationship is consummated. Of course in losing her virginity she also loses some of her illusions. "I thought being with you would be so important, it would mean so much," she says. "That afterwards two people would be as close as it's possible to get. Instead, we're just two strangers."

As Ray Carney has pointed out, the close-up of the mask that begins this coital/post-coital scene (before the camera pans down to the bed) is a tacit visual metaphor for the film's concern with appearance and role playing. If Lelia had hoped that in sex all the masks would dissolve, she has chosen badly, because the problem with Tony is precisely that there's nothing beneath his mask – in fact he told her up front, "You know, I'm not a very nice person. I'm not one of those storybook characters who's supposed to be all noble and righteous." It's only when he's confronted with his own shallowness – specifically, here, by his love-em-and-leave-em attitude; later, most dramatically, by his instinctive racism – that he desperately (and unconvincingly) assumes a more compassionate persona.

This close-up of the mask is a very rare – and still subtle – example of the camera recording external commentary on the characters. *Shadows* generally follows the convention "long shot to close up" as scenes begin, but it is also a film leery of establishing shots; the actors dictate the space, the camera follows them.

29

The live television dramas which constituted Cassavetes' main experience of film to this point were studio-bound, and directed from a control booth where John Frankenheimer, say, would cut between four or five (shifting) camera positions. It was a training ground for floor managers – in Ben Gazzara's phrase – and as Thierry Jousse comments, *Shadows* is less "theatrical" than any of the early movies by New York TV graduates Arthur Penn, Sidney Lumet or Martin Ritt. Cassavetes' camera work is freer, his editing less boxy. In fact it's surprising how heavily edited *Shadows* really is. For all its superficial resemblance to the cinema vérité school, long takes are in short supply. Even at this early stage in his career Cassavetes wasn't shy of shooting film stock: Lelia Goldoni remembers doing 57 takes of her kissing scene with Tony Ray.

To edit is, inherently, to editorialise, yet where most film-makers cut to distil and dictate meaning, Cassavetes' empathetic cutting consistently opens up and complicates a scene, by injecting close-ups of apparently "secondary" characters, for example; picking up on nuances of behaviour which might belie our first impression of an individual. Over and above this, there is an attempt to disrupt "structure," to break out of the confines of Hollywood's "moral" narrative framework. Carney: "[Cassavetes' scenes] don't exist to generate an endpoint. They capture energies continuously on the move, and in their continuous registration of movements, they honour impulses that won't be made to subserve a larger theoretical agenda or be made to trace a larger narrative trajectory."[26]

Hence, the challenge Cassavetes sets for critics: everything is up for grabs. "Meaning" becomes almost a meaningless phrase in relation to his work – or as Ben remarks at the end of the boys' debate about art in the MoMA statue garden, "It's not a question of understanding. If you feel it, you feel it."

In 'Shadows,' you can sense the tension between the liberal race drama Hollywood might have made of it, and the more slippery character piece Cassavetes came up with. The crucial revelation of Tony's racism is conveyed entirely through looks and glances; there's none of the pontification which marks analogous works of the period, like *Edge Of The City* or *The Defiant Ones*. In his commentaries on the film, Ray Carney accepts the film-maker's colour-blindness at face value, and suggests that by the second version, he had lost interest in "movie-of-the-week racial issues."[27] (Cassavetes even wrote to commend him for for focussing on the 'human,' not the 'racial' aspects of the drama). Carney, I think, gets too close to disavowing any political import. It's clear that neither Hugh Hurd or Lelia Goldoni would agree with him. Hurd noted with some irony that no-one ever imagined Benito Carruthers was really black, because the convention for casting blacks with white skins was to cast a white – like Sandra Dee in

Sirk's *Imitation Of Life*. Perversely, though, people were persuaded that the Sicilian Goldoni must be black. "America was very segregated then. Even in New York, if you mixed with people from a different race, you were considered strange or attention-seeking," Goldoni points out. "When John made *Shadows*, the fact that I wasn't at all black should have shown people that segregation wasn't possible, because, how can you tell who's black and who isn't? It didn't work, though. In California, and even in England, people believed I was black. They couldn't accept that a person who wasn't could play a black with such warmth and show such affection for someone like Hugh. Impossible. I had to be black. It hurt my career in California, because at the time, it was out of the question to employ anyone with the smallest drop of black blood alongside whites."[28]

Cassavetes referred to the influence of Italian neo-realism – he'd seen *Bicycle Thieves*, *La Terra Trema*, and – surely – *I Vitelloni* – and felt the affinity was so strong he was keen to get the film shown at the Venice Film Festival. Yet the neo-realists were inspired, at least initially, by the social deprivation of post-WWII Italy and a leftist political agenda. New York in the late Fifties was a long way from all that. It would be ridiculously reductive to read *Shadows* as a 'problem' or 'social conscience' film. (Cassavetes: "There is no problem that is not overcome and replaced by other problems.") The realism of *Shadows* is largely derived from absence: from the lack of a set script, the lack of money, the lack of stars, and the lack of all the studio artifice which goes with these things. What's left is the actor in front of the lens, the endeavour and creative imagination invested by the film-makers. Truly a step in the dark, the realism of *Shadows* is rooted in emotional authenticity, not reformist politics. Cassavetes shows scant interest in 'solving' the problem of racism; his attention is focussed on how this free spirit, Lelia, deals with it.

Like the girl in her story, she carries on as before. Unlike her creation, though, Lelia can't disguise the hurt, and her pretence – verging on self-parody in the delicious performance of female wilfulness she puts on for her last suitor – is obvious even to a stranger like Davey. Nothing is spelled out between them, but when – in the dance hall – she breaks down and puts her head on his shoulder, there's more than an intimation that the intimacy she looked for in Tony – "to be as close as it's possible for two people to get" – could be realised with Davey.

Hugh's story, too, ends on a grace note, as he consolidates his partnership with Rupert, his manager and friend, and they set off for their next gig with renewed optimism in their own potential. For Ben, the last sequence rhymes with and answers the first: he's on the town again with Tom and Dennis, drinking and picking up girls. This time, though, they run into trouble and get beaten up. The mature way he handled Tony's unwanted intrusion at home, defusing the situation more capably than Hugh, paved the way for his moment of revelation now: "If you wanna be corny about it, I've learned something." he muses, preparing to jack in his pals and find himself a steady girlfriend, "like a normal-type person." As so often, though, the certainty of the words is undermined by the ambiguity of the imagery. We watch Ben walk off alone into the night.

So as to honour the collaborative nature of the production, the new *Shadows* retained the original's now rather misleading end credit: "The film you have just seen was an improvisation."

Amos Vogel, who ran the Cinema 16 film club, was the first to screen this 87-minute *Shadows* in a double-bill with *Pull My Daisy* under the banner 'The Cinema of Improvisation.' The programme notes spared no blushes: "The most important American independent film of the decade, already a legend: John Cassavetes' pulsating revelation of the demi-world of the night people; floaters, chicks, jazz musicians and hipsters in the neon-lit desert of Times Square. Overpowering in its immediacy, this brilliant return to improvisation in the cinema etches a compassionate, violent portrayal of pick-ups and brawls, loneliness, casual affairs and search for identity. Notably adult treatment of an interracial love story reveals Negroes not as liberal clichés but as human beings in all their complexities. Winner of Film Culture's Independent Film Award."

When he saw the second version of *Shadows*, Jonas Mekas was appalled. His diary entry for 11 November 1959 reads: "At this fateful night I realised what I have to say, if I have anything to say, I'll be able to say it only as an anarchist. My realisation that I was betrayed by the second version of *Shadows* was the last stone. It helped me realise that what I was talking about, what I really saw in the first version of *Shadows*, nobody else really saw: I was pursuing my own ideal, my own dream. They didn't know what they had: a blind man's improvisation which depended on chance accidents."[29]

He used his column in *Village Voice* to condemn Cassavetes' commercial sell-out: "same title but different footage, different cutting, story, attitude, style, everything: a bad commercial film with everything that I was praising completely destroyed."[30] It made painful reading. Mekas and Cassavetes were friends, and Mekas knew full well that Cassavetes had recently accepted a contract to play the jazz-playing private investigator *Johnny Staccato* on TV and moved his family to Hollywood, in part to pay off the debts incurred on *Shadows*. He'd also recently become a father (Nicholas David Rowlands Cassavetes was born May 23, 1959): "I was so busy with the movie that not until the day I finished reshooting did I become aware that within a week [Gena] was going to give birth to our first child. A couple of days before our son Nick was born, I got a telephone call from Universal. This guy told me he had a series for me called *Johnny Staccato*, all about this nightclub piano player who caught crooks. I said 'Bullshit!' and hung up. I looked at my wife and she said 'You're absolutely right John, you can't do that stuff.' Then I looked at her belly and called the guy right back. I signed to do the series, I paid off the bill collectors and I was able to cut and complete *Shadows*."[31]

Was the new *Shadows* a sell-out? Both Cassel and Ruban are confident that the first version was nothing more than a 'work in progress.' The debate raged on the letters page of the *Voice*. Amos Vogel wrote to Cassavetes at his new home at Pacific Palisades on the Sunset Strip: he reported that the screenings had been a "personal and artistic triumph," with a packed house including such notables as Paddy Chayefsky, Kenneth Tynan, Arthur Knight and Louis Malle[32] giving "a long and pronounced ovation that continued for a longer time than I have witnessed at Cinema 16 in many a year."

Nevertheless, Vogel warned darkly that Mekas had stirred up a controversy in New York, and that a confusion existed as to which version was the 'true' *Shadows*: "You must have a very clear-cut stand on the issue. You will further confuse the issue, were you to decide to permit the earlier version to be shown. It is now being stated by certain people that Kingsley financed the new version; that it was done in accord with his wishes and that thus it constitutes a commercial 'betrayal.' You and I know Kingsley stepped out of the deal at a very [sic] stage; and that, in fact, the changes are due to your desire to strengthen the film. I showed this version because I knew this was 'the film' as far as you and your coproducers were concerned; and because I personally feel the new one is the better one. You have made a film that will live a very long time: a permanent contribution to film history and film art."[33]

At Vogel's behest, Cassavetes also wrote to the *Village Voice*, December 16, 1959. "Expression of any kind must be understood to have any meaning," he wrote. "Mr Mekas is right in that he states that this version is completely different. It was made to be understood with the understanding that comes from life, not from the opinions of others. It in no way was a concession, and in my opinion, it is a film far superior to the first. The cinematic style that was so prominent in the first gives way to the emotional experiences the characters encounter. The scenes, in my opinion, are fulfilled, the imagination of youth that sparked the first version came back stronger, clearer, and more determined to enlighten rather than prove."

It was the end of the decade. Tumultuous years in which John Cassavetes had found his vocation, his wife, and his voice. "*Shadows* will always be the film I love the best," he would reflect. "Simply because it was the first one and we were all young, and because it was impossible, and we were so ignorant, and for three years we survived each other and everything."

---

1 Quoted in Linderman.
2 AADA seminar.
3 Geoffrey Macnab unpublished interview transcript, 1998.
4 See Appendix: *Acting Out* for more on Cassavetes the actor.
5 Jack O'Brian, 'Dostoyevsky Great on TV,' *New York Journal American*, 10 August 1956, p. 12.
6 Linderman.
7 Mastrogeorge: Author's interview.
8 Seymour Cassel quotes Author's interview unless otherwise stated.
9 Russell Auwerter, 'A Talk With John Cassavetes,' *Action*, v5, n1, Jan–Feb 1970.
10 No recordings exist, but Cassavetes recounted variations of this story many times.
11 Linderman.
12 Cassel interviewed by Thierry Jousse.
13 Colin Young, 'New Wave or Gesture,' *Film Quarterly*, v14, n3, Spring 1961.
14 BBC Arena documentary, directed by Debbie Gellar, 1989.
15 Jousse.
16 John Cassavetes, 'And the Pursuit of Happiness,' *Films And Filming*, February 1961.
17 Cassavetes, *Films And Filming*.
18 Young, *Film Quarterly*.
19 Linderman.
20 Al Ruban quotes: Author's interview unless otherwise stated.
21 *Film Culture*, Jan 26, 1959.
22 Jonas Mekas, *Sight And Sound*, v28, n3&4, Summer/Autumn 1959.
23 *Film Culture*, Issue 19, April 1959, p. 4–5.
24 Ray Carney, *The Films Of John Cassavetes: The Adventure Of Insecurity*, 1999.
25 Headline and Cazanave.
26 Ray Carney, *The Films of John Cassavetes – Pragmaticism, Modernism And The Movies*, Cambridge University Press, 1994.
27 Carney, *The Adventure Of Insecurity*.
28 Headline and Cazenave.
29 Jonas Mekas, *To Free The Cinema: Jonas Mekas And The New York Underground*, David E James ed.
30 Jonas Mekas, *Movie Journal, Village Voice*, January 1960.
31 Linderman.
32 While the 'French New Wave' was already a familiar term, 'A Bout de Souffle' had yet to break and give the movement definition. In its youthful energy, its feel for the street and its disrespect for 'le cinéma du papa,' Godard's 1959 film feels like a French cousin to *Shadows* – and indeed Godard would go on to dedicate two films to Cassavetes.
33 *Wide Angle*, v19, n2, April 1997. In another letter posted after Mekas' first broadside against the film, Vogel urges 'It is clearer now than ever that the "other version" should never have been publicised and certainly should not continue to circulate. Retroactively he [Mekas] cheapens our showing and your artistic integrity. While as a critic he has a perfect right to express his opinion, we are both harmed by this.' This letter (also in *Wide Angle*) may go some way to explain the disappearance of the 60-minute 1958 version of *Shadows*.

3

Dreams for Sale:
Too Late Blues & A Child Is Waiting

'When an idealist sells himself out everybody passes judgement; the bigger the idealist, the bigger the bum. Here's a guy who talks loud about "Art" and "freedom of expression," and I think he's a phony'

Benny in *Too Late Blues*

Shortly after arriving in Hollywood, John and Gena were invited to a party thrown by her *Middle Of The Night* co-star Edward G Robinson and his wife. Too new in town to understand that no-one in Hollywood is expected at the specified hour, the Cassavetes were the first guests to show.

Edward G didn't mind a bit. It gave him a chance to show off his modern art collection – and in particular his pride and joy, one of Monet's waterlillies series. "It was staggeringly lovely," Gena Rowlands recollected.

Robinson asked his guest what he thought of it. "It's nice," said John, deadpan.

Edward G was puzzled: "What do you mean, 'nice'?"

"Do you know who painted this?" Mrs Edward G wanted to know.

"Well, yes I do," John said. "But there's something missing."

Edward G said, "What? What do you think is missing?"

"A little dog," said John. "It would be so nice to see a little dog running around with the stream and all. It would be nice."

Mrs Edward G turned purple, but her husband considered for a minute. "You're absolutely right," he chuckled. "I've been wondering what was missing in this thing!"[1]

Only two years separate the Cinema 16 screening of *Shadows* and the release of Cassavetes' second film as director, *Too Late Blues*. The two movies share an interest in the jazz milieu, some of the same actors, some of the same themes, yet *Too Late Blues* looks like somebody else's work.

One need only contrast the party which opens *Shadows* with the ritzy, black-tie affair a few minutes into *Too Late Blues*: the first a bohemian shindig in a cramped New York apartment, full of life, youth and vitality;

the second a West coast schmooze, a place to be seen, where money mingles with talent to everyone's mutual gratification. This marked shift up the social ladder is mirrored in the film's studio production work: fluid, flowing crane shots; 'invisible' editing; and none of the rough location sound recording which kept *Shadows* on the hop. Whatever was raw and ragged in the first film has been smoothed off and polished to bland non-effect.

It's not just that the first film was the work of amateurs and the second has a professional gloss; watching *Too Late Blues*, it's almost as if *Shadows* never happened. While there are a handful of black musicians loitering in bit parts, *Too Late Blues* is immediately more conventional in its focus on the travails of a lone white male protagonist: 'idealistic' jazz pianist John 'Ghost' Wakefield (Bobby Darin). Everything that was radical in form and content becomes hackneyed here. The dialogue is a self-conscious cocktail of jazz jive and hardboiled poetics – as if Cassavetes' term as Johnny Staccato had dulled his ear to how people really talk (in fact the screenplay was co-written with *Staccato* scribe Dick Carr). The narrative is a loose variation on the Faust theme and, despite Cassavetes' love for jazz music and musicians, the film betrays only the most superficial interest in the working life of musicians. To the extent that *Shadows* was an act of rebellion against the Hollywood system, *Too Late Blues* represents an uneasy capitulation. (One is reminded of Jonas Mekas' verdict on the second *Shadows*: "A bad commercial film.")

Unless you count the aptly-named *Big Trouble*, this is the least accomplished of the films Cassavetes made as director. Yet *Too Late Blues* is still of considerable interest as a preparatory sketch for the more profound explorations of sexual relations to come, and as a portrait of Cassavetes' own confusions about his art and his career at the time. Whatever its flaws, it's not an unambitious film – indeed Ghost is one of the clearest autobiographical figures in Cassavetes' oeuvre (returning to the story in the form of a novelisation – unpublished – Cassavetes dropped the nickname, to make him just plain John Wakefield). What's fascinating about the movie is how ambivalent this portrait of the artist turns out to be.

Back in 1958, Cassavetes had asked Miles Davis to record the soundtrack to *Shadows*, only to withdraw the invitation in protest at Davis defecting from the independent label Prestige to the corporate Columbia Records. Within a year, and facing debts in the region of $20,000, he'd signed a corporate contract himself, this time with NBC, to star as piano-playing detective *Johnny Staccato*. In return, he'd been promised an unusual degree of creative input, and even directed five episodes himself.[2] According to Ray Carney, these reveal a young director flexing his muscles, trying out a rich stylistic palette derived from everyone from Hitchcock to Welles, but all in the service of trite whodunit scenarios[3].

John and Gena still considered themselves New Yorkers, so they spent much of the time travelling back and forth between the coasts (*Staccato* was set in New York, but filmed in Hollywood; every six weeks they would fly back East to shoot the exteriors). Yet increasingly New York actors were heading West. According to Hollywood legend, Desi Arnez had persuaded the powers that be to let him shoot *I Love Lucy* on film so he could show it to his kids, and as soon as they realised they could recycle the shows, the extraordinary explosion of live television drama vanished almost as suddenly as it had erupted.

Slick, TV dinner noir, *Johnny Staccato* aired from September 1959 and scored high ratings, but its star became increasingly disgruntled. It was hard to maintain any quality threshold on a weekly series (they shot 39 segments in all), and Cassavetes was outraged when a show about a drug addict was pulled at the last minute at the insistence of the sponsors. They replaced it with a Christmas episode five weeks early. "It is virtually impossible to get approval on a script that has substance," Cassavetes complained to the press. "There is no limit on violence, but an honest story about a dope addict is rejected because 'it would be injurious to the sponsor's product': an underarm deodorant."

"I'm tired of pap," he said. "I'm tired of hearing my own crew say 'this is terrible.' What can I do? Fight, I guess."[4]

A father now, Cassavetes had responsibilities, but as soon as he'd paid off his debts from *Shadows*, he did all he could to get out of the series: "I even went to the sponsors and told them their commercials were in bad taste," he recalled. "One of the sponsors was a deodorant company, and one of the commercials showed their product beneath a Greek statue. I told them it was offensive to me as a Greek to put armpit soup under a masterpiece of Greek art. [But] it wasn't until I started criticising them publicly that they let me leave; I can be a despicable person! I then called my agent and said 'Look, I think I'm dead in this town for a while. Can you get me a job in Europe?'"[5]

The upshot of that was *Middle Of Nowhere*, in Ireland, with Seymour Cassel along for the ride and a screenplay by one Ted Allan, who would become a close collaborator towards the end of Cassavetes' life.[6] Gena stayed at home with baby Nick, and John contented himself with Seymour's company. "I'd go out in Dublin and try to get a girl," Cassel remembers. "John didn't do that because he was married – and he had more lines to learn for the next day. The pubs closed at 11 and I'd get back at 12 and we'd play baseball with two decks of cards, a game we'd made up – we kept scores, batting averages and all that. He was a sports fanatic – and an insomniac. We'd got to bed at one or two and he'd be on call for 6am."[7]

The film itself emerged a couple of years later as *The Webster Boy*. Like Cassavetes' other movie appearances from this period – *Affair In Havana* (1957), *Saddle The Wind* (1958) and *Virgin Island* (1958)[8] – it was a box-office dud. His acting career was effectively stalled. "I played a lot of football with my friends; I tried to get acting jobs; but mostly I just sat on my ass."[9]

Looking back, Cassavetes said, "I took acting enormously seriously, and didn't have all that much talent, which is probably why I switched to writing and directing. I had maybe a nice sound, but little else. No phrasings. I had nothing individual to say as an actor. Too slavish to the directness of the performance. It becomes easy to play what people accept you as. And I did that for a time until I got tired of it. I knew I could never go as far as I'd like to go as an actor, and I couldn't stand the idea of sitting around for a couple of years waiting for the phone to ring."[10]

When *Middle Of Nowhere* was done Seymour Cassel opted to stay in Europe for a while, and accompanied *Shadows* both to London, for 'The Beat, Square and Cool Festival,' and to the Venice Film Festival, where it won the critics' award. Under strict instructions from John to guard the prize with his life, Cassel even took it to bed with him.

To Cassavetes' delight, British Lion released the film in London, and John came over to stand in the rain and marvel with Seymour at the queues outside the Academy Cinema on Oxford Street. Seeing one customer fumbling in his pockets to come up with the ticket price, Cassavetes fished out his own wallet and declared, "How much do you need?"[11]

Its UK success swung *Shadows* into the black, and British Lion were sufficiently encouraged to mount a US release (Cassavetes claimed it was the first time a British company distributed an American film in the States). This belated recognition had two effects: it inspired the cameraman Erich Kollmar (who had fallen out with John) to sue Cassavetes for a share of the profits – they settled – and it brought the young film-maker to the attention of Paramount executive Marty Rackin. Out of the blue, he called Cassavetes and told him he'd like to see his next script.

In an interview published in the British magazine *Films And Filming* in February 1961 Cassavetes talked vaguely about a picture he was going to do for Paramount in New York: "although we have a story outline, we'll probably end up improvising the whole thing. Basically it's a story about people who get old before their time, who when they reach the age of 30 are old, and girls who reach the age of 19 or 20 and feel old and they go into the future disillusioned." (Cassavetes was 31 at the time.) He was going to use unknowns, he said. "I don't ever want to get into the big multi-million pictures where everybody is on your neck." He also mentioned "another film we're going to do. The story of a girl's suicide, caused by society's inability to educate in terms of love. Nobody in this world seems to be able to love beyond a certain point."[12]

In fact these tentative projects coalesced, as Cassavetes hammered out a script entitled *Dreams For Sale* with Dick Carr at a motel across from the pier in Santa Monica. The first draft took just a long weekend. Rackin read it straight away, and before he knew it Cassavetes had broken his NBC/Universal contract to become a producer-director on the Paramount lot.

Despite his stated preference for unknowns, Cassavetes wanted Montgomery Clift to play Ghost Wakefield, a favourite ever since *A Place In The Sun*, with Gena Rowlands as the aspiring and despairing singer he falls in love with, Jess Polanski. Rackin balked – Clift was considered trouble, he was drinking heavily and addicted to pills – and brought in teen singing idol Bobby Darin instead, then riding the wave of his hits 'Splish Splash,' 'Dream Lover' and 'Mack The Knife.' Darin had studied acting under Burt Lane at the Variety Arts Studio, and can even be glimpsed in the background of the rehearsal sequence in *Shadows*, although he wasn't someone Cassavetes knew well. Stella Stevens, at that point a TV actress, was imposed as Jess.

The rest of the casting passed without controversy, based on Cassavetes' usual combination of intuition and fraternal feeling. Ghost's band comprised Cliff Carnell (as Charlie, on saxophone) and Seymour Cassel (as Red, on bass), both from *Shadows*, Dan Stafford (as Shelley, the drummer) was an old friend from the 306 Special Services Company; Richard Chambers (Pete, on trumpet) was another pal. There was a cameo for Rupert Crosse, and Val Avery was cast as the wealthy record backer, Frielobe; Avery had a bit-part in *Edge Of The City* and was to become a long-term fixture in Cassavetes' films. The cameraman, Lionel Linden, was another *Johnny Staccato* alumnus. "Linden was a great cameraman but a sarcastic son of a bitch," Cassel recalls. "He had been doing movies for 40 years or whatever. 'Whaddaya wanna do, dig a hole in the bottom of the stage and put the camera in it?' Things like that. Hollywood is very cliquey, and back then it was even more so because the studios supplied all the work."

Rackin didn't like the idea of shooting in New York. Instead, he wanted it relocated to LA and the studio backlot, where he could keep a closer eye on a budget in the region of $375,000. At the time, Cassavetes put a positive spin on it: "I have been given the control I need over casting," he said, shortly before filming began in late March. "I chose to shoot in a major studio because of the facilities and the technical help. If I had the opportunity to make what amounts to an art film in a major studio, it would be foolish of me not to. If I am prepared to quit rather than give in to major changes, then I am safe."[13] Colin Young interviewed the director again at the editing stage, and he still sounded upbeat, even contemplating a five-picture deal with Paramount.

Ten years later, in his 1971 *Playboy* interview with Lawrence Linderman, Cassavetes had a very different perspective: *"Too Late Blues* never had a chance," he said. "I should have made the film my own way – in New York instead of California and not on an impossibly tight schedule. To do the film right, I needed six months, and I agreed to make it in 30 days – working with people who didn't like me, didn't trust me and didn't care about the film. I was so naive. I would walk into the office to see Rackin and he'd say, 'John, take off your director's hat, I want to talk to you as a producer.' I would actually put my hand on my head, looking for a hat – a perfect moron. I didn't even know which departments to go to for what and how to get things done. Not only that, but I did a disgusting thing: halfway through, I knew I wasn't making a good movie, so I did the best I could without really exerting myself. And all because I didn't know how to fight. I didn't even know you were supposed to fight. You're supposed to be a man. If you want to shoot a film in New York because that's the best place to shoot it, then you fight for that, and if you lose, you don't make the movie. You're supposed to pick your own cast and how much you want to pay them, or else you quit. I'd learned all that by the end of *Too Late Blues*."

What's curious is how this process of artistic compromise, failure and dis-illusionment reflects the key themes of *Too Late Blues*. Our reactions to them may be complicated, in part because Cassavetes was already groping for something we might call 'indeterminist story-telling' ("I want people to decide for themselves what's going on," he told Colin Young in the summer of 1961), and in part because the young director and his inexperienced lead actor aren't quite sure of themselves, but Ghost Wakefield and his group start the film as impeccable signifiers of artistic purity. They play, quite literally, 'for the birds,' Sunday afternoons at the park, with the odd charity gig thrown in. It's music for music's sake, unsullied by commercial constraints, or even by an audience – very much how Cassavetes would characterise his own endeavours in later years ("We're just exploring ideas which interest us," he would say), and a plausible parallel for the making of *Shadows*.

Into this jazz Eden Cassavetes introduces an Eve – struggling singer Jess Polanski – and then a serpent, in the form of talent agent Benny Flowers (Everett Chambers). Flowers is an ex-sideman, unable to play since an accident – a fallen angel – and Chambers plays him with a permanent grimace and an insidious sneer. Jess has already been corrupted by Benny's acquaintance; when we first see her, in the party scene, she's already numb, practically comatose. Benny's vicious criticism of her singing goes some way to explain why. It's only in Ghost's company that she starts to come

40

back to life – a long, grating drinking scene in a neighbourhood bar – but when she does, she expresses herself in the only way she knows she'll get a response: she drags him into her apartment, kisses him, and takes him into her bedroom.

Forward by the standards of the time, this seduction scene is the first of a handful of occasions when *Too Late Blues* transcends its rather thin development to achieve some of the emotional intensity which was to become this film-maker's signature. Tellingly, all of these dramatic high points feature Jess, a simpler and more poignant figure than the conflicted and ambiguous Ghost. She is the active party here, and he is quite submissive. "Your lips are soft," she tells him. Yet there's insecurity behind her bold behaviour. She lingers at the bathroom door and assures him she won't be long, and anyway, it will be worth the wait. And Ghost just sits there. He doesn't fix himself another drink, or check out the apartment, or take off his jacket. He sits there, hunched over on the bed in the semi-darkness, his back to camera in medium shot; he doesn't move, and Cassavetes leaves him there for nearly 20 seconds. Then, when Jess returns, he pushes her away. That the gesture has been premeditated only makes it more shocking. "Whoever told you that's what you had to do to reach somebody?" he demands.

She's angry too: "Are you kidding? Just where do I stand without my body, huh? Tell me that! I'm the girl with no mind, or haven't you heard? What good is talking to somebody when nobody listens? What good is falling for someone when they don't come back?"

It is to Stella Stevens' credit that she more than holds her own in this dispute (and 40 years on, it's easy to share Jessie's dismay), but Ghost is granted the moral and spiritual high ground. In effect, he says he wants more from her than sex. What does she want? he asks. She's his "Princess," and he'll give her the moon, if she wants it. "I don't believe in fairy tales," she tells him. All the same, she shows up at the park the next afternoon to hear him play. "I don't know if I can love you, because I don't know what love is," she warns.

Jess's love, then, is the prize; an index of spiritual worth. Ghost would redeem her, and Benny Flowers is pulling her back down. Returning from the park, Ghost and Jess find him waiting, perfectly at home in her bedroom. He has come through with a recording session for Ghost's band (which now includes Jess, Ghost informs him, staking his claim).

The record deal had been mooted at the party the night before, in implicitly moral terms: "Cut a couple of records, make a little loot – what's wrong with that?" Benny had asked.

Ghost's response chimes with Cassavetes' attitude to Paramount: "Nothing's wrong with that, provided you let us play what we want to play."

At the recording session, Ghost takes his best song and gives it to Jess to sing, to the initial consternation of Frielobe, who's paying the bills and isn't sure about her 'non-singing singing' style. Again, their confrontation – with Benny an unreliable middleman – articulates Cassavetes' own very real concern about 'selling out':

Ghost (to Benny): You told me this man wouldn't tell me how to play my music. He'd just listen to it.

Benny (to Frielobe): He's an idealist

Frielobe (to Ghost): But that's the way of the world. That's the way it goes. I hate commercialism too. Don't blame the poor sound engineer. Blame the world. Blame the people.

Having raised the theme, Cassavetes backs away from it. On this occasion at least, the forces of commercialism are philistine, but not fatal. Frielobe changes his mind and decides the tune ('Untitled Blues') may have something after all. He'll let Ghost record it his way.

Ghost's success – and Jess's inclusion in it – makes Benny pathologically jealous. The group repair to their favourite haunt, Nick the Greek's, to celebrate, where they are joined by the agent. This long, 17 and a half minute scene is placed at the centre of the film. In its patient and concentrated observation of emotional dynamics and social flux, its tension between repression and freedom, its unruly escalation from high spirits to violence, male camaraderie to confrontation, this is the clearest harbinger of 'Cassavetian' cinema yet, albeit in a relatively crude form. Even in its incidentals, this scene more than any other in *Too Late Blues* speaks of and for Cassavetes. There's the lusty appetite for drink (already witnessed in Ghost's vodka-whisky-what-have-you cocktail speciality). There's music and dance. And there's the insistence that America is a nation of immigrants – not only, obviously, in Nick's Greek heritage (he has the flag on his wall, alongside the Stars and Stripes), but also in his greeting for Jess Polanski ("That's great, your name is long just like mine"), and even in the couple of Irish-Americans playing pool by the door. Finally there is 'Nick': a name which will crop up frequently in Cassavetes' films. It is John's father's name, his brother's name, and his son's name.

In its way, this is a love scene. The focus is on Jess (if Gena Rowlands had played her, perhaps she wouldn't have merged so easily into the background). 'Untitled Blues' has been her triumph, and this evening marks her acceptance in the group. She dances with everyone, even Benny – who makes it clear how much he hates to have lost her: "I thought we were two unhappy people who had found each other," he whines. "I love you, Jess." Then reverting to type: "You hurt my feelings, you got an enemy for life."

Iago-like, he proceeds to drip-feed the paranoia and hatred of the Irish pool players, already disconcerted by the promiscuous dancing of the 'nutty looking girl.' He quietly confirms their preconceptions about the jazz-men's propensity for 'drugs, drink, and mixing up the races.'

But the inevitable bar-room brawl doesn't unfold in the way we might expect. Confronted by the six-foot Tommy (Vince Edwards), Ghost pushes Jess away, an instinctive reaction with an edge of panic to it, almost as if he hoped Tommy would go after her. He's practically paralysed – whether with fear or a more fundamental inertia isn't entirely clear. It's Jess who attacks ("A girl's got more guts," the Irishman offers). When Tommy makes his move, Ghost offers no resistance, no defence. He's thrown to the floor, left lying there at Jess's feet. While Charlie (another six-footer) saves the day, Ghost's humiliation is palpable. Despite his embarrassed assurances that he's unhurt, his friends pick him up and place him on a chair – he plays the remainder of the scene cut down to size, as it were, waist high to the rest of them. (It's an echo, too, of the bedroom scene.) At this moment of shame and emasculation, it's Jess who comes forward once more, takes his face in her hands, and tells him that she loves him.

This is what the scene – and arguably the film, since everything that follows feels like a postscript – has been building to: Jess's compassionate and heartfelt declaration of love, and Ghost's bitter rejection of it. "Would you leave me alone, I don't need no mother," he says, slapping away her embrace. "Take a walk!" It's a vicious betrayal, a victory for the forces of repression. Jess recoils as if she's been stung. It's not Ghost's lack of machismo which has hurt her, it's his own debilitating sense of shame.

On the face of it a dramatic *volte face*, in which the artist-idealist suddenly turns physical and moral coward, the scene brings to the surface Cassavetes' complex and contradictory feelings about Ghost, unfortunately without resolving them. If his failure to receive Jess's love here is a betrayal, does that mean his refusal to make love that first night was also an indication of weakness? And is Ghost's artistic integrity, his refusal to compromise and engage with "the world. the people," also a form of cowardice?

The film makes an attempt to render an unmacho male protagonist whose passivity can be construed either as a virtue or a flaw. It's easy to see why Cassavetes wanted Montgomery Clift for the part, with his faint masochism, ambiguous sexuality and vulnerable nobility. Pudgy-faced and unathletic, Bobby Darin does nothing to disclaim his character's inadequacies. In the baseball sequence, for example, Cassavetes photographs him unflatteringly, first pitching wide of the plate, and then being struck out. But he also generously engineers a home run for Jess. As an actor, Darin has some good moments, but there's no shape to his performance, and he lacks Clift's charisma. No matter who played the role, it's unlikely to have dispelled the film's ambivalence about Ghost, an ambivalence which confuses psychological complexity with dramatic incoherence, all wrapped up in Cassavetes' misgivings about his film-making.

Ghost sends Charlie home with Jess. In effect, he's collaborating in his own cuckolding. "You got two legs; take her home," he says. Sadly, almost reluctantly, Charlie and Jess play out the love scene Ghost has set up for them. "I'm not anybody's girl," she convinces Charlie, echoing Lelia's protestations of independence. The next day Ghost dissolves the group and puts himself in Bobby's hands. "Make me a success," he commands.

The success Benny delivers involves playing the gigolo to a wealthy jazz lover, the 'Countess' (Marilyn Clark, dressed by Edith Head in widow's weeds), and tinkling the ivories in swank clubs: easy listening purgatory. Cassavetes only sticks around long enough to register Benny's vindictive triumph – "Here's a guy who talks loud about 'Art' and 'freedom of expression,' and I think he's a phony" – and Ghost's rebuttal: "I never sold my soul – I sold me, but never my soul. I play what I like with no compromises." Even to Cassavetes, it must have sounded hollow; maybe "especially" to Cassavetes.

The cynicism, cruelty and betrayal which dominate the last half of the film contrast all too poignantly with the giddy optimism and generosity of *Shadows*. There's only one scene in the last 30 minutes of *Too Late Blues* which musters much conviction. Significantly, it's Jess who is the emotional focal point, not Ghost. Seeking to repair some of the damage he's done, Ghost finds her at Reno's bar on the verge of taking two men home. (A point of departure Cassavetes will return to at the beginning of *Faces*, while in *A Woman Under The Influence*, Mabel will also seek solace in a pick-up from a bar.) Disgusted, Ghost charges in and attacks the men, throwing them out of the bar. His physical assertiveness marks a new sense of responsibility for his (in-)actions, and it's conveyed by perhaps the single most dynamic shot in the film, a shaky handheld travelling shot as he heads down the bar, which Cassavetes manufactured by insisting that the operator ran backwards with the camera, rather than use a dolly.

Yet Ghost's hard-earned maturity comes at a cost. For all his concern for Jess, he no longer believes in fairy tales, and he won't call her "Princess" anymore. "So why did you come?" she demands. Going to the bathroom, she smashes the mirror and tries to slit her wrists on a shard. It's a shocking expression of her anguish, even if, as she admits, "I probably couldn't have done it." (Struggling with her, Ghost forces her head into the sink, eliciting what is virtually the sole spuriously ostentatious camera angle in Cassavetes' directorial career: a dramatic plug hole point of view shot which only distracts us from Stevens' convincing performance.)

44

This, then, is the "story of a girl's suicide, caused by society's inability to educate in terms of love," Cassavetes told *Films And Filming* about, but it's a story that's been compromised, pushed into the margins by Ghost's soul-searching, his belated education in adult responsibility. Perhaps that's why the director will return to it, first in *Faces*, then *A Woman Under The Influence*.

The ending is an honest but distinctly strained attempt not to cop out: Jess says she still loves him, a confession which Stella Stevens accompanies with a spasm of pain. Ghost can't reciprocate, but nor will he abandon her to her own despair ("I'm nothing," she moans). Instead, he takes her to the seedy club where his old group are playing. He apologises, but they tell him it's too late. Then Jess sings his 'Untitled Blues' from the floor, and slowly the group follows her lead. Neither optimistic nor nihilistic, the fade out is all too characteristic of this dogged but misbegotten drama.

✷　✷　✷

Released late in 1961, *Too Late Blues* was a non-event at the box-office, and was roundly criticised for its slipshod plotting and Darin's weak performance. Among the more sympathetic reviews, in *Film Quarterly*, Albert Johnson recognised "a very strange and exciting film to come from a major Hollywood studio," despite its "early perplexities,"[14] and Raymond Durgnat wrote that "the film sweeps from a casually discursive style to banging emotional scenes which combine a convincing notation of detail with almost grossly effective situations, and reach a quite exceptional intensity." Still, he admitted, it "has many errors of continuity, tone and nuance. the 'shaped' story and the discursive scenes sometimes gell dissatisfyingly."[15]

At least Paramount was sufficiently impressed to offer Cassavetes a five-picture deal, at an improved salary of $125,000 a film. "I had become a hot property – despite the fact that all I'd done in Hollywood was make one lousy picture. I subsequently learned that Rackin had to go to his stockholders and tell them I was a bright guy. He'd built me up, taken a gamble on a guy who wasn't turning out very well, and he had no real option but to go with me and hope I was smart enough to learn. And I did learn. I learned all the tricks: to get a big office and to ask for anything and everything and insist on it."[16]

According to Cassavetes, he insisted on, and was promised, artistic *carte blanche*. Although he talked about a film he wanted to do on the American Dream ("confusion has replaced patriotism; the intellect has replaced love,"[17] the only project which got so far as a completed screenplay was *The Iron Men*, another collaboration with Richard Carr, about a black air squadron during World War II. Sidney Poitier was cast to star, and

Cassavetes met with Burt Lancaster to discuss the role of a war reporter. They got on well, but Lancaster told him he was scheduled to do a film with United Artists and producer Stanley Kramer, *A Child Is Waiting*. Soon afterwards, Kramer phoned Cassavetes and asked him if he'd be interested in directing it.

The Iron Men fell through at the right time. Privately, Cassavetes was already worried that the project wasn't going to work out well – his script had already been significantly cut back at studio insistence – and he jumped at the chance to do *A Child Is Waiting*: "I wanted to work with Lancaster and both of us were convinced it would be a great film."[18]

Written by Abby Mann, who knew Cassavetes from New York, and already produced as a 'Studio One' teleplay in March 1957, *A Child Is Waiting* centred on a school for retarded children. In his autobiography, *A Mad Mad Mad Mad World*, Kramer writes, "it represented the chance to make a box office film on an important subject that everyone else was neglecting,"[19] the guiding principles throughout his career as Hollywood's self-appointed social conscience. He and Mann had recently worked together on *Judgment At Nuremberg* (1961), for which Mann had won an Oscar. Retaining Burt Lancaster and Judy Garland from that production, Kramer must have hoped lightning would strike twice. Possibly he saw a kindred spirit in Cassavetes – after all, *Shadows*, like Kramer's *The Defiant Ones* (1958) squared up to 'a problem of the races.' *Pressure Point* (1962), Kramer's most recent production, shared a similar theme, and starred Sidney Poitier, Peter Falk, and Bobby Darin, so they had friends in common too. He also seems to have regarded the project as a gamble. "I've always been frustrated in the sense that the mood and approach of young directors all over the world has far outdistanced, artistically, the American approach," he wrote in 1964. "In taking a subject that is very difficult, because it deals with retarded children, you need to make a really wonderful piece of work in order to achieve any kind of audience. so I thought I would put all my eggs in one basket and let John Cassavetes (who represented a younger school of directors) express himself in a more modern vein."[20]

The film began peacefully enough. Cassavetes went out with Mann and spent more than three months researching the subject, visiting families with retarded kids, and spending time at the Pacific State Hospital for the Retarded in Pomona, where much of the filming took place. "Getting to know those children was a moving and beautiful experience," he said.

Lancaster also threw himself into the movie. His eldest son, James, had social problems, and spent time at a private school for emotionally disturbed children, so the subject matter meant a lot to him. To play Dr Clark, the head of the Crawthorne State Mental Hospital, he too spent some weeks at Pomona, before shooting began on January 16, 1962. Judy Garland had also signed to the project before Cassavetes, and she proved more problematic. At 39, she was fighting a losing battle with drink and pills, and she was frequently late (or absent) during the shoot, which stretched from ten weeks to 14 as a result.

Garland brought with her a favourite cinematographer, Joseph La Shelle. On the first set-up of the first day of shooting, Cassavetes told La Shelle what he wanted, then returned to his office until the shot was lit. When he got back to the set, he found that La Shelle had taken it upon himself to completely change everything around. Cassavetes went ahead with the scene and didn't say a word about it until they wrapped for the day. Then he turned to La Shelle, told him he was fired, and walked away. A pleading phone call from Garland earned the DP a reprieve, but thereafter the director's instructions were followed to the letter.

If the crew were dubious about this young interloper from New York, the actors appreciated the attention he lavished on them. Cassavetes was able to cast Gena Rowlands for the first time, as the apparently neglectful mother of one of the children, Reuben Widdicombe (Bruce Ritchey). Also among the cast were John Marley, as a state inspector; Mario Gallo, who had a tiny part as a sound engineer in *Too Late Blues*, as the state medical advisor; and Paul Stewart as Goodman, Dr Clark's right hand man. All of them would reappear in future Cassavetes films.

But the kids make the strongest impression. Ritchey was the only 'professional' actor in this 9–12 age range. Two dozen of the cast came straight from the Pacific State Hospital, and Cassavetes photographs them with tender delight. He hired Seymour Cassel to work and play with them and coach them in their lines. "They were incredible," he says. "I loved them. Ramona, a little Mongloid girl who was so shy she'd never look at you until she got to know you, and then she'd start to hug you. Ah!"

Mann's screenplay was simplicity itself:

Jean Hanson (Garland) arrives at Dr Clark's school. A one-time Julliard student who wasn't quite good enough to become a professional musician, and who has lost her way in the intervening decades, Jean wants to help the children because, she says, she's looking for meaning in her life. As she gets to know the institution, she's impressed by Clark's faith in the kids, whom he treats as students, not patients – but she's also taken aback by his severity, especially towards Reuben, a healthy-looking boy who nevertheless has a mental age of five, and who refuses to participate in his lessons or even speak to the principle.

Befriending Reuben, Jean learns that his condition was diagnosed relatively late, and that after he was sent to the hospital two years ago, his parents divorced. Neither of them visits him, and Clark refuses to ask them to. Concerned that Jean's affection for Reuben might be disruptive, Clark reassigns her to another dormitory. Jean takes it upon herself to contact Reuben's mother, Sophie, and tells her Reuben is ill, to ensure that she comes. The visit backfires, though. Angry and distraught, Sophie explains her absence is because she loves Reuben too much, not too little. That night, Reuben runs away.

While the Widdicombe's discuss taking him out of the school, Jean tells Clark she's giving up. He changes her mind by showing her the fate of those retarded children who grow up loved, but not educated: they're totally dependent on others, with no vestige of self-respect. In her music class, Jean takes a firm line with Reuben. When Mr Widdicombe comes to remove his son from the school, his visit coincides with a school play, and he is moved to see Reuben taking part on stage.

The odd one out in John Cassavetes' filmography, *A Child Is Waiting* is his least personal movie, and probably a fair indication of the work he might have made if he'd been content to stay within the Hollywood system. He didn't originate the project, write it, or produce it. Nor did he edit it. During post-production Stanley Kramer lost faith in his director and recut the film. What happened next is a Hollywood legend – and there are numerous versions of the story, the violence escalating the further you get from the scene. According to Seymour Cassel, who was actually there, when he saw a preview of Kramer's version at Universal Studios, Cassavetes exploded. "We saw it and I knew John was pissed. There was Kramer and about eight of his executives, and me and John. They all applauded, but John said 'Take my name off it.' John stood up and I'm right beside him, and he says to me 'Let's go,' and I start going, but I timed it so that Kramer would catch up – I wanted to see what would happen. John grabbed him by the throat and pushed him against the wall. I knew John was just scaring him, he was too smart to ever hit him! I had to bite my lip to stop from laughing. John had these eyebrows, when he got mad he was so intense I had to laugh, it was so fearful. I remember I said to him 'John, you didn't hit him. I knew you wouldn't hit him,' and he turned to me and said, 'No, but I scared him, didn't I?' "

"There was a lot of bitterness, hostility, screaming, yelling, cursing and even some pushing. I didn't want to let him get away with what he had done to that film. I wanted him to feel the pain of my hatred for him, and I'm sure he did," Cassavetes told Lawrence Linderman.

According to the editor, Gene Fowler Jr, Cassavetes' New Wave notions didn't sit well with Kramer – or with Fowler himself: "He was trying some things, which frankly, I disagreed with, and I thought he was hurting the picture with by blunting the so-called message with technique." He cited an instance where the camera had run over a cable, causing a bump in the shot. Fowler automatically searched out an alternate take, to Cassavetes' chagrin: "My God, you damn Hollywood people," he said. "All you can think of is smoothness of camera. What we want is to get some rough edges in here."[21]

However, the real bone of contention concerned the footage of the children. "Kramer cut out the stuff with the retarded kids," Cassel says. "John found a mine there with these kids, who were so intuitive and creative, he let them have that freedom: when they were performing the Thanksgiving play and all that. One kid was having trouble remembering his lines, but it was in character for him, because he was who he was, and the kid behind him would give him the line, and finally the kid in front turned round and hit him. It was natural behaviour. That's what you want. Most actors don't have it because they're so busy acting."

Cassavetes said he "found the kids funny and human and sad. But mainly funny. I wanted to make the kids funny, to show they were human and warm – not 'cases' but kids. Stanley Kramer is a small, narrow man. He didn't understand that you can laugh at someone you love. So when he saw the film, he was incensed; I was fired and the picture was recut and it finally didn't say anything about the people we were talking about. The difference in the two versions is that Stanley's picture said retarded children belong in institutions, and the picture I made said retarded children are better in their own way than supposedly healthy adults."[22]

Burt Lancaster offered to view both cuts and arbitrate between his estranged collaborators, but by this time he was in Rome, working on Visconti's *The Leopard*.

In his autobiography, published in 1997, Kramer concedes he may have been wrong: "I've been quoted as saying [Cassavetes] didn't properly appreciate the story or do a good job managing the children we used. It seemed to me he needed more sympathy for them. I no longer feel that way. He was a fine, sensitive director who was only trying to get the best possible performances from the actors."

Even as it stands, *A Child Is Waiting* is a surprisingly effective picture. It's true that its scope is quite narrow and the score is sentimental, but for all Cassavetes' complaints, there are no shortage of close ups of the kids. The class room scenes in particular have a palpable authenticity; interacting with these children seems to strip away all Garland and Lancaster's tics and tricks – a lesson not lost on the director, who would make a habit of mixing up professional and non-professional actors in his later films. Ironically, this very element upset many contemporary reviewers. In the *New Yorker*, Brendan Gill complained, "It's almost unbearable to be made to observe the delicacy of the acting skill of Mr Lancaster and Miss Garland as they move – the charming, the successful, the gifted ones – among that host of pitiful children. Despite the purity of their motives, as actors they have no business being there; simply as moviegoers, we have no business watching them."[23]

Aside from shooting often from the children's eye-level, Cassavetes' camera style is sober and restrained. There's little vestige of what Fowler called the director's 'new wave' tendencies. The keynote is not detachment, but distance: he often keeps the adults' emotional crises at arm's length, in the same calm, authoritative manner as Matthew Clark handles them.

It is, uniquely for this director, a prescriptive film. Its educational aims are stated explicitly in the debate over funding between Clark and the state inspectors Holland and Lombardi, which allows Clark to give a speech not only on the statistical significance of the condition, but the human dignity of each and every child; it also allows him to refute the conservative agenda voiced by Dr Lombardi, who thinks that "every penny spent here should be going to our young scientists," an oblique reference to the Cold War. "You obviously believe everything you read in the papers," is Clark's stinging rebuke.

Over the course of the film, Jean learns to accept Clark's centrist, tough-love position, that "Reuben must learn the rules, so that when he does, he can at least feel part of the whole." It's not just Lombardi's callousness Clark resists, it's also the stifling compassion of Jean and Sophie Widdicombe: "Your love is not enough," he tells Jean at the end. "I'd rather fail fighting for one inch of [Reuben's] dignity than have him denatured by your love for him." And finally, "It's not what you can do for these children; it's what they can do for you," surely an intentional echo of John Kennedy's 1960 Inaugural Address, which laid the platform for civil rights reform with the famous injunction, "Ask not what your country can do for you, but what you can do for your country." (Cassavetes supported both John and Bobby Kennedy.) It's no accident that the school play in which Reuben plays an Indian at the end is to mark Thanksgiving; a rather poignant symbol of American social integration.

It's possible that Cassavetes' cut might have softened or opened up this political position, and that the problems with Garland during shooting unbalanced the argument, but the thesis is so deeply embedded in Mann's screenplay it seems unlikely that he had radical objections to it – except that, after the shooting, he seems to have developed the most radical objection of all: the film's political paternalism suddenly seemed beside the point; somehow they'd lost sight of the kids themselves. Assuredly, this would be the last Cassavetes movie where any character would be told that love is not enough.

"I discovered something about myself. I could no longer compromise," he said. "I wasn't about to make another film where we didn't say something real. *A Child Is Waiting* wasn't about a fictitious world; it's a reality for a lot of people. I had seen the great difficulty adults have in facing their children's retardation, but the kids' problems are very different. Their difficulty is finding acceptance, acceptance to do the same things normal adults do. The picture as released seemed to me a betrayal of those kids and also of their parents, who let us use their kids. At first I wasn't going to make a scene about it, because I didn't want to hurt anybody. But then I realised that truth is important; I needed to know that if I made a film about a sensitive subject like mental retardation, the people I made the film about would know I had done it to the best of my ability, with no copping out. So I really let Kramer have it. it cost me two years of work. After the noise I made, I couldn't have gotten a job with Loony Tunes.'[24]

1 Gena Rowlands seminar at the American Academy of Dramatic Arts, 1996.
2 See Appendix: Filmography as director.
3 Ray Carney, *American Dreaming*, University of California Press, Berkeley and Los Angeles, 1985.
4 Marie Torre, 'Staccato Blast Fired at Timidity of Sponsors,' December 8, 1959.
5 Linderman.
6 See Chapter 11: Love Streams.
7 Cassel: Author's interview.
8 See Appendix: Acting Out.
9 Linderman.
10 Brian Case, unpublished interview transcript, 1984.
11 Brian Case was there, and the man without sufficient funds was musician Robert Wyatt.
12 John Cassavetes, ' and the Pursuit of Happiness,' *Films And Filming*, February 1961.
13 Colin Young, 'New Wave – Or Gesture?,' *Film Quarterly*, v14, n3, Spring 1961.
14 Albert Johnson, *Film Quarterly*, Vol XV, no 2, Winter 1961–62.
15 Raymond Durgnat, *Films And Filming*, Vol 8, n3, Dec 1961.
16 Linderman.
17 Colin Young, 'West Coast Report,' *Sight And Sound*, vol 30, n3, Summer 1961.
18 Linderman.
19 Stanley Kramer, *A Mad Mad Mad Mad World*, Aurum Press, London, 1998.
20 Stanley Kramer, 'Sending Myself the Message,' *Films And Filming*, February 1964.
21 Gary Fishgall, *Against Type: The Biography Of Burt Lancaster*, Scibner, 1998.
22 Linderman.
23 Brendan Gill, *New Yorker*, February 23, 1963.
24 Linderman.

What Mr. Cassavetes Taught Me . . .
Nicolas Winding Refn

I believe the two directors responsible for creating the independent film scene in America are John Cassavetes and Paul Morrissey. In the *The Killers* by Don Siegel, Ronald Reagan, admired by Mr. Morrissey, and the future right wing President of America, shoots John Cassavetes, the most influential filmmaker in independent cinema in America. I find that rather ironic!

The first time I saw a John Cassavetes movie was when I was nineteen. At the time, I was really into Italian exploitation movies, and I had gone to see *The Killing Of A Chinese Bookie* at the Danish Cinemathèque. Prior to that, my knowledge of Mr. Cassavetes work was rather limited. I had heard about him, seen him as an actor, and when he died I paid no attention to it. All this changed when I saw *The Killing Of A Chinese Bookie*. I thought it was absolutely brilliant. The script, the directing, the cinematography, and most of all the acting were magnificent. I remember thinking: this is the kind of acting that I want in my movies. So I applied and attended the same acting school that Mr. Cassavetes had gone to, The American Academy of Dramatic Arts, since I figured that if Mr. Cassavetes had gone there I might learn something. But I hated the school, learned very little and was kicked out after a year. The only thing it taught me was: the only way to do 'it' is your own way, something Mr. Cassavetes spent his whole life practicing.

When I was 24 I had seen most of Mr. Cassavetes' films, my favourite being *Faces*, and it was time for me to make my debut as a writer/director with *Pusher*, which has a story structure and style inspired by *The Killing Of A Chinese Bookie*. My stepfather had given me one of the few books that were available about Mr. Cassavetes, and since I had no idea how to make a movie I browsed through it, hoping that it would give me leads on how to make one. However, it mostly contained very intellectual essays of Mr. Cassavetes' films and I didn't get past the first two pages. But I did learn one thing: that Mr. Cassavetes had shot his films in chronological order. It sounded like a very good idea, for this, as Mr. Cassavetes had said, and I would learn, is the only truthful way to build up a character. So I shot *Pusher* in chronological order. It gave a lot of energy and excitement as all the actors were forced to react truthfully to their surroundings, because no one could predict how the film would turn out. There was no right or wrong, just the characters' point of view and as Mr. Cassavetes had been, I became the puppet master. I also shot my second film, *Bleeder*, in chronological order and I'll continue shooting all my films that way, and that is what I learned from Mr. Cassavetes.

Nicolas Winding Refn
(Writer/director: *Pusher, Bleeder*)

4

Faces

'Faces became more than a film; it became a way of life'
John Cassavetes

John Cassavetes begins 1963 with a big new house in the Hollywood Hills, a wife and child, no work, and little expectation of getting any. It wasn't just that he'd crossed one of the most powerful and respected producers in Hollywood, he'd also crossed a protocol, or several protocols: that creative differences are kept under wraps, just between foes (he'd gone public); that ultimately the power resides with the studio and the producer (he'd refused to compromise); that your career matters more than the work (he'd committed career suicide).

His behaviour towards NBC over *Johnny Staccato* had been bad enough. Now there were suggestions that he wasn't up to scratch as a director, 'professionally' speaking; that *A Child Is Waiting* had exposed bad taste as well as bad judgement. He was unpredictable and untrustworthy. Not 'one of us.'

Fortunately Gena's career was untainted. She'd been well reviewed both for her supporting role as Sophie Widdecombe and for *Lonely Are The Brave*, a modern Western with Kirk Douglas, and she was scoring regular television work. John stayed at home with Nick, and it was in this period of enforced introspection that he taught himself how to write, he said. There were a number of screenplays and stage plays, some destined to remain incomplete; others he'd tinker with for years. *The War Horse* was one such. He attempted a novel, then abandoned it. Somewhere in this period came the first fragment of what was to become *Faces*.

Although he now considered himself a film-maker, not an actor, Cassavetes still had to make a living. Not that there was much screen-time on offer, but Don Siegel had remained a good friend since they made *Crime In The Streets* together; Cassavetes used to refer to him as his 'West Coast mother.' He came up first with a TV role, in the pilot episode of the series *Breaking Point*, (entitled 'There Are the Hip and There Are the Square'), and then, in October 1963, a movie role. Siegel had been commissioned by Lew Wasserman at Universal to produce and direct a remake of the Ernest

Hemingway story, *The Killers*; it was supposed to be the first two-hour movie to be made specifically for television. There was a catch: the schedule was tight and the screenplay only serviceable.

Siegel arrived on John's doorstep, script in hand, and offered him the title role, Johnny North.

To the director's consternation, when he handed over the script, Cassavetes refused to take it. "You afraid you might strain your hand?" he asked.

"I don't have to read the script," Cassavetes told him. "If you want me, I'll do it."

"Well," Siegel said, "If you don't read the script, I don't want you."

"It doesn't matter what I think of the script," Cassavetes explained. "I need the money. I'll memorise the lines and be a good boy."

Siegel left the script with him, feeling oddly slighted, perhaps unaware of just how badly his friend – 'a huge pain in the neck' – needed this job.[1]

Johnny North retained only the kernel of Hemingway's story: the idea of a man, knowing he's going to be murdered, who makes no attempt to escape his killers. Siegel wanted to tell the story from the assassins' point of view, beginning with the killing, then flashing back to explain North's fatalism.

Intent on off-setting the banality of the script, he cast actors he knew would bring something to the party. Lee Marvin and Clu Gulager were the hit men, one experienced and self-contained, the other a crazy kid who relishes his work. Angie Dickinson was the femme fatale, moll to Ronald Reagan's shifty crime boss, and Cassavetes was ex-racing car driver North, who is seduced into taking part in a heist as the getaway driver.

What Siegel didn't realise was that Cassavetes could barely drive. Despite hastily-scheduled lessons from one of the unit's stunt drivers, he never really understood why he'd have to shift down gears to corner; he'd drive nonchalantly, elbow flapping in the wind, "looking like an eastside punk," in Siegel's words. Cassavetes particularly resented being rocked back and forth in the Ford Cobra for the many back-projected process shots: film acting at its most mechanical.

His dialogue scenes, on the other hand, have a thin-lipped urban intensity that almost over-balances the film: there's a craving in Cassavetes' performance that the script's generic million dollar pay-day could scarcely satisfy. It's as if he knew he was out of place in this set-up.

"You're East, West, South. and my North." Dickinson tells him, cosying down in her plush apartment.

"That's the trouble: I'm Johnny North in a pad like this," he replies bitterly. "I'm a mechanic, that's all. I've got good reflexes so they let me drive. I've got grease under my fingernails, calluses on my rump and I got a wallet that wouldn't make a down-payment."

In another scene, after Reagan slaps Dickinson in front of his crew, Cassavetes storms in and slaps him right back. Moments like these tapped into the anger that was constantly percolating in the frustrated actor-director, on screen and off. They make for an effective contrast with North's ultimate impassivity.

Deemed too brutal for NBC, Universal successfully released the film in American cinemas in 1964, with Cassavetes third billed beneath Lee Marvin and Angie Dickinson, but still with his name above the title, which by then read *Ernest Hemingway's The Killers*. Reviews were good, though most agreed the stand-out performances came from the unpredictable pairing of Marvin and Gulager, and from Ronald Reagan, playing the first out-and-out bad guy in his career.[2]

Buoyed by the collaboration, Cassavetes made Siegel a proposition: a remake of a 1934 movie called *Crime Without Passion*, a Ben Hecht thriller starring Claude Rains as a lawyer concocting the perfect murder. He'd write the screenplay, for Siegel to produce and direct. Watching the film again, Siegel understood his enthusiasm. As Cassavetes had hoped, Universal were receptive to anything the maker of *The Killers* had to offer. In fact, the studio only had one reservation: they didn't want Cassavetes to write it. He's dangerous, they told him. In 1934, so was Hecht, Siegel replied. "John is young, energetic and full of talent. He is a rebel and full of brass – just like Hecht was then." He also pointed out that Cassavetes came cheap, an argument which carried the day.

Installed in an office opposite Siegel's, Cassavetes wrote furiously. Each day, the secretary they shared typed up his pages and handed them over to Siegel. "His style was terse and taut, which was not characteristic of John," Siegel wrote in his laconic autobiography, *A Siegel Film*. "The words were warm and full of fun. My criticisms were few and carefully chosen. He could get stubborn and waste three hours on a needless discussion. As the script neared its end, I noticed that John's style was undergoing a change. [His prose became] florid, rococo, flowery."

Siegel plucked up courage and remarked on this unexpected change of tone. Cassavetes demanded examples, and when they were forthcoming, he exploded: "But I didn't write that shit – I thought you did!"

Siegel considered for a moment: "Our secretary obviously figured she was a better writer than you, John!"

Secretarial revisions revised, and now bearing the title *Champion Of The Damned*, the screenplay was delivered to Lew Wasserman, 14 May, 1964. Three days later, Siegel was summoned to Mr Wasserman's office in the Black Tower, Universal's Burbank headquarters.

"Wasserman picked up Cassavetes' script and angrily slammed it on his desk. I was shocked. I had never seen, or heard, Wasserman angry. 'How could you write a script like this?'" Wasserman demanded, his voice trembling. "John I know only too well. He's capable of anything."

Siegel was mystified.

"I hate the script," Wasserman went on. "How could you submit a script, knowing NBC hates violence?"

The outburst was absurd, inexplicable. The script contained precisely two violent incidents, one of which occurred off-screen, the other an act of suicide. Nevertheless, Wasserman – arguably the most powerful man in Hollywood at the time – ordered Siegel out of his office and straight into production of *The Hanged Man*, which featured at least eight acts of violence, by the director's count.

Trying to salvage the situation, Cassavetes and his business manager went to see Mr Wasserman the following week. They offered to buy back the script he hated so much for $30,000. Wasserman listened politely, and then he made a counter-offer. It was John's for $330,000. That was the end of *Champion Of The Damned*.

A chance encounter with television executive Steve Blauner led to an offer to work for Screen Gems, a TV packaging company. Cassavetes talked it over with Gena, and decided it was time he ventured back 'into the real world.' He rang Maurice McEndree, his producer and editor on *Shadows*, and together they formed a production company to create TV shows for Screen Gems. And so, for the first time in his life, through the summer of 1964, John worked a white collar job, drawing a salary, hatching half-a-dozen shows – none of which got off the ground – and growing ever more frustrated. "After six months of that, I looked back at my accomplishments and I could find only two that I considered had been worthwhile – *Shadows* and *Edge Of The City*," he writes in the introduction to the published screenplay of *Faces*. "All the rest of my time had been spent playing games – painful and stupid, falsely satisfying and economically rewarding."[3]

He had fallen into exactly the trap he had written about in his *Film Culture* manifesto, 'What's Wrong With Hollywood.' He had compromised his integrity as an artist. "If you don't put your innermost thoughts on the screen then you are looking down on not only your audience, but the people you work with," he decided. "That's what makes so many people [in Hollywood] unhappy. They say: 'Well, I'll make a lot of money and then I'll come back and do this later on,' and the truth of the matter is, of course, they never do. These innermost thoughts become less and less a part of you and once you lose them then you don't have anything else. I found myself losing them too, and then suddenly I woke up and by accident, by sheer accident of not getting along with something, something inside, you say: 'No, I must struggle with this thing.' You fight and consequently you don't work and when you don't work you go back and reevalute your life, your relationship to the world."[4]

It was McEndree who suggested John return to a ten-page sketch he'd written a couple of years earlier, a dialogue between two men reminiscing about the good old days. Cassavetes took this fragment and in a month of 'hysteria, bitterness, mixed emotions' wrote out a 215-page unfinished treatment: "a barrage of attack on contemporary middle-class America, an expression of horror at our society in general."[5]

At first, the intention was to perform it as a play, "because I thought the only free form of expression left to the actor was the stage." Enthusiastic read-throughs with John Marley, Val Avery, Fred Draper, Seymour Cassel, his wife Elizabeth Deering, and Gena Rowlands convinced him they could do it as a movie, the way they'd done *Shadows*: independently, as a collective, beholden to no-one but themselves.[6] As the rehearsals progressed, so the material was reworked into a 175-page screenplay (still without an ending), "tailored to suit the talents of people who could turn writing into life."

The working title was *The Marriage*, although over the next three years, it went through many more: *The American Marriage*, *The Dinosaurs*, *One Fah And Eight Las* (a reference to the Christmas carol 'Deck The Halls With Boughs Of Holly'); and, late in post-production, *Faces*.

Cassavetes went to see Al Ruban in New York. In the years since *Shadows*, Ruban had gone into the exploitation film business, initially with Mo McEndree, then on his own. "In those days if you showed a woman's breasts, that was daring," he says. "It was probably the best thing that could have happened to me, because you wound up having to do everything, figuring out how to do a film on practically no budget." He invited Cassavetes to see his latest production: *Sexploiters*. "I showed him on the moviola. There was a scandal going on about housewives moonlighting as hookers so I took four instances, as bizarre as I could make them, and wove a story around them. Oh God how he laughed! John had a wonderful way of laughing: he was laughing and trying to hold it in at the same time; he would hold his nose and sort of snicker, and his face would turn beet red."[7]

Cassavetes told him he had enough money from a couple of TV roles and the Screen Gems job to start the movie, if not to finish it. Would Al like to join them? He didn't think twice. When he got back to LA Cassavetes wired him $8,000 to buy some second hand film equipment – a 16mm Arriflex camera, some lenses and lights, a Perfectone sound recorder – Ruban rented a U-haul trailer, closed up his apartment, dropped off his wife and kids to stay with the McEndree family in Kansas, and drove on to California.

Meanwhile, Cassavetes and McEndree put together their cast, and a crew of about a dozen actors and ex-actors, including George Sims, Charlie Akins and Carolyn Fleming. Originally Gena Rowlands was due to play the part of the wife, Maria Forst, but when she discovered she was pregnant, she switched to the less physically demanding role of Jeannie Rapp. To take her place in rehearsals, Cassavetes asked Lynn Carlin, a secretary who worked for another young, frustrated film-maker in the adjacent office at Screen Gems, Robert Altman. Carlin had done a little amateur theatrics, but nothing professional – on the other hand, she knew the material intimately: she had typed out the script. She came in and read, and helped wherever she could as Cassavetes and McEndree put the film together – to the irritation of Robert Altman, who eventually fired her. When she was cast as Maria, Altman couldn't believe it. "You're crazy," he told Cassavetes. "She's not even any good as a secretary!" It was years before Cassavetes spoke to him again.[8]

Nobody was paid a cent up front. "Somehow we all managed to survive. Used up our savings. Exhausted our friends. Ate spaghetti every day," Ruban says. Lynn Carlin remembers John took her out to dinner and scribbled a contract on a napkin, giving him complete control of the film, and in return, she would receive a percentage of any profits. She signed it and forgot about it – but decades later, she was still receiving regular cheques for her efforts. James Bridges, who appeared in the prologue scene, tells a similar story. He went on to direct *The China Syndrome* and *Urban Cowboy*, but while he waited in vain to see a return on these big studio productions, he was amazed to receive profits for his few hours' work on *Faces*.

"If I ask someone to do something for my gain, I shouldn't be disappointed if they don't want to do it with the same eagerness that I bring to it," Cassavetes told Joseph Gelmis in *The Film Director As Superstar*. "But if I ask somebody to do something with me for our mutual benefit absolutely straight down the line, and that is the making of a film we all care about, I think there's a good chance we will do something worthwhile."[9]

Rehearsals lasted three weeks, and Ruban used this time to teach his crew how to use the equipment, and to pick up some extra lights. John bought an Eclair camera from Universal, and because it was more suitable than the Arriflex for handheld work, this became their mainstay for 95 percent of the filming. The principal locations were Cassavetes' home (for the Forst residence), and Gena's mother's house (for Jeannie's apartment), with additional scenes at the Loser's Club.

Although the film takes place over the course of only 12 hours, the shoot lasted six months, from 2 January 1965 to July. To enable the participants to keep up day jobs, almost all of the filming was done during the evening. If John Marley found paid work in the theatre, then the shoot was post-poned until he could resume. Generally, the crew would convene at Cas-savetes' house around 5pm. They'd have dinner – spaghetti probably – and the actors would arrive about 6pm. They'd rehearse for an hour and a half or so, first on their own, then with the crew, so the cameraman could get the feel of the scene. Cassavetes never went in with a prearranged notion of camera angles or cuts. These would evolve organically in rehearsal. The actors were never given any marks to hit, and because most of the takes were sustained for minutes on end, with the camera following the actors' lead, hapless crew members were frequently diving under tables or taking cover behind doors to stay out of shot. Sometimes he'd start shooting mid-rehearsal; usually he wouldn't cut until they ran out of film (a 400' reel of 16mm lasted ten minutes).[10]

"We have to move beyond the current obsession with technique or camera angles," Cassavetes said. "How you shoot a film is a diversion. It has nothing to do with life what these people are thinking, what they're feeling, that's the drama of the piece."[11]

Originally, Cassavetes had the notion of rotating his camera crew in the same way as they had on *Shadows*, but after a couple of days Al Ruban put his foot down. "I said I'm going home, this is driving me crazy, I can't work like this. Everyone is different, you have no-one to talk to about the camera because you have to talk to everyone, and there's too much competition as to who is going to shoot. You have to have one operator. I told him, I'll be a second operator and do the lighting, but you can't keep switching around." Cassavetes relented, and Ruban became the permanent director of photography, with George Sims as the operator. Al, John, Seymour, and the rest would take turns if a second camera was in use.

To what extent was Cassavetes concerned with the nuances of lighting and camera placement? "At first I'd ask him to explain what he wanted," Ruban says. "The worst thing I ever went through! He'd always talk around a subject. Looking back after many years, he never really wanted to reveal anything. You'd be so confused you wouldn't even know what question you'd asked. So eventually I'd say, 'Okay, just give me the emotional quality of the scene, I'll light according to that, and if you don't like, we'll change it.' That's the way we worked the rest of the time, because I couldn't take all the justifications and all that. But John was always con-cerned with the camera. I would never have thought of coming in so close with the close-ups for such an extended period: he wanted to get inside the people, get them to reveal themselves. It's just that performance was every-thing with John. If he liked a take he'd use it, no matter if the focus was soft or not. And the actors loved him for that, because the performance was everything."

Shooting would last five or six hours, or until the actors' energy dropped. If a scene wasn't living up to its potential, Cassavetes would stop and return to rehearsals, rewriting where necessary. Even so, the actors weren't ad-libbing. They were expected to know their lines by heart, for scenes which might run for 20 minutes or more. "The emotion was improvisation. The lines were written," as the director put it.[12]

Lynn Carlin had trouble finding tears for the scene when Seymour revives her after Maria has tried to kill herself. "I'm slapping her on the side of the neck so it doesn't hurt her," Cassel recalls. "John takes me aside and says 'See you've got to hit her, really hit her.' And he jumped up on top of her and he smacked her! Shocked the shit out of her! And it worked. There are emotional blocks that actors can't get through sometimes, but I'm sure after that all Lynn had to do was remember that. She was totally honest in her emotions."

Carlin appreciated the quality of the work. For some of the older actors, Cassavetes' demanding methods took more adjustment. John Marley – the most successful of the cast – wasn't used to such irregular hours, the multiple takes and exhaustive rehearsals. Dorothy Gulliver, who plays Florence, was a silent screen actress who'd appeared in some of John Wayne's earliest Westerns. Cassavetes worked patiently with her in particular. There were no minor characters on this movie. "I believe that if somebody has a large part they work harder. And if their part is complete, they'll express a complete person," Cassavetes told Gelmis.

One evening, getting on for 11pm, Val Avery got fed up too – he'd had a call from his pal Ben Gazzara, who was drinking in a Hollywood bar and wanted company. Avery said he'd had enough, they'd been working for four hours, he was going. Cassavetes wouldn't hear of it: splitting half way through a scene, what was he thinking? As they had it out, Seymour Cassel – who was helping out with the crew – slipped out the front with a knife, went up to Avery's car, and slashed two of his tyres. Then he slipped back in, and whispered to John that everything would be okay, Val wasn't going anywhere. Avery was furious with his director, even if he couldn't figure out how he'd managed to sabotage his car without leaving the room – but they finished the scene.

Despite these occasional ructions, it was a joyous time. "The very best time of my life," Cassavetes would tell Lawrence Linderman in 1971. Everyone was pulling together; they all believed in what they were doing. To a great extent, the film was shot sequentially, so there was a real feeling of evolution. And the actors couldn't have had a more responsive director than John. He never dictated their actions beforehand, but watched them from behind the camera, silently laughing, or crying, his hand down his throat; or acting out the dialogue along with his cast. Sometimes – especially when he used the camera handheld – he couldn't contain himself, and voiced encouragement as if he were directing a silent movie. During the last sequence, 'the morning after,' he became so excited by John Marley's performance he kept saying "Don't look at Lynn, don't look at her."

Marley turned around and yelled "For Chrissake, John, you blew the whole goddam thing; I can't think when you're talking constantly in a stream." He'd hadn't even realised he'd been doing it. He was willing to try anything, listen to anyone's opinion, and try it again.

Money was tight, but that only strengthened their bond. Half-a-dozen of the team lived chez Cassavetes for months (Gena fled to stay with her mother to get some sleep). John and Gena both put all their savings into film stock. Lynn Carlin remembers how every morning the milkman would deliver bread, eggs, cheese and milk for everyone: "John fell so many hundreds of dollars behind in his payments, he took him aside and said, 'Okay, so how would you like to invest in the movies?' And he gave him a percentage!"[13]

After they'd wrap for the day, usually at one or two in the morning, Cassavetes liked nothing better than to sit in his old black Lincoln in the driveway, have a few beers with one of the team, and talk until the sun came up.

As Cassavetes saw it, *Faces* "became more than a film; it became a way of life, a film against the authorities and the powers that prevent people from expressing themselves the way they want to."[14]

Over the course of six months, they shot in the region of 150 hours of film. Even for such a long script (about 320 pages when all was said and done), that suggests an extraordinarily high shooting ratio. Much of the first month's work was discarded – it took that time for Cassavetes and his actors to reach the pitch he was after. Even then, almost every shot would go through at least half-a-dozen takes, often twice that many. Cassavetes liked to quote one of his favourite directors, Frank Capra, who always said that once you're making a movie, film stock is the cheapest commodity you've got.

The footage was processed on a daily basis during the shoot, however they held off transferring the sound to save money. It wasn't until they'd got the movie in the can that they discovered their second-hand Perfectone was running at the wrong speed, throwing off the synchronisation. The labs they consulted couldn't help, and suggested writing off the film as an experiment. Instead, Al Ruban, Cassavetes and McEndree spent four months going through the soundtrack, cutting it up word by word, until each syllable was in synch with the images – and all traces of Cassavetes' unconscious injunctions had been excised.

That accomplished, Ruban had to return to New York for a year to earn some money. Cassavetes elected to train up four novice editors to work – separately – under his supervision on the Moviola installed in his garage. According to Ruban, when he saw the result a year later, the movie was a mess: "It was horrible. Nothing like what I'd remembered. I looked at John and said 'What have you done?' He said, 'Well Mo did reel one, and Jennifer did two, and so on.' I said but where's this and this and this. So we went back to the dailies and started over."

With the birth of Alexandra – Xan – in the summer of 1965, and more than $50,000 out of pocket on *Faces* – the total cost of which would come to $225,000 – Cassavetes had resumed his acting career as best he could. He did three TV dramas for the *Bob Hope Chrysler Hour*. According to Seymour Cassel, they paid $10,000 a show (top dollar then), but Cassavetes wangled $100,000 for the three by agreeing that one of them would be a pilot – you were paid more for pilot shows. Crucially, he got to pick which shows he'd do. "He chose three plays there was no way anyone would want to do as a series," Cassel says. "John was a businessman too: he knew you had to screw the other guy before he screwed you, and the last thing in the world he wanted was to do another TV series." He was top-billed in the lurid biker exploitation pic *Devil's Angels*, and in a couple of Italian gangster movies, and Robert Aldrich cast him in his macho war movie, *The Dirty Dozen*.[15]

Al Ruban moved in with John and Gena, Nick and Xan. Every morning, he and John would discuss the day's work, then Cassavetes would go off to make *Rosemary's Baby* with Roman Polanski, and Ruban would cut *Faces*. In the evening, they would review the edit together.

Even then, it was another eight months before the work was finished. It was this period that cemented their friendship. Ruban remembers one evening in particular, some months into the work, as a make-or-break moment. He'd been editing on 16mm – like "spaghetti," he said – and there was a mountain of film all over the editing room. He was missing his family back East, and Lady Rowlands, Gena's mother, was coming over for dinner, along with the old dog she took everywhere with her – a French poodle which Al hated vehemently. After they finished their meal, they found the dog in the editing room, in a pool of diarrhoea, with excrement all over the film. It was the last straw for Ruban: "I said 'That's it! I can't take it anymore! I'm getting my suitcase and I'm going home right now!'

John said, "No, Al, you can't go. I'll clean it all up, everything will be okay." And he did: he cleaned it all up with his bare hands. I still wasn't convinced, but I was wavering now. He picked up the soiled film, and he ran into the bathroom, and I could hear the tap running – and then he began to laugh. He came out and held the film under my nose to show me

– somehow the excrement had erased the emulsion from the film. He said, 'Look, even the damn dog's a critic!' I had to laugh too – I loved that. I thought 'How can I leave, here's a guy who'll truly go through shit for his film'."

The rough cut clocked in at six hours. They cut it back to 3 hours 40 minutes, and Cassavetes held his first private screening, a women-only affair. Seymour Cassel remembers his wife Betty coming back from it in a sombre mood: "I said 'What's wrong? Isn't it any good?'

'Yes, yes, it's magnificent. But it's so honest and real, it's overwhelming'."

He had to wait for the second, men-only screening, to see for himself that it was true.

In order to see how the film played outside Hollywood, they took it to Montreal and Toronto, and arranged free midnight screenings. 'John bombarded them, he did every TV and radio show – and he was a great salesman,' Ruban says. "We hyped the hell out of it and invited everyone in the world." In Toronto, they ran it with people sitting in the aisles and standing at the back, and when that screening finished at 3.40am, they had to persuade the projectionist to stay and show it again for the people who hadn't got into the theatre. Both screenings met with standing ovations.

Still, Cassavetes felt it was too long. They cut it down again, this time to 1 hour 50, and screened that version at the Music Hall in Beverly Hills, March 1968. According to Ruban, "everyone claimed they liked it, but it wasn't the same kind of response we had gotten before. The difference was that the people in the audience were satisfied to walk out and keep right on going, while at the showings of the previous version they'd felt compelled to stay around and talk about the film. We knew we had overcut, so once again we went back to editing."[16]

What they hit upon, in this long, slow process, was the discovery that trimming and tightening sequences tended to weaken the film's impact. Better, they found, to delete whole episodes, and respect the integrity of the remaining scenes. Hence, the opening 40 minutes in the Losers Club, (described in the published screenplay), now lasts a mere 40 seconds, as Richard, Freddie and Jeannie leave the club. Gone too was a prolonged sequence in which Maria is consoled by her friends after Richard has demanded a divorce. "I loved that scene and the interference of those women," Cassavetes said. "But we found that the whole half-hour scene wasn't really necessary. It just wasn't necessary to explain why all of a sudden we find this woman going out with a bunch of broads we've never seen before."[17]

The final version runs two hours nine minutes – and there's no suggestion that Cassavetes was unhappy with this running time. In fact, Lynn Carlin remembers accompanying him to its London premiere at the NFT.

They were supposed to go and meet Gena and some guests for dinner, but an hour into the movie John still couldn't tear himself away from the screen. "This is the best movie I've seen in my life," he whispered to her. "I can't leave before the end!"

* * *

A prologue in a commercial screening room establishes Richard Forst (John Marley) as a powerful businessman. Then – after a single title credit – we're plunged into a bar scene, just as Richard and his colleague Freddie (Fred Draper) are leaving with Jeannie (Gena Rowlands). Their spirits are high; they have all been drinking. Freddie most of all. They go back to Jeannie's place to continue the fun. There's more drinking, singing, horseplay. The men are old friends, but also rivals here. They're reliving their bachelor days, trying to forget the wives and kids they have at home. Jeannie, it becomes obvious, is a pick-up from the bar. When Freddie senses an attraction between the others, he insults Jeannie by asking how much she charges. The mood is broken. Freddie leaves and Richard follows him.

At home, Richard's incessant fooling and Maria's gossip about Freddie's infidelities can't disguise the void between them. Tiring of all their hollow laughter, Richard announces that he wants a divorce. He gets on the phone, calls Jeannie, and asks her to meet him back at the Losers' Club.

She's entertaining two businessmen, Jackson (Gene Darfler) and Jim McCarthy (Val Avery), along with her friend Stella (Elizabeth Deering). She wants to leave, but finds she's trapped. When Richard shows up, he sees a reflection of his own boorish hijinks with Freddie. Eventually, they are alone again.

Meanwhile, in her own bid for freedom, Maria has gone out to the Whisky-a-Go-Go club with her friends Florence (Dorothy Gulliver), Louise (Joanne Moore Jordan) and Billy Mae (Darlene Conley). They meet Chet (Seymour Cassel), and return to Maria's house, where they dance and flirt, nervously. Chet is young and uninhibited. The women belong to an older generation. They're married and repressed. Chet has his pick of them, but he doesn't want to hurt anyone. Even so, one by one the women leave, embarrassed and humiliated. Drunk and desperate, the oldest, Florence, begs Chet to take her home, and he agrees, leaving Maria alone. But as she begins to tidy up for the night, Chet reappears, and takes her to bed.

The next morning, Richard wakes up beside Jeannie, and they reestablish their playful intimacy. When Chet wakes up, he discovers Maria lying on the bathroom floor, over-dosed on pills. He drags her into the shower, slaps her, pours coffee down her throat, until she wakes up. It's at this point that Richard comes home. Chet leaps out the bedroom window and runs off down the street. Richard is angry and disgusted, Maria quiet and unhappy. They sit apart on the stairs, smoking, speechless.

Cassavetes' first mature film, *Faces* represents a quantum advance on anything he'd done before, and still stands as one of his greatest accomplishments – for many, it is his masterpiece. For all his 'democratic' instincts, *Faces* is unmistakably Cassavetes' personal vision, and owes very little to what was going on in cinema either among the old guard, or – a couple of moments aside – the various European new waves.[18]

It was in exile that Cassavetes found himself at home. Excluded from Hollywood, he was emancipated from convention, the artificial ir-reality of studio production design, musical cues, soft lighting, and all the other paraphernalia that transform actors into movie stars.

There's none of that here, and *Faces* feels raw and real in comparison. With lights flaring in the lens, the handheld camera continually adjusting the frame to keep the actors in shot, grainy 16mm film stock, no external musical commentary (until the blues playing under the final shot), and numerous subliminal and not-so subliminal jump-cuts, *Faces* has the rough-hewn immediacy of 'cinema-vérité.' Cassavetes claimed to be uninterested in form, but even if it were only a by-product of the process, the free-form aesthetic of *Faces* serves a radically different purpose to the received vocabulary and grammar of Hollywood's manufactured language, so complacent in its passive adherence to the romantic myth of individual heroism sustaining the common good.

If the shooting of *Faces* became 'a way of life,' it also allowed a new way of looking at life, of relating to society on screen. While Hollywood struggled to reflect the great social turmoil of the Sixties (John Kennedy's assassination, upheavals in civil rights, women's rights, the war in Vietnam, the Youth movement and the growing popular suspicion that the common good wasn't well served by the establishment), Cassavetes caught the mood by turning the camera back on the very people who embody the status quo, the middle-aged, upper-middle class.

The Forsts and their friends have realised the American dream: they're wealthy and successful, cultured (the Forsts' home is covered in posters from galleries and theatres) and safely paired off in marriage. The trouble is, they hate their lives. *Faces* echoes with hollow laughter, with jokes, classroom schtick, singing and dancing; a shrill and desperate hysteria. Everyone's fooling, but nobody is fooled. Husbands and wives are titillated by the prospect of adultery; their own sexual attraction long-since dried up. Richard and McCarthy's oneupmanship, Richard and Freddie's banter and the hijinks, these are mating rituals and courtship displays; camouflage for their loneliness, and their inability to communicate with the opposite sex.

Like actors in a play, these people are continually performing: making an exhibition of themselves; acting or reacting. More than once, the camera seems to be giving us the view from the stalls, squatting down beside Jeannie, for example, as we watch Richard and Freddie do their vaudeville act. Yet there's nothing passive or complacent about *Faces*. Cassavetes doesn't want you to watch this film; he wants you to experience it, to feel it, to be 'in the moment.' We're continually having to catch up with the characters, because – prologue aside – we're never formally introduced. Consisting of essentially just eight dialogue scenes, the screenplay doesn't hold to a conventional narrative structure; indeed it resists supplying even backstory. We never hear about Richard or Maria's childhood, or how they met. There is no psychological key to their predicament. More like a Harold Pinter play than an American movie, *Faces* opens up a hall of mirrors in which characters are doubled, scenes echoed, and each action inspires its own reflection. When Richard returns to Jeannie's apartment, for example, he is confronted by McCarthy and Jackson, a mirror image of himself and Freddie just a few hours earlier. His adultery echoes Freddie's dalliance, and is in turn echoed by Maria's one-night stand. If we are to make sense of these equations and come to some understanding of the characters, Cassavetes insists we spend time with them – something very close to 'real time.'

Initially, it seems that understanding will be hard to come by. The disenchantment of *Too Late Blues* is as nothing to the virulence of *Faces*. Carney suggests that the character of Richard Forst was inspired by Stanley Kramer and studio executives like him (at different times, Cassavetes described both Kramer and Forst as 'narrow' men), and the pre-credit screening room sequence inevitably suggests a studio boss, even if it transpires that Forst is chairman of a finance company. There's even a passing resemblance between John Marley and Lew Wasserman (coincidentally, Marley went on to play a studio head in his most famous role, in *The Godfather*). In the end, though, Forst is a businessman, and it makes no difference whether that business trades in movies, metal, insurance (or travel and immigration – like Cassavetes' father). Marley also looks strikingly like Cassavetes himself towards the end of his life: the same emphatic dark eyebrows under thick silver hair, the same dimpled chin and grimace-like smile.

Business – 'the brutish existence,' Cassavetes calls it in the introduction to the screenplay – has boxed in and programmed these men so that they no longer relate to the world on any terms beyond power and prestige. "I'm a road man. I've been in every toilet in 50 states," McCarthy proudly announces to anyone who'll listen. When he discovers that Richard is a CEO, he becomes pally and deferential. "Did you tell Jeannie about the board meetings?" he asks. "I was about to," Forst replies, dryly. At least Richard has an inkling of the division between work and life.

Even when he's closest to self-knowledge, alone with Jeannie in her bedroom, McCarthy blithely supposes that his commercial success stands for something: "You know what it is to be a promo man in a firm like mine? I tell you, you meet more millionaires, more presidents than you'd dream could exist. That sounds like a big thing to you, huh? So what have I got after all those years? A big house and a kooky wife and a kid who wears sneakers."

It's part confession, part complaint, but not a truth McCarthy is prepared to live with. Immediately, he leaves the room, tousles up his hair, and makes a great show of zipping up his trousers in front of Jackson and Stella, just so as they know what kind of a guy he is.

Outside their natural environment, and especially in the company of women, the only recourse for these 'dinosaurs' is to drunken 'grade school theatrics,' infantile tongue-twisters and silly jokes. The Forst's marriage is an antic charade consisting of nothing but these mindless verbal digressions. "Don't get serious," Richard commands Jeannie. When they're serious, the men betray their resentment and antagonism. Freddie, McCarthy, Richard: each of them calls women whores, but they speak more out of self-loathing than misogyny. The men are the mercenaries. They're getting old and they know it. They're used up and they don't like it. "My God, Dickie, you're getting old and grey and I'm getting fat and grey," Freddie says.

"You think I'm one of those gross businessmen?" Richard asks Jeannie. "I've buried eight relatives in the last six years, I'm just a mild success in a dull industry and I want to start over again."

It's in moments like these, when they're 'off-stage,' no longer playing to the crowd, that these men momentarily transcend their own banality, and perhaps redeem the bitterness in Cassavetes' original conception. For all the flood of words in *Faces*, all the horseplay and hysteria, it's not in being seen, but in seeing for themselves that these people approach some kind of recognition. And this is important: Cassavetes was a writer with a profound distrust of words. He knew they rarely tell the truth. *Faces* is full of fleeting impulses, unspoken thoughts and repressed desires, diligently registered in literally hundreds of searching close ups, the *Faces* of the title.

The use of the close up in this film reveals Cassavetes to be a more engaged, innovative and 'interventionist' director than he might at first seem. While cinema-vérité documentary purported to record reality as it unfolded, sacrificing visual lyricism for transparent actuality, Cassavetes' vérité is a construct, a fiction restaged many times from many angles. (Most of *Faces* was shot with only one camera.) His direction isn't neutral observation; it's emotional resonance weighed and measured in feet and inches across the screen; relationships balanced in space and time. Each shot is a barometer of feeling, and the close up, especially, is an emotional notation, a nuance of character – manifold in *Faces*.

Case in point: look at the gradations of cruelty, pain and compassion as Freddie, excluded by Richard and Jeannie's dance, breaks the mood:

Medium shot: Freddie: "By the way, Jeannie, what do you charge?"

Medium shot: Jeannie and Richard dancing. She stops and look over at him.

Long shot: over Freddie's shoulder, as Jeannie comes up to embrace him.

Medium close up, reverse angle: Jeannie (hugging him) "Oh, Freddie, don't spoil it."

Close up: Freddie (pulling back): "Spoil what? Honey. I just want to know how much you charge?'"

Close up: Jeannie

Three shot: Freddie pontificating now, "I know I have to pay."

Close up: Freddie (to Richard): "Shocked aren't you. What do you think she is, a clean towel that's never been used?"

Close up: Jeannie (recoiling)

Extreme close up: Richard (wincing)

Extreme close up: Jeannie

Extreme close up: Richard

Then a three-shot as Richard moves to strike Freddie.

It's not simply that the close ups carry the emotional weight of the scene, they also tell the story. The silent exchange of sympathy and solidarity caught in that rapid double-beat of tight close ups between Richard and Jeannie anticipate his decision to spend the night with her, and not his wife. It's never stated whether he's already considered divorce, and his attraction to Jeannie isn't spelled out verbally, but we see what they see in each other; we sense what they sense. Thus, a romantic visual subtext plays out underneath all Freddie and McCarthy's coarse and prosaic bluster of money and power.

"We did 52 takes of that sequence," Al Ruban remembers. "We seemed to shoot forever, with two cameras going, an enormous amount of film being used up. Fred Draper was going crazy. He was John's best friend – a brilliant actor. He'd say 'Tell me what you want. Tell me!' And John would just say, 'Do it again. Let's try something different.' He would drive actors crazy with the repetition. He was looking for something, couldn't find it, wouldn't tell Freddie. Back in the early days in New York it was Freddie who worked all the time, then he just sort of faded into the background and became a teacher. I think John wanted more for him. It was one of the rare instances when I thought he hurt the actor – just by wanting more."

✳   ✳   ✳

For all the despair in *Faces*, all the desperation and the cruelty, it's ultimately a compassionate film, and even, arguably, an optimistic one.

Cassavetes told Ray Carney that all through the shooting he was puzzled by these characters, men like Kramer whom he knew from the other side of the desk, and who had dealt such a blow to his confidence, but, he went on to say, a strange thing happened as he made the movie: "His bitterness and rage dissipated, and he began to feel a deep compassion for these men. He started to realise things that he hadn't before. He let his film teach him, and he gradually changed his mind about these men. He still saw how awful they were, but where he had begun by despising them, he began to feel sorry for them. He saw how they tortured themselves even more than they tortured other people. He saw how unhappy they were, how emotionally needy they were, how insecure, how desperate for love and approval. In short, John eventually came not only to understand the men who had ruined his life, but almost to love them."[19]

There's no question that Cassavetes finds the wives more sympathetic than their husbands. It's true that there's just as much jockeying going on between the women for Chet as there is between McCarthy and Richard for Jeannie, but they're not on some power trip, it's their own sexual and social inhibitions which hold them back. It's a curious scene: four middle-aged women drinking heavily with a cavalier young man in a middle-class home. Richard's desertion has given them all license to flirt with sexual promiscuity – they're there as moral support for Maria, as witnesses, allies and even rivals. It could be grotesque, but Cassavetes isn't judgmental. As Carney says, Cassavetes "is attracted to moments of imbalance because they are also moments of possibility. Asymmetrical, awkward moments offer possibilities of personal exploration and expression."[20] Social gatherings distort behaviour, but also challenge it.

Singing and (especially) dancing is almost always a touchstone for truth in his films, a mark of vitality, emotional-expression and connection; Chet is a sexy, graceful dancer, utterly at ease with himself, free in a way these women can't even remember. "You're definitely an individual type," one observes, anxiously. He bestows his liberation like a blessing on each them – "You've got nothing to worry about, none of you" – and challenges them to keep up with him (Louise and Billy-Mae fail of course, beating a retreat back to the conformity and inertia of their domesticity, tails between their legs).

The drunkest woman is also the oldest and the least desirable: Florence. She's all over Chet, and again, it could be grotesque, but it isn't. Cassavetes never moralises about alcohol. Quite the opposite: if it loosens people up, then that's a victory. Chet isn't embarrassed. He's happy if he makes her feel young. She begs him to kiss her, and he obliges. She wants him to drive her home, it's the least he can do. "I get a lump in my throat every time I see her," Cassavetes remarked about Florence. "She tries everything and she doesn't care how ridiculous and pathetic it is. The point is that she tried. She fought for it, tied herself up in knots. And isn't it better to fight to realise your fantasies, to fight and lose, than to gripe and pine away."[21]

There's hope, at any rate, in the young. Jeannie may not feel young – she lets slip she's 28 – but she hasn't allowed herself to be hardened by her experiences any more than Chet has. Far from it. Her face – Gena's face – is lovely in this film: it's the first thing we see after the title, Jeannie slowly turning to look round at Richard, at the camera, at us. Perhaps this is when he falls in love? She's a listener, but an acute listener. The role is scarcely on the page, she doesn't have many lines, but Cassavetes watches her watch devotedly: rueful, patient, sympathetic, amused, concerned. Her responses are invariably generous and heartfelt. (Years later, Gena joked that it was because she was pregnant that she got so many close ups.) She plays along with men, she draws them out of their protective shells; they have fun. There's no moral backtracking the morning after, either: it's a sunny, intimate, playful scene. neither of them regrets anything, except that Richard knows how hard he's working just to be relaxed. In his notes to the script, Al Ruban reveals that this sequence was shot on a slower-speed plus-X reversal, "without any appearance of grain. At no time in the film did Gena look more beautiful."[22]

But there is cause for regret. "You get laid once and everything is solved. Get all the soldiers in Vietnam laid and all the Middle East problem is solved." Ostensibly Richard is talking to Maria, but he might as well be remonstrating with himself. His erstwhile high spirits were as evasive as his wife's suicide attempt. In Cassavetes' words, "There is no problem that is not overcome and replaced by other problems."

The ending was written and blocked after the rest of the film had been shot and long discussions with John Marley and Lynn Carlin. "What would you do?" Cassavetes asked Marley. "I'd walk out," he replied. So they tried it, but Marley found he couldn't leave.

There's a surge of anger: "You want violence?" he runs up the stairs, and pushes his wife against the wall. Because Carlin was pregnant, Marley held back, and Cassavetes stepped in and illustrated how it should be done: "He threw me violently against the wall, to show him. He'd been very gentle with me until then. John was attentive, but that didn't stop him from telling his story."[23] It's Maria – eyeliner streaking down her cheeks – who strikes out, slapping Richard: "I hate my life. I just don't love you."[24]

And then the beautifully choreographed impasse on the stairs, Forst slumped at the foot, Maria at the top. "Throw me a cigarette, please." He tosses one up, a step or two short. "A light." Again, it falls just short so she has to bend for it. He needs the lighter back. They both sit and smoke, and cough. He turns so his back is against the other wall. She does the same. Then he rises and wearily climbs up, and steps over her, and out of shot, and Charlie Smalls' blues begins to fade in on the soundtrack, "Never Felt Like This Before." She gets up and follows Richard out of shot, but no sooner has she left the frame than he's back, and he resumes his position, sitting across the stairs. She comes down, but he's blocking her way. She waits. He moves. She passes out of frame. And he gets up again, and climbs up, and leaves an empty staircase. Banal and polite, intimate and remote, it is a devastating ending.

Nevertheless, there is hope. Hope in Jeannie, and Richard's exposure to her; hope in Chet, and Maria's exposure to him. Even as she cries and vomits up her pain, Chet cheers her on: "Cry! That's it, that's life!"

Bringing her back, just babbling to hold her attention and make a connection, Chet articulates something close to the moral of the film: "Nobody cares. Nobody has the time to be vulnerable to each other. So, we just go on. I mean, right away our armour comes out like a shield and goes around us, and we become like mechanical men."

1 Don Siegel, *A Siegel Film*, Faber and Faber, 1963.
2 Seymour Cassel has an unbilled cameo as a hotel receptionist.
3 John Cassavetes, *Faces*, introduction to the screenplay, Signet, 1970.
4 John Cassavetes interviewed by David Austen, 'Masks and Faces,' *Films And Filming*, September 1968.
5 Cassavetes, *Faces* introduction.
6 In the event, the production history of *Faces* also echoed *Shadows* in unintended ways, not least in its three-year gestation.
7 Al Ruban quotes, Author's interview unless otherwise stated.
8 Ironically, Carlin also discovered she was pregnant just as filming began.
9 Joseph Gelmis, *The Film Director As Superstar*, Doubleday, New York, 1970.
10 For a detailed account of the lighting and film stocks, see Al Ruban's notes in the introduction to the published screenplay.
11 Gelmis.
12 Gelmis.
13 Headline and Cazenave.
14 André Labarthe, 'A Way Of Life: An Interview With John Cassavetes,' *Cahiers du Cinéma* (aka *Evergreen*), March 1969.
15 See Chapter 5: Husbands.
16 Al Ruban, 'Faces from My Point of View,' *Faces* published screenplay.
17 Gelmis.
18 The exceptions would be the conspicuously 'arty' pre-credit sequence in which Richard Forst sits down in a

projection room to watch an industrial film, 'the "Dolce Vita" of the commercial field,' which turns out to be the movie we're watching; and an ironic reference to the European film-maker Cassavetes would most often be compared to: Richard refuses to take Maria to an Ingmar Bergman movie, because 'I don't feel like getting depressed tonight.'

19 Ray Carney, *Moviemaker* 26/27, 1999.
20 Ray Carney, *The Films Of John Cassavetes – Pragmaticism, Modernism And The Movies.*
21 Bruce Henstall, ed, 'Dialogue on Film no4: John Cassavetes and Peter Falk,' AFI 1972.
22 Most of the film was shot on 4-x negative, a grainy, high-speed stock which doesn't require much light.
23 Headline and Cazenave.
24 The comparable speech in the original version of the script is far longer and more accusatory.

The Most Daring Film
Jeremy Kagan

I think *Husbands* is the most daring film, and in many ways has the most to say about the human condition, because it begins with loss, how do you deal with loss? But it's bigger than that: what do you do with the time that you have in the body that you are? These three men as friends struggle with that for the rest of the film. That's profound, I think, because we're all doing that. The excesses, the adventures, the connections, fulfilled and unfulfilled desires, the relationships, the frustrations. It's all in there. And daring. That famous bar scene that everybody likes to be critical of, it's an incredible sequence: you're there with all these people, and if you allow yourself to open up to them it's not a long sequence, it's painful, it's raw - which is one of the things I always have respect for with John, because I feel like he stripped away a level of the film experience and exposed a nerve for the people who were on the screen, and the people watching the screen too. For some people it's really uncomfortable – it's not why they go to the movies. *Husbands* is quintessential Cassavetes to me. I like many of the others, *Faces* and *Shadows*, certainly *Woman* for the performances, but just for resonance there's nothing can beat that one.

Jeremy Kagan
(director: *Heroes, The Big Fix, The Chosen,
The Journey Of Natty Gann*)

5

Husbands

'Til the tune ends we're dancing in the dark/And it soon ends/We're living in the wonder of why we're here/Time hurries by; we're here/Dancing in the dark'

Harry in *Husbands*

Surprisingly, for such a tough and confrontational work, *Faces* found a receptive audience. Ten years earlier, Cassavetes had written that "Hollywood isn't failing, it has failed." Now the critical consensus had caught up with him. In 1968 the Hollywood studios were all struggling. Audience attendance figures seemed to be caught in an irreversible slump (from 4060 million in 1946 to 820 million in 1971), and while the moguls were looking back – gambling on big budget musicals to recreate the success of *The Sound Of Music* – everything that was dynamic and relevant in cinema emanated from Europe: Godard and Truffaut, Bergman, Fellini, Antonioni, Richard Lester, Lindsay Anderson, Milos Forman. This list seemed endless.

And it was in Europe that *Faces* first made an impact, when it played in competition at the Venice Film Festival. Although it screened without subtitles or dubbing, the European press was quick to pick up on both its anti-Hollywood form and what they interpreted as anti-American sentiments. The film came away with five prizes, including a Volpi Cup for John Marley's performance, and those American critics who crossed the Atlantic penned enthusiastic dispatches. When the New York Film Festival asked to see the film, Cassavetes instructed Al Ruban to demand the prestigious closing night slot – and forbad him to submit a print. (Ruban went behind his back and sent it anyway: "Of course they loved it, and they selected it for closing night," he remembers.) American art-house distributor Walter Reade-Continental struck a deal with Cassavetes which paid him $250,000 outright, and a percentage of the profits on top. The filmmaker embarked on a whistle-stop publicity tour to generate interest in the picture. That wasn't hard. In the years since he embarked on *Faces*, John Cassavetes had become a movie star.

It happened very much against the odds, and almost by accident. Hoping to bankroll post-production, and still persona non grata with the majors,

Cassavetes took any job he could. In the first instance, that meant *Devil's Angels*, one of a rash of low budget biker flicks rushed into production to cash in on the notoriety of the Hell's Angels. Directed by Daniel Haller, it co-starred Mimsy Farmer, Beverly Adams, and Leo Gordon (lurking further down the cast list, we find George Sims, the camera-operator on *Faces*, and Maurice McEndree, playing 'Joel the Mole'). Cassavetes had the leading role, but even in the less than illustrious annals of the genre, this was strictly for the drive-ins.

At least *Devil's Angels* played the drive-ins. *Roma Come Chicago* (*Bandits in Rome*) was an Italian gangster movie destined solely for local consumption. On those terms, it was sufficiently successful for Cassavetes to be invited back in 1968 to make another, *Machine Gun McCain*.

It took Robert Aldrich to cast Cassavetes in a Hollywood studio release, his first since *Saddle The Wind* in 1958. Not that Cassavetes was grateful. He owed Universal money, and they decided to loan out his services to MGM for a picture called *The Dirty Dozen*, to be shot in England in the early summer of 1966. "John didn't want to do a war film," Al Ruban says. "They threatened to take him to court, so he did it. It worked out because of Aldrich: a super-super tough guy, but a straight shooter."

In later years, whenever he was asked about working with other film-makers, Cassavetes would cite Don Siegel and Aldrich as his favourites. They had much in common: both began their careers while the studios were still at their peak in the Forties (Siegel cutting montage sequences for the likes of *Casablanca*; Aldrich working as an assistant director to Jean Renoir on *The Southerner* and Abraham Polonsky on *Force Of Evil*), made their names with spare, violent B movies in the Fifties (*Invasion Of The Body Snatchers*, *Kiss Me Deadly*), and came into their own as audiences grew more cynical about America in the late Sixties (*Madigan*, *The Dirty Dozen*). They had a similar independent streak, tempered with pragmaticism, irony, and a very male nihilism. It's easy to imagine what they liked about Cassavetes: his bloody minded anti-authoritarianism, his idealism, his anger and his refusal to compromise, attributes he shared with many Aldrich and Siegel heroes.

The Dirty Dozen told the story of a group of military misfits: sociopaths in uniform who are released from military prison to mount a murderous raid on a German command post in France. Shot at the Boreham Wood studios in England between April and October 1966, this was a WWII story with a Vietnam war sensibility: unheroic and anti-Establishment. Cassavetes was cast as Victor Franco, a smalltime hood with big chip on his shoulder. Alongside him, there was Charles Bronson, Telly Savalas, Donald Sutherland, Trini Lopez, Jim Brown, George Kennedy, Robert Ryan, Ernest Borgnine, Lee Marvin as Major Reisman, and, in a smaller role, Ben Carruthers from *Shadows*.

"Aldrich liked me a lot, and it made me very free," Cassavetes said. "Working with people like Lee Marvin, Charlie Bronson, Telly Savalas, you can't fail to have fun. We were all greedy: there aren't going to be that many big parts in a picture, so you all fight for some screen time. Bob used to call us 'the animals,' more like a football coach than a maestro. He'd say 'Who wants to do this? Step forward.' Everyone would just look at each other, too afraid to move, and I'd jump forward and someone would shout some obscenity. I didn't care. I started off with three lines and ended up with a lot more."[1]

Aldrich even allowed the actors to devise their own death scenes. Cassavetes chose the least dramatic, and probably the most effective: his head simply slumps forward onto his chest. Dead.

Cassavetes clearly relished Franco's truculence and outspokenness; the character is such a malcontent, he unwittingly does the major a favour by uniting the dozen in opposition. The performance proved a linchpin of the film, and earned Cassavetes an Oscar nomination for Best Supporting Actor. It was the highest grossing film of 1967.

Did he like the picture? "Yeah, I liked it," he told Brian Case in 1984. "I didn't like the ending. I tried to ditch out of the end, actually. I copped out, pretended I was sick, wouldn't step forward anymore. Bob threatened to sue me! He said you get there and you do what I say. I just didn't care for killing 90 million Nazis stuck in a basement, throwing a bomb in and burning them up alive. I didn't care for that very much. I didn't see what it had to do with acting."

The very qualities which made Cassavetes right for *The Dirty Dozen* worked against him in Roman Polanski's horror film *Rosemary's Baby*. He played Guy, Rosemary's husband, a stooge for the devil. Ira Levin's novel painted Guy as an all-American type, which Cassavetes clearly wasn't. Warren Beatty and Robert Redford were both offered it, but Beatty felt it was too much the supporting role, and Redford was in dispute with Paramount at the time. According to some accounts, Cassavetes suggested himself for the part to producer William Castle; perhaps his attention had been caught by the name of Guy's next door neighbours and fellow Satanists: 'Castavettes.' Polanski met him in London, and they got on well enough that he persuaded Paramount's Robert Evans to overlook the actor's 'difficult' reputation.

Director and actor collaborated fruitfully during rehearsals on an empty stage on the Paramount lot, but once they got on set, in late 1967, the two men's antipathetic approach to film-making quickly became apparent. For Polanski, the actors' work was settled. His whole attention now was with the camera and the mise-en-scène. He instructed the actors precisely where to stand, how to move and how to speak, and he expected them to follow his direction to the letter. For Mia Farrow this wasn't a problem, but Cassavetes felt like he'd been tied in a straitjacket.

On set slanging matches mutated into public mudslinging. Polanski suggested that in playing a soulless careerist actor Cassavetes had been cast to type. Cassavetes countered he was only trying to survive the shoot. "Cassavetes isn't a director, he has made some films," sneered Polanski. "Anyone can take a camera and make a film like he made *Shadows*."

"Ask him why he's so obsessed with the bloody and gruesome," Cassavetes responded. "Behaving like some kid in a candy store."

Years later, Polanski still hadn't forgiven the feud. "I quickly discovered he had no gift for characterisation, could only play himself, and was lost without his beloved sneakers," he wrote in his autobiography.[2]

"Polanski is an artist, but yet you have to say that *Rosemary's Baby* is not art," Cassavetes told a group of students in Chicago in 1975. "It is a dictated design. People are used within that design to make a commercial product to sell to people. *The Dirty Dozen* in its is way more artistic, because it is compulsively going forward, trying to make something out of the moment without preordaining the outcome."[3] Despite all the bad blood, the movie was a big hit – indeed, Cassavetes is probably more famous for this film than any of his own.

In 1968, Cassavetes was nominated for an Academy Award for a second consecutive year, this time for the screenplay of *Faces*. He didn't attend the ceremony. According to Seymour Cassel, he didn't want to take any attention away from Cassel and Lynn Carlin, both nominated in supporting actor categories. It was extraordinary recognition for a movie made outside of the system, non-union and no-budget – a film that everyone had told them they would have to scrap and forget about. *Faces* turned up on the ten best lists of the *New York Times*, *New York Magazine*, the *Los Angeles Times*, *San Francisco Examiner* and *Chicago Sun Times*, among many others. "Phenomenally good," said *Newsweek*. "A picture so good one can hardly believe it. Far and away the strongest, bluntest, most important American movie of the year," said the *New York Times*. In addition, the National Society of Film Critics cited Cassavetes' screenplay and Cassel's supporting performance as the best of 1968. In New York, *Faces* played at the Little Carnegie theatre on 57th Street for 20 straight weeks – it made over $400,000 at that venue alone. Never again in his lifetime would Cassavetes receive such widespread acclaim and popular recognition.

Husbands – 'a comedy about life, death and freedom,' according to its opening title card – came out of ideas about ego and responsibility, individualism and maturity, love and marriage which can be traced at least as far back as *Too Late Blues*, and which would obsess the film-maker throughout his life. But there was a more painful spur too: John's older brother Nick had died of a heart-attack at the age of 30 in 1957 (all the more poignant that Gus, Archie and Harry's dead friend Stuart should be 'played' by Gena's brother David Rowlands in the photo-montage which opens the film). Before he fashioned the screenplay, Cassavetes found he had amassed four hundred pages of notes. It was difficult to get the screenplay right, and he rewrote it obsessively throughout 1968 (one sequence up to 200 times, he claimed). It helped somewhat that he had the three lead roles cast in his mind: he wanted to co-star alongside Ben Gazzara and Peter Falk.

Why these actors? According to Al Ruban, Cassavetes expressed an interest in working with them before he'd even settled on what his follow-up to *Faces* would be. "John wasn't sure what he wanted to do next, so we decided who we'd like to work with. I remember sitting in his kitchen talking about all these actors for hours, and it came down to agreeing that the most exciting guys were Ben Gazzara and Peter Falk." There was evidently an impulse, after the claustrophobia of *Faces*, to break new ground and work with new people. All three of them were New Yorkers, born within a few miles and a couple of years of each other, Gazzara of Sicilian heritage; Falk, Jewish. Those dynamics would prove useful for a movie about three New Yorkers mourning a close friend, 'forty-year-old kids' who impetuously take off on a binge which ends in London, 5,000 miles away. (Why London? Presumably Cassavetes' 16 weeks there with Aldrich and company had something to do with it.)

Husbands *begins with Gus (Cassavetes), Archie (Peter Falk) and Harry (Ben Gazzara) escorting a white-haired old lady to the funeral of a close friend (we deduce it's the guy we've seen horsing around with the three of them in the snapshots under the opening credits). They're middle-class, middle-aged New Yorkers, married, settled. but rocked by this premature death. They don't know how to express their emotions, or even what those emotions might be, but they're determined not to let this moment pass unmarked. So they go on a bender: a wake in Stuart's memory. Twenty four hours into their binge they conduct a beery, boorish singing competition in a downtown bar which ends with them puking their guts out.*

They stumble home at dawn. Harry wants to shave and shower and change and get to work. Archie and Gus just sit outside his house and wait. Inside, Harry's marriage falls apart. He aggressively protests his love, but gets nothing back from his wife. His friends have to come in and pull him off her. They commute back into town and go to their workplaces drunk as skunks. But it's not enough. They get back together and decide they have to take off for London immediately, for Stuart, and for Harry.

79

London: after a few hours sleep they smarten themselves up and head for the nearest casino. They successfully pick up three girls and bring them back to their hotel, where each embarks on a clumsy seduction, torn between sensitivity and cynicism. The next morning Archie and Gus decide they must return to their wives straight away before they lose themselves and fall in love. Harry will stay behind. As Gus approaches his suburban home, he sees his young son Nick, who tells him in he's in for a roasting.

Ben Gazzara remembers that the first he heard about the project was a chance encounter on a studio lot in Hollywood. In New York in the Fifties Gazzara had mixed in the same circles as John and Gena, prior to electrifying Broadway with a hat-trick of hits: *End As A Man*, *Cat On A Hot Tin Roof* and *A Hatful Of Rain*. He was on nodding terms with Cassavetes, no more than that, though he'd been invited to a special screening of *Faces*, and loved it. On this occasion in mid-1968 John honked him from his Lincoln and shouted over, "Ben, have you called Marty?" (Marty Baum was their mutual agent.) "We're going to do a picture together; call him!"

Gazzara thought little of it, but a month later Cassavetes took him out to lunch at the Hamburger Hamlet on the Hollywood Strip, and told him about his idea. It was, Gazzara remembers, the first time he and John had sat down head-to-head and had a real conversation.

Cassavetes had met Peter Falk at a ball game a few years before; what's more, Falk's wife Alice Mayo was an old classmate from Port Washington. But again, they knew the work better than each other: Falk had been Oscar nominated in 1960 for *Murder Incorporated*, which featured Seymour Cassel in a small role, and again a year later for *Pocket Full Of Miracles*, the last picture by Cassavetes' favourite director, Frank Capra. Falk was friendly with the comic writer and performer Elaine May, and he was keen to talk to Cassavetes about co-starring in a movie May had scripted, *Mikey And Nicky*.

Both were established stars at least on a par with Cassavetes, but both were also disillusioned with the business: neither of them had been able to build on the promise of his early work. Gazzara was coming off his two-year stint on a television series, *Run For Your Life*; Falk had made a string of uninspired movies (*Robin And The Seven Hoods*, *The Great Race*). They were hungry to do something they believed in. Working with the man who made *Faces* was a step in the right direction. "He was the most fervent man I ever met," Falk recalls.[4] They both agreed to work for a percentage of any future profits, and in return Cassavetes promised them a genuine collaboration.

In Prague, shooting *The Bridge At Remagen*, Ben Gazzara watched the Russian tanks roll in. The next morning he got a call from Cassavetes:

"Ben, don't get killed; I got the money! We're gonna make *Husbands*." An Italian Count, Bino de Cirogna, had agreed to invest $1 million.

The Bridge At Remagen relocated to Rome, where Cassavetes was shooting *Machine Gun McCain*[5] with Peter Falk and Gena Rowlands, and they got down to work on the script.

At first the three of them were cagey of each other. "We were all terrified that the three of us would get into a boring conversation and cease to be friends," Cassavetes said. One evening in a bar, as the conversation began to ebb away, Cassavetes suggested each of them should name his own character (in the first draft, they were simply Benny, John and Peter). Falk came up with Archie. "C'mon, you can't be an Archie," Cassavetes complained. To which Falk responded, "Jesus Christ, John, first you tell us to choose our own names, then when we do it, you say we can't. This is freedom?" Archie it was.

Gazzara wanted Harold, after a New York bar: Harold's Show Spot. Cassavetes liked Gus: "because it was Greek and a good name."

"By the end of the evening, we were really able to talk to each other, and when the picture began shooting, we were buddies."[6]

Tristram Powell's BBC documentary, *The Making Of Husbands*, provides a valuable record of the rehearsal process after the team had relocated to New York in January 1969: Cassavetes, Gazzara and Falk working through the script scene by scene, line by line, intent not simply on clarity and motivation, but reaching towards the realisation of the moment in all its ambiguity and confusion. What's striking and unusual is how rewriting seems integral to the proceedings; more than fine-tuning the lines, Cassavetes is on his feet writing, not with pen and paper, but with actors, nicotine, laughter, and – yes – improvisation.

Peter Tanner, the English editor Cassavetes had hired, was already on the production. "John would go into a room with Peter Falk and Ben Gazzara and a secretary, and they'd improvise. I mean, we had a script, but it didn't bear much resemblance to the final film. The secretary took everything down in shorthand. They'd work all day with a break for lunch and the next day, the secretary would have typed it up. They'd read it through and change it all. That's my recollection."[7]

Powell captures the genesis of the first scene, as Cassavetes struggles to come up with a reason for the three friends to arrive together at Stuart's funeral – and has the inspiration that it's to escort the dead man's grandmother. There's a secretary in the corner, taking shorthand. (Al Ruban remembers with amusement one of John's secretaries who sat there through a morning's work, assuring the director that "Yes, she was fine – she had an excellent memory," but – it turned out – not writing a line. "Oh, was I supposed to write it down?" Of course she'd forgotten everything.)

Gazzara, especially, is a sounding board; Falk is less voluble, almost bemused. As both actors have subsequently confirmed, during this phase Cassavetes subtly incorporated aspects of their own personalities into the characters: bullish, pugnacious Harry; philosophical, private Archie. "John wanted to get away from conventional dialogue and well-written stories," Gazzara told Thierry Jousse. "He was looking for emotion. and not just one quality, but three, four, five – the complexity of people's reality. That's why he wanted to rehearse, and it was during the rehearsals that he really wrote '*Husbands*'."[8]

There's footage of Cassavetes with Jenny Runacre, who plays Mary, the tall English girl Gus brings back to his hotel room. Straight out of drama school, Runacre's line readings are stiff and self-conscious. He tells her to laugh for a full 30 seconds before the speech. She manages ten, and it helps, a little. Holding her tight, he whispers in her ear: "You're terrific, you're terrifically attractive. I think you're beautiful, really wonderful. Wonderfully terrific. You want to go somewhere?" and it's not clear, 'til they break and he cackles, that this from the script, and not a director seducing his actress. ("I really mean it," Cassavetes observes with wry detachment.)

"It was a terribly intense process," Runacre remembers. "That day I think I smoked about 500 cigarettes. I thought they were all mad. It was my first film, virtually my first acting, and I thought it was all too much. John and Peter and Ben were so bonded and macho. In real-life on the set they were just the same as in the film: playing lots of dice and gambling and laughing and rolling around. Little in-jokes between them. I got incredibly paranoid. I'm sure that's what John wanted me to feel. He wanted it to be so real that you couldn't act."[9]

That kind of tension between play and reality Powell captures in rehearsal survives in the finished film. Take the very physical scene where Gus romps with Mary on the bed, grappling her, tickling her, playing the fool. As she fends him off, are we hearing Mary's protestations, or Jenny Runacre's? When he instructs her to cover herself up – an attack of pure Cassavetian prudery: "I can see everything, I hate that!" – is Gus directing the scene? "I'm schizophrenic," Gus/John confesses to Mary/Jenny.

The effect is voyeuristic, but not sexual. It's the frisson of watching something dangerous, unpredictable, and alive. The scene's reality is double-edged; playing on a deeper comprehension that a film is a construct, that it's supposed to be actors acting, not people behaving.

Runacre's scenes with Cassavetes were largely improvised, she says. "That scene in the coffee shop was improvised: when I slapped him it was totally instinctive, from nothing, not even in rehearsals. John was completely taken aback. But he kept it in. And the fight on the bed was improvised. When we came up to his bedroom, we'd ordered drinks and come in (which came off improvisation in rehearsal), and that whole thing about how much I hated him I made up. I had terrible flu and I was actually feeling like that at that point. Then I had a couple of days off, and we had no idea how he was actually going to get Mary Tynan from that position – that aggressive, seated position on the chair – on to the bed with him. That fight sequence just evolved, thinking and working at it."

Did she feel used at all – that Cassavetes had overstepped any professional boundary lines? "No I would rather have gone like that than some straightforward love scene, which at that point I wouldn't have been able to do with him at all, because I was in such turmoil. His greatest skill was in this manipulation. When the fight scene evolved, I don't think he had any more idea than I did about how to shoot it, how to get the couple on to the bed. But his brilliance was in perception; seeing how people work and gauging your reactions, he could manipulate the situation so it would work. There was always a slight antagonism between us which he used. I was always terribly defensive about everything."

Cassavetes loved to cook up this kind of uneven tussle. Runacre looks about six inches taller than Cassavetes, a disparity they both comment on in the movie (in a scene cut from the final print, Mary and Gus dance together, she towering over him in her high heels). Noelle Kao (Julie) plays her long bedroom scene with Falk in perfect silence; the presumption is, she can't speak English, but we're never sure and nor is Archie ("You're inscrutable," he tells her).[10] Runacre and Jenny Lee Wright (Pearl) were actresses, but neither had much experience; Kao was a dentist's assistant. The seduction scenes draw out the professional American actors, who are compelled to over-compensate for their co-stars' inexperience, to come on too strong. As fellow film-maker Jeremy Kagan notes, "With non-actors, what happens is you can only get the truth that they can give. Sometimes it will be amazing, because it is what they are, they're not acting it, they are it; other times there will be this awkwardness, and sometimes that might put the other actors off-kilter and bring up a truth for them as well. Because the moment is true: they can't look into the eyes of the non-actor and see another actor, all they can see is the person who is there, which forces them sometimes to be who they are."[11]

"There are things done by extras, who come in just to be background, and all of a sudden John's working with them, and they'll give performances that will stun you," Gazzara comments in Powell's documentary. "Better than any actor could [come up with], the preplanning and setting actors do."

He's describing the most famous – indeed infamous – scene in *Husbands*. The bar scene comes on day two of Archie, Gus and Harry's odyssey, some

20 minutes into the film. By now well and truly oiled, the threesome conduct a rowdy wake with a bunch of barflies, each of whom is cajoled and bullied into singing a song; another of the men's childish contests.

The sequence has no beginning; we can only imagine how the scene started (or not: Pauline Kael complained, "The people around the table wouldn't sit there while these clowns bully them unless they were paid for it."). The songs are bittersweet evergreens, sentimental, and trite; the singing tremulous and greeted with jeers, cheers, catcalls or hysterics.

It's a dark scene, sombre as a Rembrandt; all the illumination is on the faces of the gathering. The set-up resembles a last supper: a long, oblong table, Harry more or less in the centre, Gus and Archie at his right. The pals' white shirts set them apart from the dozen or so 'disciples.' It's shot in long, hard takes; Cassavetes used two cameras for the scene and let them roll. The visual signature is strongly vérité, in that it scarcely seems edited; the camera respects the space and time of the mise-en-scène. It's an upsetting sequence: the characters seem to gang up boorishly on the singers, in particular the last one, Leola (Leola Harlow). What makes it more disturbing, the actors (Cassavetes/Gazzara/Falk) seem to gang up on Harlow. With their cigars and their repeated exhortations for 'more soul, more feeling,' the trio resemble casting directors at an audition. "Too cute," Harry admonishes her as she launches into "It was just a little love affair" for the umpteenth time. "We're not criticising you, you're just not speaking to us," Gus tells her. The alienation is compounded by the scene's length (ten minutes) which makes it seem both indulgent and pitiless. Tristram Powell's film takes us further into the mire; his behind-the-scenes footage is virtually indistinguishable from the movie: that is to say, there is no clear distinction between what is a take and what isn't. We can't see how complicit Leola Harlow was in her character's humiliation. "All you have to do is not pretend. Shove it on the line," Cassavetes (or Gus?) tells her. (In fact, Harlow told Ray Carney that she didn't know what was going on, and was genuinely hurt and confused by the abuse.)[12]

In Powell's film, the scene ends with the three friends singing to Leola, and when she tries again, she finally earns their approval; there's a tear in her eye. Instead of cutting to the men's room, the bar owner, Red comes in and unleashes a genuinely poignant rendition of 'Brother, Can You Spare A Dime?' This was indeed how the original cut of *Husbands* played. Mysteriously, since 1970 the film has lost eleven minutes from its 141 minute running time, with this excision and further cuts to the subsequent scene in the gents' urinal. As it now exists the scene's climax is less gratifying, with Archie promising to take his clothes off if Leola sings better. The shirt comes off, then his trousers – "Here they come, baby!" – and the film cuts on Leola's genuine shock. It's still a release, but harder and less sentimental. Few films are less sentimental than *Husbands* as it now stands. Ironically, the theme Cassavetes first proposed to his collaborators was this: "Whatever happened to sentiment in the world today?."[13]

Cassavetes was well aware of how tough this scene was for audiences, and there was considerable pressure on him to cut it at the time. Resisting it became a matter of pride. There was a serious split with Al Ruban over it. "I thought there should be less picking on the woman – but he wouldn't let me touch it, not even to show him. We had a big fight over it," Ruban says.

Cassavetes told Lawrence Linderman that both Falk and Gazzara had 'anxieties' about the length of the film. Even when it was released, "Columbia would call me up to report that 52 people had stormed out of one theatre in one day. But I still say our bargain was with purity and not with success. *Husbands* is an extremely entertaining film, in spots. Like life, it's also very slow and depressing in areas. The one thing it's not is a shorthand film. I won't make shorthand films, because I don't want to manipulate audiences into assuming quick, manufactured truths. If I had my way, *Husbands* would be twice as long as it is and everyone could walk out if they wanted to."

✳ ✳ ✳

"We know the sequence is supposed to reveal something that 'ordinary' movies don't. But what does it reveal except the paralysis and humiliation of the bit players?" Pauline Kael wanted to know.[14]

Well, the paralysis and pain of Gus, Harry and Archie, for starters. The very opposite of 'indulgent,' this sequence consciously serves to distance us from the protagonists. With very few cutaways, the camera is trained on the three 'ring masters': drunk, sniggering and insensitive, they're hardly seen at their best. Later, as they leave the bar, Red (John Kullers) will tell Harry, "You know you've got an awful lot to learn. You know absolutely nothing about people; you really screwed up tonight." Typically, Harry doesn't want to hear it.

The duration of the scene is another disruptive technique. To this point, *Husbands* has been characterised by open spaces and short, pointed scenes: the empty street at night, the empty subway car, the empty basketball court, the swimming pool. Unusually for Cassavetes, each scene has led into the next; a straightforward, linear progression, which takes us from the funeral, Harry's declaration "I don't want to go home. I'm gonna get very drunk," to their drunken all-nighter; early morning on the El, and Gus's sentimental observation that he'll never be a pro basketball player, which leads to the sports club. The film's title card announces itself as a comedy, and so far, the pointedly ironic editing has delivered on that promise.

Husbands appears to be a much more comfortable movie than *Faces*. It's shot in colour, in 35mm, anamorphic; it features movie stars and locations and technical finesse.

The bar scene wipes the smile off our faces and rewrites the rules before our eyes – or rather, it throws away the rule book altogether. It's as if the comfort level afforded by a $1 million budget made Cassavetes uncomfortable. "The problem with having a professional crew is, they take advantage of you," he complains in Powell's film. "Too many technicians." Shooting in colour "caused me a lot of pain," he told a journalist shortly after they wrapped. "But Sam Shaw [who served as associate producer] assured me if we shot it in a certain way it would look as 'hack' as anything else I've ever done."

This was the first feature shot by Victor Kemper; while the lighting in *Husbands* is quite conventional, the long lenses and mostly static camera (with occasional pans) create an observational, chanced-upon aesthetic that's the visual correlative of the actors' repetitions, hesitations and cross-talk. Writing in *Cahiers du Cinéma*, Sylvie Pierre and Jean Narboni delineated Cassavetes' 'natural expressionism': "edginess, doubts, hesitations, illuminations, fleeting and contradictory expressions, lassitudes, irritations, idle moments and bursts of activity succeeding one another as they do in life. A war waged by tremors and pauses on meaning in its living inexactitude."

In a sense the bar room scene is contrived and artificial; but on another level it expresses a real pain. ("John wasn't interested in realism; he was interested in spontaneous emotion," Falk insists.) What it tries to do – to go back to Kael's question – is to shake the audience out of our paralysis, and remind us – if only in displacement – of what Archie, Gus and Harry have been working up to: contemplation of what Stuart's death means to them. When they bully Leola for more feeling, more sincerity, more soul, the men are really beating up on themselves, trying to find an emotional response commensurate with Stuart's loss.

"John wasn't afraid to torture his audience," Al Ruban says. "If he wanted them to feel pain, he'd make it painful. He wasn't afraid to do that."[15]

It makes sense that what follows is, in Gus's phrase, a "private moment," as Archie, throwing up, tries to figure out what his life is about. "I want to tell you how I really feel," he tells Gus. "What's really wrong with me. It's a tremendous need. An anxiety. It's a – that's what happens, I forget what it is. What is it? It's got to be important right?" The speech is rambling and inarticulate, funny and heartfelt, punctuated with retching, and with Harry, excluded and paranoid as ever, banging on the cubicle door: a deeply Cassavetian confusion of comedy and anguish, for characters, actors and audience alike.

Husbands is explicitly a film about men; men with wives – although those wives are, save for the opening photo montage and the one sequence when Harry goes home, kept off-screen. It's a film of noisy desperation. Like *Faces*, it's about the realisation that life slips through your fingers. Marriage – Harry's marriage, at any rate – is a trap and a sham. "I'm uncomfortable with you. Nothing personal," his wife tells him. Not for the last time in the films of John Cassavetes, a man's need for love is expressed with intimidation and force: Harry forces his wife to her knees until she relents. He's furiously beating wife and mother-in-law when Gus and Archie interrupt.

Then he goes to work.

He's going through the motions, one of Chet's mechanical men, or as Archie would have it: "a phony": "Harry, you get to work on time, you fawn over your wife, you're absorbed by yourself, and you have no sense of humour."

Harry's defence is reasonable – "I have responsibilities. I'm a man who is responsible" – a rationale most people live by, most of the time. But it's not enough. Archie, contrarily, declares that "If I wanna stink I'll stink. You have to be free. You have to be an individual." That Harry's boss is played (in an unbilled, wordless cameo) by Fred Draper hints that, if he doesn't instigate change, he could end up like Freddie, Draper's character in *Faces*, in ten or 15 years.

So is Harry's flight to London, Gus and Archie in tow, a legitimate escape – or an irresponsible escapade? There can be no definitive answer, because Cassavetes never made up his own mind on this point. He told *Life* magazine, in a cover feature published in May 1969: "The job that has to be done here is for three men to investigate themselves – honestly, without suppression. The minute you settle down and say, that's it, I'm closing shop, I know what I am, then you're a man, no longer a man-child. Is it really better to be a man-child than a man? I don't know."[16]

Husbands is not performed in the spirit of criticism that *Faces* was, in part because for all their faults, the men are friends; in part because Cassavetes identified more closely with his characters. Gus makes much of his Greekness; his wife is called 'Jeannie,' and his kids are played by Cassavetes' children, Nick and Xan. *Faces* had addressed the middle-aged, high middle-income bracket. 'The white American society,' in the director's own words. "One day I woke up and realised that I'm part of that society and almost everyone I know is."[17]

The trio's endless game-playing and competitiveness might be read as juvenile, but it was a childishness Cassavetes cherished in himself and encouraged in others. Youth is vitality. To live without exuberance is not to live at all. His cousin Phedon Papamichael was a pro football player (and later art director on John's films), and Peter Falk remembers being out on the town with them at three or four in the morning, and John would decide they'd have a race: Papamichael to start from 51st Street, Falk from 48th Street, and the first to 46th Street wins! "Walking races like the one in '*Husbands*' he loved even more. John was incredibly competitive. Imagine: for seven years we argued about how tall Muhammad Ali was!"[18]

The gambling scene, when they visit a casino, was inspired by an incident during the shooting of *The Dirty Dozen*. Cassavetes was on a tight per diem, and it looked like Gena was going to have to fly back home with Nick and baby Xan. Instead, he decided to go for broke, and disappeared with his old friend Sam Shaw, in town in similarly strapped circumstances on another project. They headed for the Pair of Shoes casino. "He was a great player," Shaw recalled. "He had a perfect memory, for dialogue, or events, or for cards. We played blackjack, and he broke the bank. It was enough money for us keep our families with us in London, and buy $800 coats for everyone. That gave birth to the scene in *Husbands*, a scene where they were really playing for money: everyone forgot the camera was there."[19]

This spirit of bravado infected everything Cassavetes did. Just as the de Cirogna money was running low – just $40,000 in the bank – John instructed Ruban to build a vast nightclub set in the Chalk Farm Roundhouse. "I want a bar that runs 60 feet, and the taps have to work, the beer has to flow," he said. "And I want a big stage, and a runway coming out another 30 feet, and tables over here, sawdust on the floor, and up top a net with balloons in it."

Ruban said "What are you talking about? We only have $40,000 left."

John said, "Oh yes, and I want a trapeze, acrobats, the works." He gave him a wink. "Al, Paramount is coming here. Universal is coming. Columbia is coming. They're going to buy it when they see the set."

"I swear that's what we did," Ruban says. "We spent all the money on that set, had people swinging on the trapeze, drinking Whatney's real ale, and I think there's one shot of that scene in the finished picture: Peter trying to make his way through the crowd. But they bought it on that – in fact they competed against one another and Columbia won. They paid $3.5 million for it. Peter, John and Ben came out great, they split a million dollars between them."

According to Peter Tanner, the director printed an amazing amount of footage, four or five times as much as he was used to (Tanner cut *The Cruel Sea* and one of Cassavetes' all-time favourites, *Kind Hearts And Coronets*). The rushes frequently ran to over two hours a day. He'd often shoot until the film ran out, 1,000 foot takes, of which three or four would be printed. Each one would be a master shot, but each would be a new variation, in angle or the tempo of the scene.

"Film-making for John was a completely different process from that of other directors," Tanner says. "I soon saw I had to throw away everything I'd normally do editing a film and start all over again. With John you would go with the actors, like in jazz with the soloist."

Tanner worked closely with Al Ruban on the first cut; Cassavetes kept a discreet distance. "He said after *Faces* he never wanted to set foot in a cutting room again," Ruban says. "My only mistake was I put it together the way he shot it." When they screened the movie for close to a thousand people at two screening rooms at Universal, everyone loved it. "They said it would win Ben Gazzara an Oscar. It was a comedy, with Benny in the lead role. The other two didn't have their own narrative line, and it was more overtly comic, but it was faithful to John's script." The only person who didn't like it was John.

"It wasn't emotional enough," Ruban speculates. "Too comic. And it didn't play off Peter or John's characters."

"It was much funnier," Tanner confirms. "Maybe John got tired of it? I thought they ruined it."

In the fall-out, Ruban headed back for New York nursing a bruised ego. "He was always so changeable, that was his nature," he reflects. "We would disagree about many things, and he would win me over to his point of view – and an hour later he would come over and have changed his mind. Flip-flopping. I would be so angry. He was a Greek all the way. Adversarial about everything. When you had a discussion, he would take the other side all the time just because he loved to debate. And with Falk and Gazzara: all these New York types would like to speak their mind. It was invigorating – but you had to be able to take it."

Cassavetes locked himself away in the cutting room and started recutting.

Bo Harwood was a new recruit in Cassavetes' editing team. As he remembers the film was already supposed to be out on release, but John had artistic control, and he was going to reedit it. "Columbia went crazy. He had threats. John could live through that kind of turmoil and power struggle. He wasn't afraid of it. He had a wonderful knack of being able to walk into the office of a studio head with Al Ruban and he would get these guys so off-balance they didn't know if they were coming or going. They knew John wasn't afraid of them – they were terrified of him! So John spent the next six months putting this film together, screening it at least every week, and every week it was different. Maybe a million feet of film, two or three cutting rooms wall to wall with 35 mm reels, huge, wonderful scenes that never ended up in the picture."[20]

Gazzara reckons the best version he ever saw ran for nearly four hours (Tristram Powell's documentary suggests that much more material was shot in London: scenes on the Underground, scenes in a plush ballroom with the three men, Mary and Pearl; a scene in which Archie picks up Julie). Seymour Cassel says that he saw a version in which Gus never appeared again after the funeral. "But Benny's great in it, isn't he?" John purred. A week later, Cassavetes invited him to see another cut: this time the film was all Falk's. "I thought it was supposed to be the story of three guys," an exasperated Cassel complained. "Yeah, but isn't Peter good?"

"He loved to find different ways to tell a story," Cassel reflects. "When it was released, he couldn't touch it anymore. He was always sad to have to abandon one of his films."

There is a temptation to suppose that Cassavetes wanted to include more of his own performance: certainly there is more of Gus and Mary than the other two couples. It may be though that Runacre was the real attraction. Gus is not a particularly flattering self-portrait. "I think it's a very illumi-nating picture of machismo," Runacre says. "They were macho, the three of them, but I don't think John set out to make them likeable. My charac-ter you do feel a bit of sympathy for at the end. So many women have said to me how much they relate to that character. So many older women come up to me and say they remember it, and how they felt the same way at that age. That's where his brilliance was."

There is distance here: *Husbands* may not have many laughs, but it's cold intelligence justifies the term 'comedy.' It's a film virtually without point-of-view shots, a subjective technique Cassavetes deeply mistrusted as inherently facile and dishonest. In the casino scene, there are no cutaways to the table to draw us into the game. Returning to the hotel with their pick ups, the men's dreams of sex without strings don't work out as they plan: Harry can't stop talking about the wife he's left; Archie recoils in disgust from a French kiss (something he's never experienced before, apparently); and Gus's over-bearing charm is just another form of evasion, frankly exposed by Mary's lack of affectation. To cap it all, much to their alarm, Gus and Archie both fall in love with their one night stands – an eventu-ality which propels them back to their wives in a spin.

It's one of the film's many ironies that Archie and Gus ultimately resume their conventional lives, while Harry instigates a real and decisive break. Another of those ironies: the last time we see him, singing 'Dancing In The Dark' in his London hotel room, he's picked up what appears to be a sur-rogate family: wife, mother and daughters.[21] It's like the fable of the man named Flitcraft in Dashiell Hammett's *The Maltese Falcon*: a happily married man who took off after a beam had fallen from ten storeys up on to the sidewalk beside him; recognising that life is chaos, he'd embraced chaos. Yet when Sam Spade caught up with him a couple of years later he had settled down again, and married the same kind of woman he'd married before. "But that's the part of it I always liked," Spade said. "He adjusted himself to beams falling, and then no more of them fell, and he adjusted himself to them not falling."

Husbands is a difficult film. No less than its protagonists, the film seems to be groping for a clarity which never comes, and which, in fact, the film-maker could never accept: "It's never as clear as it is in the movies," Ray Carney quotes him as saying. "People don't know what they are doing most of the time, myself included. All my life I've fought against clarity – all those stupid definitive answers. Phooey on a formula life, on slick solutions. It's never easy. And I don't think people want their lives to be easy. In the end, it only makes things more difficult."[22]

For Cassavetes, making a film was an exploration, a journey of discovery. The exploration may even have been more important than the discovery, if we accept that exploration is a working model of engagement with a world in constant flux, while discovery could lead to closure and complacency. Much more than the closed and contained world of *Faces*, the expansive and elliptical *Husbands* allowed Cassavetes room to experiment.

On set, he'd keep his options open. He wouldn't let his actors 'direct' the non-actors, nor would he give specific directions to the professionals. It drove Falk crazy: "About three weeks into shooting, I was getting angry and frustrated, because I didn't know what was going on. We were all in the back of the car, and I turned to him and I said, 'John, I will work with you again as an actor, but never' – and by this time I was beginning to shout – 'Never! Ever! Again! As a Director!' He just laughed his ass off."

"It was very funny," Gazzara confirms. "John would never give you a simple direction. He'd go off on a long discourse, and Peter would look at me and say 'What does he want?' And I'd say, 'He wants you to turn to move over there'."[23]

"He kept you in the dark because he feared that if he articulated things clearly you might turn it into a cliché. What he wanted from you was yourself. He wanted to get some part of your feelings and emotions that were too varied to be reduced to words," Falk says.

It seemed that Cassavetes couldn't let go of this film. With its great oscillations of feeling, a definitive rendering seemed to miss the point. Even as he was recutting, Cassavetes wasn't satisfied, and he wrote a novelisation of the film: Falk couldn't believe it, here were all the answers he'd been asking for. Cassavetes didn't feel the need to have it published.

Even the ending, on the face of it utterly desolate (a shock cut to black as Gus returns to a roasting from his wife, bribes in hand for his screaming kids) may not be as bleak as it first seems. We don't know enough about this marriage to be sure, but we know that Gus's wife was sufficiently understanding to dig out his passport when he asked her to, and do the same for Archie. "I'm really unable to interpret it," Cassavetes said. "I've talked to people who liked *Husbands* and some who think it's the saddest movie they've ever seen. I find that hard to understand. In the last scene of the movie, the fact that Gus is about to get some kind of heat from his wife. It's kind of flattering. It's an indication that there's something there, that we're living, that people care, that our silly endeavours have some meaning."[24]

In the autumn of 1970, *Husbands* premiered at the San Francisco Film Festival. The screening was a disaster. "Everyone yelled 'Fascist!' They were booing and going crazy," Cassavetes remembered. "Here is this whole row of Columbia executives and their wives, and the wives turn to the executives and say, "What is wrong, why are they booing?" The audience got worse. They got hostile. Eighteen hundred people really booing."

He went up and asked them how they liked it. "Absolute silence. Finally, one guy said, 'If you guys were making a satire about the middle class and how piggish they are, that is one thing. But if those guys depicted on the screen are really like you, that's another.' And I said, 'It's us. It's us,' and Peter said, 'That's right.' Well, we thought we were going to be killed. It was getting terrific. The only friends we had were Gena and Seymour. Any time anybody said something, Gena would shout 'Sit down!'"[25]

Yet another edit brought the length down from 154 minutes (the version shown at the festival) to 141 minutes for the release version. It wouldn't be the last time that the reception of Cassavetes' work would be distorted by the political mood of the time. Reviews were mixed (although *Time* raved "one of the best movies anyone will ever see. Certainly the best movie anyone will ever live through"). Many were beginning to complain about the director's supposed 'self-indulgence.' Cassavetes tried to bar Pauline Kael from seeing the film. She had been one of the few to slate *Faces*, and after Gazzara persuaded Cassavetes to relent she was just as vicious this time round.[26]

Box-office was barely satisfactory, about $1.5 million in the US.

Seymour Cassel remembers flying from LA to New York with John at around this time. "Have a look at this," he said, and pulled a cheque out of his pocket. It was made out to John Cassavetes, to the sum of $975 000. "He said to me, 'Let's go to Brazil'," Seymour remembers. "He knew I'd go anywhere, any time. I said "Right, let's go!" And John said, "We should just make some phone calls, let our wives and kids know we'll be back in a few weeks."

"He'd always put you on like that. And I'd fall for it every time. 'We can't do it,' he said. 'One third is Benny's, and another third is Peter's; it's the money for *Husbands*. Let your hair grow. I'm going to write a movie for you and Gena, a romantic comedy, a love story'."

---

1   Brian Case interview transcript 1984.
2   *Roman By Polanski*, Heinemann, 1984 .
3   Anthony Loeb (ed), *A Conversation With John Cassavetes*, Columbia College, Chicago, 1975.
4   Peter Falk, Author's interview (1999) unless otherwise stated.
5   See Appendix: Acting Out.
6   Linderman.
7   Peter Tanner, Author's interview (2000).
8   Jousse.
9   Jenny Runacre, Author's interview (2000).
10 In fact this scene was pieced together out of next to nothing in the editing. Cassavetes sent a young guitarist he'd met – Bo Harwood – to remix it with some new lines Falk recorded in the studio.
11 Jeremy Kagan, Author's interview (2000).
12 Ray Carney, *The Adventure Of Insecurity* programme.
13 According to Cassavetes in Austen, *Films and Filming*, September 1968.
14 Kael, *The New Yorker*, VXLVI, n46, January 2, 1971.
15 Ruban, BBC Arena on John Cassavetes, 1989.
16 Ann Guerin, 'Dead-on Dialogue as the Cash Runs Out,' *Life*, 9 May, 1969.
17 *Cinema*, v4, n1, Spring 1968.
18 Headline and Cazenave.
19 Headline and Cazenave.
20 Bo Harwood, Author's interview (2000).
21 'There was a scene with Ben Gazzara dancing with a girl, and she really wasn't any good. John started going at her, and he said "Even our continuity girl could do this scene better than you can. In fact she will!" So he fired her and called over Peggy Lashbrook and she did it – and she wasn't bad either.' – Peter Tanner.
22 Quoted in Carney, 'The Adventure of Insecurity.'
23 Gazzara in the documentary To Risk Everything To Express It All.
24 Linderman.
25 Loeb.
26 Seymour Cassel remembers an incident circa the release of *Faces*: 'We were going downtown, and we'd been drinking in some bar, and Pauline told us about some party in the Village. We were heading there in a cab and she started pontificating about some film, and John said "Jesus Christ, something stinks in here," and then "You know what? It's these shoes!" And he took her shoes and threw them out the cab window. Pauline didn't care – she went barefoot.'

6

Minnie And Moskowitz

'The movies are a conspiracy. They set you up to believe in . . . everything.'
Minnie Moore

If *Husbands* expresses a yearning for freedom, then *Minnie And Moskowitz* is about loneliness, the need for love and commitment. But it's also Cassavetes' most optimistic and romantic movie, an affirmation of marriage and family, scored to a sunny Louis Armstrong scat.

After the years of struggle, Cassavetes was embarking on the most creative period of his life. He wrote the script for *Minnie And Moskowitz* in two and a half weeks, and while that was still in rehearsal he was developing a screenplay, *Two Days In Rochester*, for Ben Gazzara – a loose follow-up to *Husbands*. A backstage drama, *Opening Night*, was also taking shape in his mind. "Unbelievable as this may sound, I'm doing just what I want to with my life and on my own terms, without any hassling whatsoever," he affirmed to Lawrence Linderman in the spring of 1971. "Never have I felt so correct about myself, so secure in myself. I believe in miracles."

Whatever anyone else thought about *Husbands*, Cassavetes knew he was hitting his stride, coming into his time. Rocked by the seismic changes in American society during the late Sixties and early Seventies, even Hollywood was slowly coming into step. The studios didn't pretend to understand why students, draft-dodgers and drop-outs flocked to *Easy Rider*; all they knew was that profits were to be made.

At Universal, Lew Wasserman set up a youth unit under the control of Ned Tanen. A young, smart executive, Tanen commissioned adventurous film-makers: he offered studio resources without studio interference; a low-ish budget of between $750,000 and $1 million, and final cut. Dennis Hopper signed on to make his second film, *The Last Movie*. Frank Perry's *The Diary Of A Mad Housewife* (1970), and Milos Forman's *Taking Off* (1971), starring Lynn Carlin, were the first to reach cinemas. Neither of them were big commercial successes, but they garnered plenty of critical prestige. Peter Fonda's *The Hired Hand*, Douglas Trumbull's *Silent Running*, Monte Hellman's *Two Lane Blacktop*, and John Cassavetes' *Minnie And Moskowitz* were all put into production under the auspices of

Tanen's youth unit between 1970 and 1972. Sadly only its final production, George Lucas's *American Graffiti*, would prove a hit with the target youth audience, several months too late to save the initiative.

Tanen liked Cassavetes' screenplay; a modern update on the screwball comedy, it suggested a tentative rapprochement with Hollywood:

Seymour Moskowitz is a happy-go-lucky romantic, a New York car park attendant who likes his job and loves women. Minnie Moore holds a responsible job at a museum in Los Angeles. She's cultured, intelligent and beautiful, but beginning to fear that she's destined to go through life alone (she's currently embroiled in a sometimes violent affair with a married man, Jim).

Seymour impetuously relocates to Los Angeles, and meets Minnie by gallantly interceding on her behalf when a blind date arranged by her friend Florence goes horribly wrong.

Moskowitz is immediately attracted to her, but Minnie has had it up to here with men – and then some. Nevertheless, he's persistent, and she reluctantly agrees to go out on a date with him. It does not go well. She's cool and distant, he's nervous and cheap. And anyway they've nothing in common. He's just some schmuck with a good heart who doesn't know anything. Then again, maybe she knows more than is good for her. He seems happy, which is more than she can claim. A second date goes even more awry than the first, with Seymour getting into a fight with one of her acquaintances from work. Yet she can't stop herself from pouring out her heart to him, and the next thing you know they're phoning home to tell their mothers about the impending nuptuals. And they live happily ever after.

Universal's only disagreement was over casting the eponymous Moskowitz. Tanen wanted Jack Nicholson, who'd made such an impact in *Easy Rider*, and was fast-becoming *the* anti-establishment star; Cassavetes wouldn't hear of it – he'd written it specifically for Seymour Cassel, even giving the character his Christian name.

Minnie was for Gena. Save for her few scenes in *Machine Gun McCain*, she hadn't acted in a movie since *Tony Rome* in 1967. In 1970, she'd given birth to their third, and last, child, Zoe, the Greek word for life. It was time to get back to work.

With Women's Lib so high on the social agenda at the beginning of the Seventies, Gena was often stereotyped in the press as an actress who had sacrificed her career for her family. "I haven't given up anything. I'm able to act and I have the same husband I started out with," she protested. "I didn't want to waste my youth being a movie star anyway."

According to Cassavetes, as their family grew, his wife repeatedly threatened to give up her career, and each time he threatened to leave her if she did.

After *Faces* and *Husbands*, Cassavetes had to get used to dealing with the assumption that his own marriage was rocky – a suggestion he always repudiated. It was only as time passed, and he was able to look back on it, that he admitted to difficult periods in the relationship. Describing the genesis of *A Woman Under The Influence* to journalist Brent Lewis in 1975, he confessed: "For years I claimed the artist's right not to be headed down by anybody or anything. I made films, got drunk, stayed away from home. I destroyed my wife yet she stood by me through child after child."[1]

At much the same time, he told another reporter, "I don't know whether it has anything to do with my age or experience, but at this point in my life. I've come to recognise the errors of my own ways, perhaps, the selfishness and the insensitivities of my past – but mind you, I'm not putting these down. From an actor's and a director's point of view these are wonderful things – his art is forged from them. It's just that now I recognise things I had eliminated from my life . . . those other values in familial and social relationships."[2]

It was true that he and Gena fought often and passionately. Their fights were legendary among friends, yet seemed only to intensify their intimacy; they had promised each other from the off that they'd never hold back. "I believe that any two people who disagree should really go as far as they can, and I think we do: screaming, yelling, petty acts of hostility and cruelty," Cassavetes told *Playboy*. "It's all meaningless. It's always meaningless if that essential love is there."[3]

(Asked if she'd ever considered divorce, Gena would joke, saltily, "Only every day!")

"Both of them were headstrong. I think that was what attracted them to each other," says Seymour Cassel. "Their relationship was fantastic. The passion in it was great. But Gena had to stand up for herself all the time. John was very open and unstructured. Gena was a lady with class. She would want to go out to dinner or something, and John would rather go to a basketball game. And yet they had the same passion for the arts, he loved to go to plays with her, and music. Sure there were arguments. They would get into arguments about the silliest things. He would provoke her, he loved to provoke people, to get a reaction and play out of themselves. He liked to see a little craziness in people. He was a workaholic. He wanted to play ball, shoot film, make movies and cut 'em. And he could survive on five hours sleep. John was not an easy person to live with."

"I remember one time I asked to borrow John's car because my bike was in the shop," Cassel goes on. "John said okay, but I had to drive them both to the studio first and pick them up later, because they were co-starring in some TV show together. So I'm driving them, and not even a mile from their place, turning onto Laurel Canyon, they're arguing over whatever and Gena says 'Pull over, I want to get out.' She gets out, and John says 'You know what, you're making a big mistake, because I'm going to show up at work and you'll be late'."

"Go to hell!"

So off we go and he's giggling to himself.

He calls me about two hours later and he's found out that Gena has gotten on a plane and gone to New York. Gone to New York!

He said "C'mon Se, you got to pick me up, they let me off early, I'm going to New York. I know where she is: the Plaza. I already sent fucking roses and I got tickets for a show tomorrow night."

I said, "Are you nuts?"

He said, "No, she's the one that's nuts. But you can have the car for the weekend!"

Gena liked to say the model their domestic life most resembled was the screwball set-up celebrated in Frank Capra's *You Can't Take It With You*. Anarchy ruled. An avid collector of all kinds of ephemera, Gena had closets built in every room in the house to store her bric-a-brac. Her hobbies over the years included diamond cutting, studying languages (she experimented with a record supposed to teach you as you slept), and mechanics so she could fix her car.

Because her eyes were especially sensitive to light, the interior walls of their house off Laurel Canyon were painted dark colours: warm browns and violets. Even so, downstairs they eschewed curtains, safe behind the protective cover of the fruit trees and shrubs John cultivated in the garden.

While her husband and her son shot hoops or went to ball games, Gena preferred to read, or to paint, sew and write with Xan. Even when she was working and John wasn't, it was Gena who did the cooking. "The only time I've ever seen her hysterical is when she's cooking," John noted.

"John's forceful, Gena's soft," Cassavetes' mother Katherine said. "Her softness blends well with John's enthusiasm."[4]

Superstitious, Gena consulted an astrologer about all her important decisions. Nearly ten years into her marriage, the astrologer told her John was the wrong man for her. On that occasion, the stars were over-ruled. Another time, though, she ducked out of an interview with the *New York Times* because the reporter was a Capricorn and the stars were not auspicious. Amused, John gallantly stood in for the journalist, and profiled his wife himself, albeit with interjections from Gena: "She's a woman who believes in forces and is afraid of the unknown," he wrote. "To make her personality more clear, she and her mother went to the Bornstein Memory School because Gena felt her memory was failing her and she was misplacing things. After the two-month course was over, she was convinced she had an air-tight memory and when she said good night to Mr Bornstein she called him Mr Bernstein."

"John that's terrible. I mean, it's so clumsily written. I don't mean to be rude, but . . . Anyway, I've always had a terrible memory, except for scripts. By the second time I read a script, I can remember it nearly verbatim. My memory isn't getting any worse, it was always awful. It runs in my family."

"She can handle important matters that would crumble the Queen of England, and yet petty irritations send her into dizzying headaches," he continued. "She's a great mother because she's gotten the children to take care of her, to understand her moods and laugh about them. She's a great mother because she delights in the progress of her children. 'What do you mean the children take care of me? Why, they do not. I think they regard me as a kind of dizzy mother, but I don't think they take care of me. I mean, they may help me add up the bill at the market, but that's different. You make it sound as if I sit around eating chocolates, and they come and fetch for me. You have to take that part out'."[5]

Cassavetes claimed not to like the institution of marriage, but then so too did Gena, and in much the same terms. Most people get married for the wrong reasons, they'd say: because everyone else is doing it, or to escape, or to be sensible. The only valid reason is because you're crazy about each other.

"Love is a bondage," Gena said. "It is the exact opposite of freedom. But the greatest, most important thing is committing yourself to someone. And when you don't, you're really outsmarting yourself. It gets to be a bunch of momentary titillations, and we're bigger than that, we're deeper than that, all of us. When you love someone, you want to do something hard. You reach a point in life when you want to give everything."[6]

In *Minnie And Moskowitz*, Cassavetes wanted to work back from the male solipsism of *Husbands* to explore what it was that still compelled people to marry in an era of sexual liberation and 'free love,' and, perhaps, to explain the validity of his own marriage – if only to himself. He wrote the script in double-quick time, but then he'd been mulling over the idea for months, talking to Gena and Seymour about it, talking to anyone and everyone in fact. "Eighty percent of the time we talk about scripts and ideas and why people do things," Gena said. "The other 20 percent we talk about the children."[7]

Cassavetes' secretary at the time was Elaine Goren (she became Elaine Kagan when she married the film-maker Jeremy Paul Kagan in the mid-Seventies). "John used to dicate his scripts," she says. "We had an office in the motel that was across the street from Universal. We used to walk over every day and eat on the lot and make trouble. John loved to make trouble. And he instilled in all of us that it was great fun to make trouble. We'd watch old movies there – *Gun Crazy*, *In A Lonely Place* – and we'd write. He dictated the scripts, and he'd do the voices, because he was always an actor as well as a writer. I'd read them back to him, and he would call anyone around, anyone who was in the hall, the Sparkle Water guy, the delivery person, the people at Universal who were delivering your desk. 'Sit down, listen to this.' He wanted to hear how it rang. He was always observing, always interested in everybody."[8]

Gena never participated directly in the writing except in this capacity as a sounding board and a fellow observer in the field, as it were (she complained that he jotted down every word she said in his notebooks). She never read the scripts until John was ready to show them – but increasingly over the years Cassavetes wrote films for his wife. He'd ask her what kind of role she'd like to play, and they'd kick over certain possibilities that suggested themselves. After *Husbands*, only *The Killing Of A Chinese Bookie* would not centre on Gena's presence. According to Seymour Cassel, it was John's proclivity for card games which produced such vivid female characters: "He used to play bridge with Gena, Gena's mother Lady Rowlands, and Don Siegel's wife, Do. He told me, 'They think I'm one of the women. They just talk, and I hear all these great stories!'"

Gena encouraged her husband to write a comedy. They both loved Capra and the popular cycle of screwball comedies he initiated with *It Happened One Night* in 1934. The screwballs took their name from a baseball term for a fast, spinning pitch which fools the batter into expecting a different trajectory (in a 1934 All-Star game, New York Giants pitcher Carl Hubbell struck out five Hall-of-Famers in a row, including Babe Ruth and Lou Gehrig, all with screwballs). At around the same time, in the mid-Thirties, the noun came to be used adjectivally, for insane or eccentric – derived from 'screwy,' an early nineteenth century English phrase for drunk.[9]

In the movies, screwball comedies were also pacy and off-kilter, 'madcap,' in another popular expression of the time. A reaction against both the Depression and the Production Code, they revelled in a high society world of Deco and decadence, where social constraints existed only in order to be travestied by the genre's real subject: sexual animus. In Andrew Sarris' phrase, these were sex comedies without the sex. The suppressions of the censors fuelled a hysterical sublimation: screwball couples didn't make love, they waged war. And the more they fought, the closer they became. As the tin-pot psychiatrist observes in *Bringing Up Baby*, "The love impulse in man frequently reveals itself in terms of conflict."

With their worldly-wise repartee, antic farce and slapstick, classic screw-balls by Howard Hawks, Preston Sturges, Ernst Lubitsch and Frank Capra thrived on class division and sexual antagonism – and, unusually for Holly-wood, almost always granted their heroines parity with the men-folk in wit and resourcefulness.

Making his first studio film for a decade, it seemed fitting that Cassavetes should be attracted to this genre from his youth. He understood sexual antagonism and social travesty very well; the crazy inventions and charades of characters like Jean (Barbara Stanwyck) in *The Lady Eve* and Hazel (Carole Lombard) in *Nothing Sacred* chimed with his own perceptions of spontaneity and flux in all human relationships.

One staple screwball plot device saw poised, rational heroes played by Cary Grant, William Powell, or Joel McCrea sent reeling by the irrational force of unconventional women like Katharine Hepburn, Claudette Colbert, or Irene Dunne. In *Minnie And Moskowitz*, Cassavetes merrily reverses the gender roles, so that it's the serious and self-contained Minnie who is besieged by lunatic men – and especially by Seymour Moskowitz, a long-haired social misfit with a ponytail and a Yosemite Sam moustache.

We first meet Seymour at work in a New York car park, delivering a vehicle for an unbilled Mario Gallo (Dr Lombardi in *A Child Is Waiting*, and Mr Jensen in *A Woman Under The Influence*). Knocking off, he goes to an old movie, *The Maltese Falcon*, and drops in to a cheap all-night diner, where he orders a hot dog, a coffee and a beer. He falls into conversation with a derelict who introduces himself as Morgan Morgan (Timothy Carey). And immediately the film is off on a five-minute tangent, unthink-able in classical Hollywood, even in as eccentric a form as screwball comedy.

In plot terms, this sequence has no function at all. Screenwriting gurus would excise it immediately. Yet it's one of the most memorable encoun-ters in all Cassavetes' work, and an enduring testament to the high regard in which he held Tim Carey, a tall, deep-eyed actor who worked with Kazan in *East Of Eden*, Brando in *One-Eyed Jacks*, and Kubrick in *The Killing* and *Paths Of Glory* (during the making of which he staged his own kidnapping in a bizarre ransom stunt). Carey then spent decades making and remaking his peculiar independent films, *The World's Greatest Sinner* – which he began at much the same time as Cassavetes began *Shadows* – and then *Tweet's Ladies Of Pasadena*, in which he played Tweet Twig, odd job man for an old maid knitting society, animal lover, and husband to a British female wrestler (Cassavetes held a fund raiser for it in 1969). John also tried to get Ned Tanen interested in Carey's script, *Al*, and regularly leant him money and equipment over the years, to the consternation of some of his friends, who found Carey hard to take seriously. "Carey was

100

out there, operating on a whole other world of ideas and experiences. You had to be ready to take a trip into outer space to talk to him. He freaked everybody out because he was so strange; but John was excited and comfortable to be working with this dangerous spirit. John just used it, played with it, delighted in it," Jeremy Kagan observes.[10]

"There wasn't a negative bone in John Cassavetes' body," Carey marvelled. "You could call him up anytime and he was always there to give you a helping hand."[11] The scene was written specifically for Carey, and Cassavetes allowed him to extemporise for hours. When the scene was over, the director hugged his friend and told him, "You've made the film, Tim."

It's virtually a monologue, in which Morgan holds forth, rambling to Seymour about his contempt for humanity ("Everyday people, that's what's wrong with the world"), and for movies ("I don't like cinema, bunch of lonely people going in, lookin' up."), and – three times – how his wife is dead.

Hollow-eyed and unshaven, right from the off Morgan casts a shadow over the film; he's a spectre of loneliness, embittered, broke and evidently broken. If he calls Seymour his son, it's an adoption the younger man might prefer to resist. There is a kinship between them – as we discover in the next two bar scenes, Seymour can also be socially intrusive, to over-compensate for his sense of exclusion – but he has a long way to go before he becomes as sorry as Morgan. While Morgan talks – and is utterly self-absorbed – Seymour listens and is capable of responding generously. Even at his most exasperated, Seymour has a twinkle in his eye. Morgan is beyond romance, both on screen and in life ("Buffalo Bill's defunct," he recites, from ee cummings' poem), whereas Seymour is still an ardent believer in both Humphrey Bogart and Love: the two being sufficiently confused in his mind that he relocates to Los Angeles – Philip Marlowe's old stomping ground – to find happiness.

This tension between romance and anti-romance, cinema and reality, plays throughout *Minnie And Moskowitz*. Cassavetes' most movie-centric film, it makes at least half-a-dozen specific allusions to Hollywood, including clips from *The Maltese Falcon* and *Casablanca* (twice), and verbal references to Bogart and Bacall, among others. The allusions aren't simply sentimental 'hommages,' although that's part of their appeal – they stand for dominant conceptions of masculinity and romance against which the characters must measure their own lives. The clips from the Bogart movies both hinge on his noble renunciation of love, for example. The theme is articulated explicitly by Minnie in her drunken conversation with her elderly friend and colleague, Florence (Elsie Ames):

"I think that movies are a conspiracy. I mean it. They set you up from the time you're a kid to believe in everything; to believe in ideals, and

101

strength, and good guys, and romance. And of course, love. Love, Florence. So, you believe it, right? You go out, you start looking; it doesn't happen, you keep looking. You get a job, like us, and you spend a lot of time fixing up things, your apartment and jazz, and you learn how to be feminine – you know, 'quotes' feminine – learn how to cook. But there's no Charles Boyer in my life, Florence. I never even met a Charles Boyer. I never met Clark Gable. I never met Humphrey Bogart. I never met any of them. You know who I mean. They don't exist, Florence, that's the truth. But the movies set you up. No matter how bright you are, they set you up, you see?"

Coming immediately after a discussion about female sexuality, the sort of thing, Minnie points out, that the movies never talk about, this critique sums up Cassavetes' ambivalence about Hollywood, and explains the counter-Hollywood aesthetic operating even in this LA story: the casting of non-stars, use of real locations, elliptical editing strategies, a sound mix which doesn't downgrade ambient street noise, and the natural lighting style derived from cinema vérité. (Cassavetes used Arthur Ornitz as his cameraman here, a veteran who had worked with documentarian Joris Ivens in the Thirties then collaborated with Lionel Rogosin and Shirley Clarke; unfortunately, despite their respect for his work, the film-makers had to replace their cameraman when he kept disappearing for cat-naps, it seemed he suffered from narcolepsy – hence the film's three cinematographer credits.)

Yet Cassavetes doesn't reject Hollywood out of hand – after all, if there's one thing Moskowitz and Minnie have in common, it's Humphrey Bogart. John never lost his love and respect for the idealism of a Capra or a Lubitsch, despite his determination that American cinema had profoundly lost its way in the interim.

"Maybe there really wasn't an America – maybe it was only Frank Capra," he wrote in an anniversary edition of *Daily Variety* in October, 1970. "Our children are dying for lack of guidance and, more importantly, ideals. The majority of the audience hang in disbelief, stand on line with expectancy and see films geared solely for exploitative use [so often that audiences begin to accept this exploitation]. They find themselves laughing at what isn't funny, angered by what they don't care about, and influenced and contaminated by hours of unfelt unmotivated propaganda. The cause of motion pictures should not be a dehumanising one. Give the audience the vaguest permission or cause to feel, and they will take the challenge."[12]

It was the insincerity of most contemporary movie-making he really objected to. He went on: "What's wrong with our industry? The answer to this question has always been dependent on what kind of people are in our industry. What are they made of? And, do they have anything to say that they themselves would listen to?"

If Hollywood and the establishment didn't believe in the values they espoused – 'Buffalo Bill's defunct' – on what grounds could the independents open up a meaningful debate?

For Cassavetes, the debate which counted wasn't cerebral or political, at least in the institutional sense, but always emotional. It's Ray Carney's thesis, elucidated in his books *American Dreaming* and *The Films Of John Cassavetes: Pragmatism, Modernism And The Movies*, that the film-maker belongs in the American philosophical tradition of Walt Whitman, Ralph Waldo Emerson and William James, with their revelations of direct, sensory experience, life lived out, stripped of conceptual and intellectual abstraction. Poles apart from the established pantheon of Welles, Hitchcock and Ford, their contained and institutionalised virtuosity, their elaborately metaphorical artifice, Cassavetes plunges into the flux of common social exchange, asserting endless creative, performative possibility as a liberation from unduly inhibited, inherited notions of identity and behaviour.

It sounds complicated, but boils down to an idea as simple as it is radical. It holds that art shouldn't be objectified and fetishised, but incorporated within our daily lives. Emerson: "The true romance which the world exists to realize will be the transformation of genius into practical power." The implications lead Carney to turn film scholarship on its head and reject *Citizen Kane* as the apotheosis of kitsch (his own pantheon includes Dreyer, Capra, Elaine May, Barbara Loden, Paul Morrissey, Jim Jarmusch and Robert Kramer, and also crosses over to Charlie Parker, George Balanchine, and Henry James).

"In my opinion, these people and these small emotions are the greatest political force there is," Cassavetes told Jonas Mekas in December 1971. "These small emotions, these character disagreements are of vital necessity. Judgements have to be left to the audience. The majority of 10,000 people that I've come into contact with personally in my life, I've never seen anyone go and blow somebody's head off. So why should I make a film about them? But I have seen people destroy themselves in the smallest way. I've seen people withdraw, I've seen people hide behind political ideas, behind dope, behind the sexual revolution, behind fascism, behind hypocrisy, and I've myself done all these things. So I can understand them. We have terrible problems, but our problems are human problems."[13]

Minnie And Moskowitz is about the primacy of feeling. Minnie Moore has all the accoutrements society prizes: she's attractive, cultured, sensitive, sophisticated – she has a job in the Los Angeles County Museum – but she's lonely and afraid. Unmarried at an age when that's becoming a cause for concern, she's seen the back of 30 (it's hard to believe, looking at the film, but Rowlands must have been around 40 at the time). It's not that Minnie doesn't feel – "I get more aroused, I'm more willing to give of myself [than ever]," she tells Florence – it's that she bears the emotional scars of her past relationships and is physically abused by her current boyfriend, a married man (played by an unbilled Cassavetes).

If Seymour might see a version of his future in Morgan if he looked hard enough (and he never would), the prospect must be much more acute for Minnie looking at Florence. "Are you still romantic," she asks her. "Do you still do it?" ("Yes," comes the reply, "But I get very frustrated, I don't know whether it's the sex thing or being alone.")

For all that it's the lightest of his mature films – "an entertainment,' Cassavetes called it – *Minnie And Moskowitz* is surprisingly violent and hard-edged. Returning to her apartment after her evening with Florence, Minnie finds a man there, Jim, who introduces himself with a smack across the face. Her blind date with the apoplectically needy Zelmo Swift (Val Avery) like-wise degenerates into verbal and physical abuse in another of Cassavetes' most memorable scenes. Such is their desperate fear of rejection and lone-liness, the men in Minnie's life cling to her, and get angry if she makes an independent move, as if proximity alone gives them possessory rights. Even Seymour has a threatening edge: driving after her in his pickup, right onto the sidewalk; or later, brawling with Dick Henderson (Jack Danskin), when he inadvertently lands a punch on Minnie. Small wonder she takes cover behind her enormous sunglasses whenever a man gets too close.

Yet it's Minnie's caution and reserve the movie breaks down. Under-neath it, she's all alone. In another beautifully written and acted speech, she finally unburdens herself to Seymour:

"I'm having trouble being myself. I'm having trouble feeling what it is that's right, what it is to do. Like being alone. Should I go out or should I just relax to it. What do you think? Everything used to make me feel like smiling – I notice I don't smile as much as I used to. Did you ever notice that? Did you ever notice it's an effort to breathe sometimes, because the air just isn't light enough? You see, my friend – Seymour – I don't have any real problems of any size. It's mainly being alone that makes me so irri-tated. Do you know? I hear room tone when I'm alone. I hear frequencies. Noises like the bathtub running, or the sink, or distant traffic that irritates me. God knows why, because when I'm with somebody I want to get away. There are not too many people that thrill me. I'm not too sociable. Some-body light bores me, somebody heavy depresses me. So you're right, I do look down. I look at you, I look at you and I think what can this poor guy want with someone like me?"

It's a mark of Cassavetes' astonishing facility with tone in this film that this speech segues effortlessly into a giddy, screwball embrace, as Seymour takes her in his arms and carries her up the stairs ("Would you like a cup of tea?" she asks. "Some eggs?"), and then to tears as he puts her down on the bed and promises to watch over her as she sleeps.

In contrast, Seymour is a life-force who coasts on his emotions: he breezes into a bar and tries to pick up every woman in it. Sometimes he gets a beating, sometimes he gets lucky. An extrovert, he leaps before he looks. In his introduction to the published screenplay, Cassavetes describes him as "the new symbol of hope in America. When life achieves sameness he gets bored and moves on. He's a footloose, practical, uncomplicated American dreamer who sees romance in a cup of coffee and pretty eyes. A Seymour Moskowitz has his own style. He's been tugged at and pushed like the rest of us and has emerged like we all wish to be – a guy that knows romance is better than loneliness."

Seymour is the film's crazy comic motor, the loose screw which gives it such a quirky rhythm. Leaning over backwards to impress Minnie, the girl of his dreams, he takes her to a chili dog stand, bitches about the parking fee, and spills relish all over himself. "I usually eat alone," he explains. "In fact I usually eat in my shorts."

You could almost say that *Minnie And Moskowitz* is as much a love-letter to Seymour Cassel as it is to Gena Rowlands. "I think our attraction to each other was our ability to surprise one another, whether it was acting or playing ball or testing a woman," Cassel says. "Part of what we loved in one another was that craziness, like kids: 'I can't believe you did that man, you're crazy!' John encouraged unpredictability. That's what makes you interesting in life. I loved that in John and I think he loved it in me too. My behaviour as a person is probably a little more open and erratic and unpredicable [than most]. We're all like that in private, I think, we're just scared of what other people think, but who cares? Go out and enjoy life!'

"It's not that complicated for Seymour Moskowitz, he knows it's this woman," Cassel says. "I love that about him: the simplicity of his approach to life. He liked cars. You don't have to have these huge ambitions. The most fulfilling one is to have a relationship which lasts."

From Minnie's perspective, Moskowitz is a perfect mismatch: she's refined, he's crude; she's affluent, he still goes to his mother for money; she's introspective and guarded, he's utterly unselfconscious; she's WASP, he's Jewish; she's poised and good looking, he's kind of embarrassing. "He eats sideways," as his own mother helpfully puts it.

The obstacles are plentiful. One thinks of the movie Seymour watches right at the beginning, *The Maltese Falcon*, with Bogart itemising all the many reasons he won't play the sap for Mary Astor, and then looking at the other side of the equation and coming up short: "All we've got is the fact that maybe you love me and maybe I love you." Not enough for Bogart, but more than enough for Seymour.

"I'm just trying to project a week from now; a day from now," Minnie tells him on their second date. "I just can't see myself here."

"I only know I feel something," he replies. "What do you have to think for? I get to thinking I go crazy, man, so I don't think. If it overloads me I run." And off he sprints to prove it. He truly loves her, that's the point. "I think about you so much I forget to go to the bathroom," he avows, one of the cinema's finest romantic declarations.

Minnie shies from the embarrassment, the turmoil and the pain: "There's some kind of craziness going on here that's not right. Every time you come near me you get beaten up; every time I come near you I get cut or I get punched or something. It's not right, Seymour. It's just not there, don't you understand? It's a pretend place that people get to. They just never say it, but it doesn't exist; it's not there, Seymour, it just isn't not there. It's nothing." She doesn't say the word, but it's love she's denying.

It's not Seymour's protestations which turn her round, but when he threatens suicide by nail scissors he unthinkingly snips off his moustache – a comic illustration of his own depth of feeling and love's power as a catalyst for change. They're married four days after their first encounter in the car lot, and the movie ends on an unclouded vision of family harmony: Mr and Mrs Moskowitz at play with a brood of kids and their grandmothers.

"These people are terrific," Cassavetes enthused. "They're going to get married so they call their mothers. The fact that they call their mothers is so fresh and so incredibly emotionally true, to me. I mean the girl calls her mother, she wants to protect her mother and not let anything happen to her, despite the fact she's getting married, because marriage means divorcement from your parents. It's the same thing with Seymour, and . . . they meet, and they don't want their children to get married. They behave politely, but they're not open and happy and warm for their children, even though they're in their thirties and attempting to cure their loneliness. Still, I love Seymour and Minnie because they accept these people, understand what they are. And we can look at them with delight, not distrust."[14]

In contrast to Cassavetes' previous films, *Minnie And Moskowitz* was turned around remarkably quickly. Cassavetes wrote the script in January 1971, but Ned Tanen gave it the go-ahead almost immediately, and Al Ruban and Universal production executive Paul Donnelly set it up fast enough for shooting to begin in New York March 23.

Al Ruban: "He came to me and said 'Look, I'd really like to prove to these guys – all I ever hear is, "You take all the time in the world to shoot it, you have no-one to be beholden to, so what?" I want to show them that I can exist in their world, that I can make my kind of picture on their kind of timetable.' I said, 'Let's do it.' We had a budget that was close to $900,000, we came in $100,000 under budget three days ahead of schedule, and delivered the picture three months early. And it didn't mean anything to the studio. To them it was just a low-budget picture that was competing with their big stuff."

They shot a week in New York, then took a week off to relocate the production to Los Angeles. They wrapped June 17 and the movie was released in December. Comparisons between the final shooting script and the finished picture reveal minimal changes (a bedroom scene between Seymour and the Irish girl he tries to pick up in the bar was cut by Universal for length after the first release). "John wrote the first line of *Minnie And Moskowitz* and I took it with a pencil on a piece of paper," Elaine Kagan says. "I gotta tell you what an extraordinary trip that is a year later, when you sit in a darkened room and some actor up there on this coloured celluloid is saying this thing you wrote in a little squiggly line. That's amazing, how it just comes to life. And John absolutely made you feel part of it. There was a feeling you were all in this together."

✳ ✳ ✳

Gena hadn't especially enjoyed making *Faces*. "The first day you realise your husband doesn't love you anymore," she told an interviewer in 1968. "The second day that he never loved you. The third that he hates you. And after that it gets bad."

The pressure was less intense this time, not only because they'd been through it before, but the professional production made less demands on them, economically and physically; it didn't invade their home in the same way either (although their kitchen and drive did double for Jim's in the brief scene when he returns to his wife and kids). And of course this time Gena wasn't pregnant.

The only time they really fought was when it came to shoot the swimming pool scene, when Gena suddenly announced she couldn't and wouldn't swim. As scripted, it was supposed to be a race between Seymour and Minnie – Cassel speculates that Gena didn't want to lose to him. But Cassavetes was outraged. "What do you mean you can't swim?"

"I can't swim," Gena insisted, "And John, you've never seen me swim."

"Goddamit, Jesus, don't tell me you can't swim."

"John, don't talk like that, if you're going to swear, I'm going to leave."

For once, Cassavetes was dumbfounded. With this woman, you never knew where you were. It was ten years into their marriage before John discovered she knew how to play the piano. He'd been so upset, he refused to speak to her for days. Now, with a movie crew waiting, he simply told her to dive in, and Seymour would save her (judging by her expert dive in the film, Rowlands must have been a quick learner).

Gena also played a trick on him in the scene where John's character, Jim, beats up Minnie. As he feigned the swinging punch, she pulled the old stage trick of clapping her hands behind her back. The camera crew were convinced he'd really made contact and leapt to her aid. "But I wasn't within two feet of her," he complained, as they helped an apparently groggy Rowlands to her feet.

As for Seymour Cassel, he relished what would prove to be the most substantial role of his career. "I got to kiss Gena – and I'd wanted to do that for 12 years," he jokes. His only run-in with John occurred in the romantic scene outside the dance hall, when out of the blue Cassavetes asked him to do a handstand to impress his date. At first Cassel refused, he thought it was crazy and unmotivated – exactly why it works, in effect, as the actor eventually admitted.

In keeping with the spirit of the piece, the movie was very much a family affair. Seymour Cassel's wife, Elizabeth Deering, played the girl he picks up after a fight with Minnie, and her mother, Elsie Ames, played Florence. John's mother Katherine played Seymour's Jewish mother, Mrs Moskowitz. Minnie's mother was played by Gena's mother, Lady Rowlands, and David Rowlands played the preacher who married them. Of course the kids in the final scene were little Cassels and Cassavetes too. "I believe totally in nepotism," John cracked. "It impresses the hell out of my family and friends."

The family casting goes further: associate producer Paul Donnelly's sister, Kathleen O'Malley, played the waitress in the New York diner, and his son played the young car park attendant with the throwaway one-liner, "Sorry about the wall, sir." Eleanor Zee, from the dentist scene in *Husbands*, pops up as the mother on the aeroplane, and Jack Danskin, who played Dick Henderson, was actually the boom operator on the shoot, pressed into service when Cassavetes sacked the actor who'd been cast originally.

According to Seymour Cassel, when Lew Wasserman saw a preview of the finished movie, he was moved to remark, "Terrific picture. Too bad you didn't make it with stars," a comment made within earshot of Seymour and Gena. He missed the point, of course. This movie was no less personal to Cassavetes than *Faces* or *Husbands*, even if its overtly comic register allowed him more lassitude. Casting his wife and his best friend as a couple should be signal enough, and the casting of his mother as Seymour's mom, and Gena's mother as Minnie's (and their grandchildren as their grandchildren) surely clinches it: this picture is a free comic elaboration of

Cassavetes' own whirlwind courtship of Gena Rowlands: John the brash New Yorker, college dropout, and immigrant son; Gena the shy senator's daughter from Wisconsin and Washington. Seen this way, the film becomes a celebration of his wife's power over him, with clumsy, inadequate Moskowitz more or less throwing himself at her feet. The marriage ceremony in the film was in fact based on their own marriage, when the priest really did forget Gena Rowlands' name, and bride and groom couldn't stop themselves cracking up. It may be a fairy tale ending – this 'Happy Ever After' – but it also happens to be true.

✷ ✷ ✷

Universal created a poster campaign with Gena and an upside-down Seymour joined at the head. Cassavetes so hated it that he produced his own fly posters, featuring a still from the wedding scene, and as the movie opened in New York, he and Cassel cruised around Manhattan in one of the studio's black Cadillac limousines, jumping out to plaster their posters on telephone booths and doorways, and laughing uproariously, to the general bewilderment of passers-by – few of whom felt compelled to check out the movie itself.

"John and I went down to Cinema 2 or 3 to check out how it opened," Al Ruban remembers. "When we got to the street it was completely clogged up with people. We were delirious, we thought we had a huge hit. But when we got closer, we couldn't even get in to see *Minnie And Moskowitz*, even though it was empty, for all these queues waiting to see *A Clockwork Orange* which was playing next door. That was a little defeating. Universal wouldn't put any money into promoting it. They said it only cost this much, the advertising is commensurate with the budget."

Critical reaction was mixed but generally positive. Cassel remembers one particularly perplexing response: "Andrew Sarris was critic at *Village Voice* at that time. A wonderful writer, but rather overweight, balding and what hair he has sticks up a little bit. He looked like a porcupine. I know Sarris and I like him, but he married a beautiful woman, Molly Haskell, who came to New York as a model and who became a writer, and was a critic for *Harper's Bazaar* and others. Tall blonde, 5'10" marries short Jewish guy who looks like a porcupine. She loved the movie, he didn't. He didn't believe that Minnie and Seymour would get together. I said 'My God, Andrew look at yourself! It's Molly and you!' He said 'Oh, but that's life and this is a movie.' Impossible!"

In *Newsday*, Joseph Gelmis rated it "The best American movie of 1971," and *Time* also rated it one of the year's best. In *The New Republic*, Stanley Kauffmann called it "Cassavetes' worst film," which was strong condemnation, coming from him. The film-maker could shrug off bad reviews: "It doesn't matter whether they like it, it matters whether they feel something," he said. "We only have two hours to change people's lives."[15]

Gena Rowlands got great reviews; she also received an unusual Christmas present from Seymour: his ponytail.

1 Brent Lewis, JC Recalled, *Films And Filming*, April 1989.
2 'A Director of Influence,' *Film*, v2 n26, May 1975.
3 Linderman.
4 The *New York Times*, Sunday, February 13, 1972.
5 John Cassavetes, *New York Times*, February 13, 1972.
6 Marni Butterfield, 'Gena Rowlands: Portrait of a Happy Actress,' *Show*, v2, n12 February 1972.
7 Judith Crist, 'Take 22,' *Continuum*, NY, 1984.
8 Elaine Goren (Elaine Kagan) Author's interview, (2000).
9 Ed Sikov, *Screwball*, Crown Publishers Inc, 1989.
10 Jeremy Kagan, Author's interview (2000). Kagan met Carey on the set of *Chinese Bookie*.
11 Ara Corbett, 'Rebels with a Cause,' *FilmFax*, n56, May/June 1996.
12 John Cassavetes, 'Maybe There Really Wasn't An America – Maybe It Was Only Frank Capra,' *Daily Variety*, Oct 27, 1970.
13 Jonas Mekas, 'Movie Journal,' *Village Voice*, December 23, 1971.
14 'See With Director John Cassavetes,' *The Herald*, January 9, 1972.
15 *The Herald*, January 9, 1972.

'Never A Safe Place.'

John Sayles

It might have been *Shadows* or *Faces* or *A Woman Under The Influence*. A kid in his teens or early twenties sits in a little art house or college auditorium watching the screen, and it dawns suddenly – "This is an American movie, but I know these people. It isn't a Technicolor dream or a cartoon with live actors; it doesn't drip with studio mood music or theatrical problem-drama dialogue. There is recognizable human behavior, adult human behavior, happening up on a movie screen. What gives? Who did this and how?"

And in that dawning came the realization that this was something else an American film could aspire to, that the Europeans weren't the sole proprietors of the natural moment. And for some the question: "Where do I sign up?"

Working both in the mainstream and on independent films, I meet lots of those kids, older now and working as directors, producers, writers, editors, cinematographers, actors. When the early promise of Brando and Dean seemed bent on recycling tired dreams, John Cassavetes jumped in head first, armed with an actor's sporadic wages and the nerve to be an amateur in a game rigged for professionals. His early movies were on-the-job training, with most of the seams showing, but they managed to hit notes the slicker movies couldn't approach.

Actors love John Cassavetes' movies because he respects the human process, the struggle to communicate confused emotions. His characters repeat themselves, contradict themselves, paint themselves into verbal corners – but always keep plugging, keep trying to break through to some understanding or human connection. His characters don't get to be cool, knowing, detached.

For an actor, he offers the thrill of true engagement with the other actors, you lock into each other and truly don't know the emotional direction (though the lines may be scripted) your partner in a scene is going to take you. He directed and edited, made choices, shaped his movies, but you get the sense the actors involved had the time and freedom to try anything without fear of ridicule, that the only way you could fail was by being lazy.

Above all, it was raw cinema, no place to hide a performance in a tricky cut or camera move, risky business for an actor. When it didn't come alive, the actor's technique was laid out naked, all vanities exposed. But when it did work, the audience felt the anger and tentativeness, the discomfort and

111

sometimes even the desperate caring that other movies tried so hard to objectify and make safe.

Watching a Cassavetes movie was never a safe place to be; it always threatened to come and get you. *In A Woman Under The Influence*, Gena Rowlands made audiences queasy with embarrassment for her mad house-wife, a mass of moviegoers breaking out in sympathetic flop sweat as she began to unravel in public. If the traditional Hollywood hero is 'the man who knows,' Cassavetes' heroes were the men and women who doubted.

Our media culture is so pervasive, so prolific, that influence in the arts is three-dimensional rather than linear. Cassavetes must have had his own influences, movies he'd seen or actors he'd worked with. But his most important source seemed to be our own doubting, inarticulate, love-hungry lives – a source mainstream movie culture needs a shot of from time to time.

Cassavetes' other legacy lies not in the content or style of his films, but in the mere fact of them. Their existence proved that if you were willing to pay the price, this can be done. It was never easy, and you were likely to get your head handed to you critically and financially, but you could make movies outside the mainstream industry. And if that system was not interested in distributing those movies, you could try to get them seen on your own.

Many of today's leading distributors of foreign and 'Off Hollywood' pictures cut their teeth stumping for a John Cassavetes movie. Fresh from their college film societies or wandering in and out of the audience, they had to create their own system, to develop a personalized, labor-intensive technique for selling a film that is still the only answer for most low-budget, 'word-of-mouth' movies. Cassavetes did it and kept doing it, not to chase the brass ring of a 'breakthrough' hit, but to tell the stories he wanted to tell the way he wanted to tell them. His career as a director was a great, subversive act, and you never got the feeling watching his movies that he expected any thanks for it.

I never met John Cassavetes, but I saw most of the films he directed. A lot of people making movies in America today are deeply in his debt. Many of these people have never seen any of his work, but for others that debt is an obvious one. I hope his movies find a place in our theaters, become readily available on cassette, get seen. Not for any academic, history of cinema purpose, but so the watchers can meet the people in them, can come up against Cassavetes himself in one of his intense, passionate family dramas. I hope there will be more kids who sit in theaters or school auditoriums or in front of video screens and experience that dawning, "My God, I know these people." And for some, "Where do I sign up?"

John Sayles
(Writer/director: *The Return Of The Secaucus Seven;*
Baby, It's You; City Of Hope: Matewan;
Passion Fish; Lone Star; Limbo)

7

A Woman Under The Influence

'There's the outside world and there is the inside world. The inside world is your home, your family, the things that create emotions within you. The outside world is you: where you are going and how you move and where you fly. I really believe – after making the picture, not before – that the inside world really holds you, really contains you, can cause you pain that you don't show outside, and that is why no one ever talks about it.'

John Cassavetes discussing *A Woman Under The Influence*

Mike Ferris had mustered out of the service in 1968. A life-long movie fan, he had been in New York, "inching my way toward Hollywood," as he puts it, when he saw *Faces*. "I thought why am I here doing this when I could be out there doing that?" he remembers.

Ferris had made it to Los Angeles by 1970. Within three months his friend Gary Graver gave him a gig as a camera assistant: they went out into the desert and shot *The Other Side Of The Wind* with Orson Welles – an on-again, off-again production which would resume every so often over the next seven or eight years. He picked up other work too, *Boxcar Bertha*, Corman stuff, but he was still a novice when, driving up Laurel Canyon in the summer of 1972 he spotted Seymour Moskowitz stopped at a light on his motorbike. Ferris had seen *Minnie And Moskowitz* fourteen times already, it was his favourite movie. Seymour felt like a friend. So he gave him a shout: "Hey, Seymour!"

To Mike's surprise, Seymour yanked the bike around and came up alongside him. "Hey, man. What's up?" he said. He looked just like he did in the movie.

Ferris blurted out how he'd seen it fourteen times and how he loved *Faces* and what he was doing in Hollywood.

"Well, man, your timing is great," Seymour told him. "John's just gearing up to do another film. Why don't you call him?" And he gave him the number of Cassavetes' new office over at CBS Studios.

"So I raced home and I looked at the phone and I picked it up and I called," Ferris says. "I didn't know how I was going to get past the secretaries when a pert lady's voice answered the phone and said 'Faces

International.' I said "Hi, this is Mike Ferris, can I talk to John Cassavetes?"

"Yeah, hold on." Just like that. It didn't take 15 seconds, "Hi this John."

I blurted out everything I had told Seymour and he just listened. I told him I would do anything to be part of his gang.

"He said 'What are you doing Friday? About five o'clock. Come down to the office we'll have a chat.'

"I got there at five, he had a pass waiting for me at the front gate. He had a big open-plan office on the second floor, like the big newsroom in *The Front Page*. There was nobody there except this little group in the corner: Ben Gazzara walking around with a cigar, kind of boisterous; Peter Falk, just sitting on a couch, talking. And over on the right there's John Cassavetes talking to this lady who's writing furiously on a note pad. He's dictating a script to her. He stops what he's doing, he comes over and shakes hands as if I was a visiting dignatory. Very open, very friendly. Takes me over to Peter and Ben and introduces me as if I was one of them. Then takes me into the back, into one of the glass partitions, sits behind a desk, reaches out a script that's half the size of the phone book and tells me it's the script to *A Woman Under The Influence*. And he talked to me for an hour and a half about the characters and the story. That's how I met John Cassavetes."[1]

A Woman Under The Influence started out as a play. "John and I had been talking, as usual, about stories and ideas – and just life, generally," Gena Rowlands told Judith Crist. "I thought that I'd like to do a play, and John was interested in writing a play – which he had never done. He asked what I was thinking of, what kind of play. I said I didn't know, I would like to do something that relates to women right now, some modern problem that people are struggling with – and at the same time, I'd hope it was a problem that women have always struggled with. It was some time before he wrote the play, but he finally brought it to me and said 'See what you think.' So I read this play – and I just couldn't believe it. I couldn't believe John wrote it. I was astounded and moved by it – and at the same time I realised that I couldn't play that on stage. I couldn't last two nights playing that – and in a week I'd have to be hospitalised. Then I felt like the basest ingrate in the world. We talked about it and he said he understood, and then he said 'I think I have another idea'."

"He went away, mysteriously – and actually I would have stopped him if I had known what he was doing. He wrote two other plays with the same characters – and if you saw all three plays on successive nights it made a whole, or you could see each play individually of itself. In the two new plays the other characters had more to do, but my role would still have been quite substantial. Well, if you think I felt like an ingrate the first time – I said 'I don't think you really understood what I meant. Doing three plays is not going to be easier than doing one play.' We talked seriously about it for a while, trying to see if there would be any way to do it. Finally he said, 'Well, then, I'll write it as a screenplay'."[2]

Cassavetes' relationship with Universal had soured again – none of Tanen's movies were working at the box-office – and the other studios were playing it safe. "Nobody wants to see a crazy middle-aged dame, anyway," one executive told him. John couldn't agree. This was something he just had to do. Like *Minnie And Moskowitz*, *A Woman Under The Influence* deals with love and marriage, but it probes far deeper. Its characters are more sorely tested, and in some important ways they are found wanting. Friends who had participated in read-throughs of the plays at Woodrow Wilson Drive (including Peter Falk, Elaine May and the Cassels) were enthusiastic about it, and after all, they'd made films their way before, lived to tell the tale, and even turned a profit. Cassavetes sat down with Sam Shaw, and worked out that they could produce it themselves for about $800,000. John resolved to mortgage his house, and Falk agreed to come in with him – and he had another suggestion: why didn't John come in and co-star in an episode of *Columbo*?[3] The series was a huge hit, syndicated in 35 different countries – Falk had even made the cover of *Time*, with his stogie and his dirty old raincoat – and John's salary could go straight into the movie.[4]

By the time the film started coming together Peter Falk was entertaining a lucrative offer to star in *Day Of The Dolphin* for his friend Elaine May's old partner, Mike Nichols. After *Who's Afraid Of Virginia Woolf*, *The Graduate* and *Carnal Knowledge* Nichols enjoyed a golden reputation, but it was too late to switch allegiances, they were all in this together: "By the time we were done with *Husbands*, it occurred to me that maybe this guy Cassavetes was on to something and I didn't know it," Falk recalls. "I had to give it another shot." He told John he'd match any funds he put in.

Cassavetes decided they would start shooting in two months, in the fall. He assembled a crew. There was no money, they'd be working for the love of it. Caleb Deschanel would be the lighting cameraman – he was a bright young USC graduate. Deschanel brought Fred Elmes with him, also from USC, but he didn't take to Mike Ferris much. He thought he was too green to be trusted. Elaine Goren was pressed into service as the script supervisor.

Most of the action would be centred around a single location: the home owned by Nick and Mabel Longhetti, an ordinary working class couple. "We looked at maybe 150 houses," Cassavetes said. "It was really hard to find something in the right price range that would make you feel you were in a real house and also depict the kind of blue collar existence we had in mind. Some of the houses we scouted had plastic covers on everything, plastic pictures on the walls, and most of the family's money went into electrical appliances. That's a very real thing, but we didn't want it. So we decided we needed a hand-me-down house and finally found one that that had been given to the Nick character and still had all the old furniture and old woodwork."[5]

It was big, old fashioned looking place on Taft, in the depths of Hollywood. The production offices occupied the second floor, and Cassavetes set his crew to cleaning up the downstairs, washing and scrubbing and painting. "It was like Judy Garland and Mickey Rooney: let's put on a show in the barn!" Mike Ferris says. "John was there too, on his hands and knees. And by the time it was done he knew everyone's personality, and how to use them. He only wanted to work with people who were interested in looking for the same truths he wanted, and willing to pay the price you pay for that: hard work and giving up whatever your life is for four or five months. And he was able to do that. Those kinds of people were drawn to him."

Cassavetes told Bo Harwood, who had supervised the music on *Minnie And Moskowitz* and helped out on the editing of *Husbands* that he'd like him to compose a score. Harwood was a guitar player, a hippie out of Haight-Asbury, the Summer of Love. "He told me we were going to start shooting in a month and a half, and he wanted me to compose a theme on piano. I said 'I'm a guitar player, I don't play piano. I don't even read music.' So he said 'We'll rent a piano.' We rented a piano, and he moved me into Peter Falk's bungalow on the Universal lot, which Peter didn't use much, and I started working on a theme for *A Woman Under The Influence* and trying to play the piano."[6]

Three weeks before shooting was due to start Cassavetes called him over from where he was working on the house. He said, "Bo, you record all your own music on tape recorders and stuff, why don't you do the sound on the movie too?"

"I was like, 'Are you out of your fucking mind?' I didn't have a clue. He'd had one of the best sound men in the business, but he didn't like his energy, so he let him go. He told me, go rent a Nagra, learn how to use it. And that's how I started mixing. I found a boom guy who could carry me for the first couple of weeks, and I learned everything I could. I don't mind telling you the first week we started I had to go for a walk and barf every morning I was so scared I'd screw up."

"When I first got caught up with this guy Cassavetes, I thought he was a square from New York," Harwood says. "It didn't take me too long to realise I was the conventional one and he was the freak. He made me feel conservative. He was always breaking my patterns, putting me on uncharted ground."

Two days before the shoot was due to start, Michael Lally, the production manager, called everyone in for a meeting of cast and crew and announced that they would have to push the start date back. They had no money, no film stock.

Cassavetes went crazy. "I don't give a fuck if we don't have any money. I don't give a fuck if we don't have any film in the camera, in two days time we are going on that set, the actors are going to be in front of the lens, we are going to be behind the lens, and we are going to go!"

Somehow, the next day, Cassavetes got his hands on 10,000 feet of film and they were up and running.

Nick Longhetti is a blue collar worker employed by the city engineering department. Nick's a straight-ahead guy, good at his job (he's a foreman), but mindful of his family responsibilities: he has an elderly mother, Margaret (played by Katherine Cassavetes), a wife, Mabel (Gena Rowlands), and three kids under the age of ten: Tony, Angelo and Maria (played by Matthew Cassel, Matthew Laborteaux and Christina Grisanti, respectively). Nick's not particularly religious, not political or intellectual, he's just a well brought up working-class guy who wants to be liked and respected, and genuinely tries to behave in a likable, respectable manner.

Nick's done one brave, foolhardy, individual thing in his whole life. He married Mabel. Mabel who loves him more than anyone will ever love him; Mabel who is beautiful and wild and unpredictable. And Mabel who is 'unusual,' eccentric, and maybe – though Nick won't stand for it to be spoken out loud – maybe a little bit crazy. He's crazy about her, too, if it comes to that.

The film's principal action unfolds over just a couple of days, in which time Nick will commit his wife to a mental hospital; and then the last act takes place over the course of an hour or two, six months later, on Mabel's release. It begins with Nick standing up his wife after she has packed their kids off to her mother's for a promised night of love. He's called in to fix a burst watermain, there's nothing he can do.

Mabel listens, she hears him, but she cannot bare to be alone. She goes out to a bar for a drink, and there she picks up a man, Garson. Drunk, she brings him back home, and is unable to resist when he forces himself on her. The next morning he's freaked out when she insists that he is her husband. Shortly afterwards, Nick shows up with his entire crew for breakfast. Mabel makes them welcome, sits them down for spaghetti and makes conversation. But she is too solicitous. It becomes embarrassing to

117

Nick, who smacks her down. They argue, and his colleagues make their excuses and leave. Despite everything, Nick and Mabel are able to make up and make love.

That afternoon, Mabel anxiously waits for their kids to come home from school. She is springing a surprise party for them. Harold Jensen arrives with his kids. He doesn't know Mabel and her uninhibited spontaneity makes him uncomfortable. He is worried about leaving his children with her. Nick phones up and it sounds like chaos to him. He rushes home and finds Jensen in his bedroom – he reacts violently as if it were Mabel's lover.

That evening Mabel tries to make her husband see that he's been a fool, but that it doesn't matter: they still love each other. Nick is angry and humiliated. He has called his mother over for reinforcements and the family doctor, Doctor Zepp. Rejected and afraid, Mabel suffers a nervous breakdown. Zepp gives her a shot and she has to be committed.

The next day at work Nick cannot take the reproach and concern of his workmates. He lashes out blindly and one of the men ends up hurt. Nick pulls his kids out of school and insists they all go to the seaside together. He wants to make it up to them; wants them to forgive him.

Six months later: Mabel is coming home. Nick has arranged a huge welcoming party of family and friends. Then, before she arrives, he gets cold feet and sends everyone away save for the family. Mabel is cowed and overwhelmed and not herself. She wants to be alone with her husband and her children. Nick hates to see her like this, but tries to force good spirits on the occasion. It only sends Mabel back to the brink: she gets up on the sofa and begins to dance.

At last Nick throws everyone out. He and Mabel scuffle and she tries to cut her wrists. Only the intervention of the children brings them back to their senses. Tenderly, lovingly, they put the children to bed and follow suit themselves.

Consider Mabel, packing off the kids with her mother (Lady Rowlands) for the night, a blur of anxiety, agitation and excitement. Already it's clear that this will be an intensely physical performance from Gena Rowlands: free-wheeling a child's bike down the driveway, or hopping on the lawn after a sandal has gone astray. Yet what follows is an enforced stasis: Mabel in her large, old fashioned, suburban house, waiting.

The kids gone, it's clear she doesn't know what to do with herself. She fools with a box for a minute, claps her hands, mutters something, switches on the radio. Cassavetes' camera adopts an unusually formal distance, static and locked off, as Mabel stands in the shadowy hallway, alone with her thoughts. It's a faintly theatrical set-up, and a tellingly rare instance, up to this point, of a Cassavetes character in solitude – one thinks of Maria Forst, putting her house in order for the night before Chet surprises her, or Minnie Moore, again, surprised to find Jim in her home. Here, Mabel is in for a disappointment; her date doesn't show. A burst water main will keep Nick busy all night. Mabel's more akin to Reuben Widdicombe, neglected every visiting day in *A Child Is Waiting*.

It makes sense that Cassavetes found his métier in film-making, the most collaborative of art-forms, because for him, to be alone is to be already a little dead; it's only in communion with others that we can amount to something. "The nature of living is defined not by money, political power and the like, but by virtue of the fact that we are social beings," Cassavetes said.[7] He would agree with Martin Buber: "The uniqueness of man proves himself in his life with others. For the more unique a man really is, so much the more can he give to the other."

Yet there's an element of denial in such a philosophy, as the maker of *Faces* surely recognised. In their very different ways, *Husbands* and *Minnie And Moskowitz* are explicitly flights of fantasy; with *A Woman Under The Influence*, a more contemplative artist emerges, readier to confront existential ideas and fears. Loneliness is precisely Mabel's problem, and this is one of the reasons *A Woman Under The Influence* had a mixed reception from feminists, who welcomed the film's implicit criticism of the housewife's constricted role in society, but not Mabel's self-insufficiency or her emotional fragility. On the face of it, she's no feminist role model. For Cassavetes, 'Women like Mabel can go mad simply because they are isolated in their homes. Mabel must find out what others are thinking just so that she may gain a feeling for life. It is only by interacting with them, by engaging in some sort of a competition with others that she feels alive.'[8]

She wilts some, in her floral print dress, but Mabel isn't entirely negated in her solitude: the aria playing on her radio is allowed to continue even as night falls around her on the porch; the music – a duet from *La Bohème* – bestows its own grace and gravitas on her, and this too is a sign of Cassavetes maturing as an artist. While jazz, singing and dancing were clearly always important to him, the music in *Faces* and *Husbands* is used with puritan restraint, and mostly confined to the diagesis in time-honoured vérité style. That began to change with Bo Harwood's cautiously sparse trad jazz arrangements in *Minnie And Moskowitz*, and markedly here, with Harwood's subtle but emotionally expressive sound design incorporating his own original score – notably a melancholy, pensive piano blues, sometimes augmented with wordless vocal harmonising – appropriations from opera (Puccini, in keeping with the Longhetti's ethnic background) and *Swan Lake*, associated with Mabel in particular, a dying swan herself.

"Listening to the music in all of John's films there are several places where I break out in a cold sweat because musically it's so bad," Harwood confesses. "The meter is bad, or the sound is bad. John loved the music in *Woman*, he said it was the best film music he'd ever heard – and I believe he meant it. But I don't agree with it."

"The premise was, I would do a rough track of the score in the office (apart from a little orchestrated stuff): the piano stuff, the guitar stuff, the la-la-la, all that was recorded in my little office with an inexpensive tape recorder. It was temp music. And John fell in love with it. I was supposed to rerecord it, to orchestrate it, but we didn't have the money or the time to do it, and the truth was John didn't want to: he wanted to keep it raw and innocent, and that's where he kept me. And the films we did after it was basically the same thing: a lot of things you hear are temp recordings for a pre-mix. Often he'd let me go into the studio and record it properly, and I would think it sounded great, but then when we came to the final mix he'd listen to both, give me a look and my heart would sink. He double-crossed me lot like that."

Like Jess Polanski and Maria Forst before her, Mabel seeks solace in a bar and male company. In the synopsis he wrote for the press book, Cassavetes says, "For the first time we recognise this is a woman who's incapable of handling the dangers of the outside world. The talk with the new man at the bar is strange, she drinks too much and too fast, she sings a few strains of an old song and leans heavily upon the man trying to gain comfort and love."

Drunk, she agrees to take the man, Garson (OG Dunn), back to her place. There, she tries to fend him off, but he takes advantage; rape is implicit. The next morning, she wakes in her bed and hears a man getting dressed in the next room, talking softly to himself, and she shouts out for her husband. Garson is courteous and gentlemanly, but he's not Nick. She knows it and she refuses to know it. She slept with a man, therefore that man is Nick. QED. At the same time, she whispers to herself, "Mama, what do you think of him? I know you can't like him, because he's not your son, but." It's a scary non-sequitur, and proof, if it's needed, that Mabel's not playing games with Garson, she really has lost her grip on reality. (Bo Harwood even puts a faint, neurotic electric guitar pulse under the scene.)

So, there is madness in Mabel. It's referred to first when Nick talks to his work mate Eddie (Charles Horvarth) at the scene of the burst water main. It's pointedly Eddie whom Nick confides in, excusing another worker from the cab of their truck – granting Eddie a respect which the audience may remember after Mabel is committed, and his silent reproach proves too much for Nick to bear. Eddie tells Nick he has to call his wife, to let her know he can't come home. "Mabel's a delicate, sensitive woman," he says.

"Mabel's not crazy," Nick retorts. "She's unusual, she's not crazy, so don't say she's crazy. This woman cooks, sews, makes the bed, washes the bathroom, what the hell is crazy about that? I don't understand what she's doing, I admit that. She's not like a normal person. Jesus Christ, I don't know what she can do."

Judged by social norms, Mabel is 'unusual'; yet she cooks, sews, performs those tasks routinely allotted to a working class wife and mother in America in the early Seventies. And more: when Nick brings home his entire work crew – a dozen men – after they've worked through the night (as protection against his wife's wrath? Or confident in her hospitality?), Mabel's only thought is to make them welcome. That's her problem, Cassavetes told an audience of students after a screening of the film at Chicago's Columbia College: "Her problem was that she was doing everything to please someone other than herself. When Nick wanted her to go to bed with him, she'd go to bed. If he wanted her to apologise, she'd apologise. He wanted her to be nice to ten guys coming in at 8:00 in the morning – ten guys for spaghetti – well, that is a man's dream. She really is under the influence of family and Nick."[9]

'Tell me what you want me to be. I can be anything you want'
Mabel Longhetti

The famous spaghetti scene is superficially analogous to the bar scene which occurs at roughly the same point in *Husbands*: again, we have a dozen or so figures sitting at a long table, this time eating as well as drinking. Again, there is a strong improvisational feel, with characters speaking off camera, speaking over each other, blocking sight-lines, and the sequence plays out in real time over ten minutes or so. The result is a deep grounding, a foundation on which the film's sense of reality rests. As Ray Carney has pointed out, there are very few social signifiers to be found in the Longhetti household – one plain wooden crucifix – compared to the talismanic Italian-American treasure troves you find in *Raging Bull*, or *The Godfather*. As this film makes clear, Cassavetes' 'realism' is not a question of diligently accumulated props and exemplary art direction, except at the most elementary level; his authenticity is above all temporal, and based on a strict philosophical commitment to the present tense, the actor's perpetual realisation of the moment.

Such assertions sound pretentious, but in fact they come down to practical technique. Unlike the wilfully excessive wake in *Husbands*, the spaghetti scene is acted by a mostly professional cast (including Hugh Hurd and Cliff Carnell from *Shadows* and *Too Late Blues*, as well as John's close friends James Joyce and John Finnegan), and if it wasn't strictly scripted, it was at least rehearsed a dozen times ("30 times," Cassavetes told one interviewer), on and off camera. (It was well rehearsed in another sense, too. The cast frequently sat down together at the very same tables for their meals. "A lot of spaghetti got eaten," as Peter Falk remarked.)

In what had become Cassavetes' standard operating procedure, *A Woman Under The Influence* was shot as near as possible in continuity – all the scenes at the house were shot in order – in long, undisrupted takes, often running until the film ran out. The camera crew mostly used long lenses on a 35mm Mitchell so as not to intrude on the actors' space, with neutral camera set-ups to avoid any obvious editorialising (the movie is almost entirely shot at eye-level).

Cassavetes would shoot a scene perhaps a dozen times from a different angle, but each time in full, as if it were the master-shot. In a sense, every shot is the master-shot. "Usually the actors don't know what's being shot. Even though we sometimes shoot very tight, they never know when the camera's going to swing on them, so everyone has to play every moment," he told *Film-makers' Newsletter*. "If you set up a formalised shot, the tendency is for the actors to let down when they're not on screen. So the fluidity of the camera really keeps it alive and allows the operator to make his selections emotionally." It was, he accepted, "more like documentary work" than the traditional Hollywood model, and it led to a bust-up with Caleb Deschanel, who took aesthetic pride in what he was shooting.

An aspiring film-maker himself, Jeremy Kagan was a vistor to the set: "John encouraged freedom, but he knew what he was aiming at. It wasn't amorphous; he knew where he wanted to put the camera and could even be argumentative about it. There were real disagreements with the young cinematographer at the beginning of *Woman*. He had a lot of forethought about what was needed; he understood the medium very well."

Mike Ferris remembers turning up for work one day and being ushered in to see John. "He told me he just fired Caleb and we were going to shoot the rest of the movie between us. He said 'Mike, anybody can shoot,' and he thrust the camera in my hands. He was fearless. He didn't believe you could make a mistake, didn't mind breaking the rules – I don't think he ever knew there were any."

"John was much more interested in the atmosphere for the actors than the camera. He didn't rehearse like everyone else. Mostly people let the actors work out where they're going to go, but don't hesitate to move them around to hit certain marks to the camera's advantage. That's the traditional Hollywood way, and it's why they look so good. If you don't go where the light is, you won't look good. John couldn't have been less interested in that. We would light the rooms with photofloods, because you couldn't be stopping the action once it started. So we lit for what was going to happen in every room, which is why it has a harsh, stark look. We would try to get a feel of what was going on as he would set things up. Then we'd put the camera here and another camera there, and the actors would start to go and we'd get what they did documentary style."

On *A Woman Under The Influence*, Cassavetes estimated they shot 700,000 feet of film (Ferris reckons a million feet), upwards of 100 hours of footage, a shooting ratio wildly in excess of studio practice.

Between a quarter and a third of the film was shot handheld, and invariably Cassavetes operated these shots himself on a 35mm Arriflex. "Once there's a handheld camera up there, the actors go much faster," he noted. "When I'm shooting, I think nothing of saying to the actors 'Get the hell out of there, move, move!' But I don't think the camera operators would dare to take that privilege." Again, this broke with the established Hollywood norm at the time, where the handheld camera was deemed to be disruptive and alienating, except in rapid-fire action scenes.[10]

Quite often, he'd use two cameras at the same time. "He liked the fluidity that it provided. That the actors would be all on camera rather than [separated in] individual shots or over the shoulder shots," Al Ruban says. "It made the actors more energetic, but it also provided something for John. It kept the scenes alive, kept things flowing."

You only have to watch the films to know the value of these techniques: they are alive in a way few movies can match (hence, surely, the prevailing myth that they were improvised). For all that *A Woman Under The Influence* started out as a piece of theatre, and could also be said to have been acted out in a theatrical manner, the effect is theatrical only in as much as it preserves some of the immediate connection felt between actors and audience. Cassavetes works constantly to break down the mental proscenium arches with which most film-makers frame and rhetorise their material.

The spaghetti breakfast is crucial because it brings together the two sides of Nick's life: work and home. "James Turner. I work with Nick," one of men introduces himself. "Mabel Longhetti. I live with Nick," rhymes Mrs Longhetti. Work and home: the dichotomy cuts deep through Cassavetes' films, most explicitly in *Faces* and *Husbands*, and reveals itself in myriad aspects in *A Woman Under The Influence*, including public and private realms (signposted, literally, by the 'Private' sign prominently displayed in the Longhetti home on their bathroom door, and which happens to appear directly above Mabel's head in this scene); also rational and emotional;

male and female. "I think all of us have at least two selves, and one of the selves is full of duty and responsibility, and the other is a personal self full of drama, emotions and dreams," Cassavetes once said, adding: "An actor is really representative of the conflict between those selves." In his early forties, Cassavetes was reaching a balance in his own life between the two: a reconciliation inspired more than anything by the example of his wife and star, Gena Rowlands.

With Nick at one end of the long, narrow table, and Mabel at the other, the gap between them speaks volumes. What's striking is the degree to which Cassavetes is prepared to indulge the 'personal self' of drama, emotion and dreams, epitomised by Mabel, over and above the dutiful, responsible Nick.

Mabel instinctively treats Nick's workmates as family. She cooks for them, toasts them, asks after their wives and kids; she tries to put them at ease. When Vito starts singing, and then Willie (Hugh Hurd) takes up the aria, it's a spontaneous seranade, a heartfelt tribute to their hostess. Moved (again, quite literally, as if transported by the music), Mabel wants to dance with Billy Tidroe, or Vito, or any one of them; such is her own emotional openness, her need to share and sustain the goodwill around her. This to Nick's growing irritation, embarrassment and, finally, anger: "Get your ass down!" he yells, firmly putting his wife in her place, and the men too, visibly cowed and embarrassed both by her surfeit of spontaneity, and his crushing sense of propriety.

This contretemps sets the pattern. Mabel is uninhibited to a point where those around her feel threatened – and Nick most of all, so mindful of keeping up appearances that he becomes a coercive and oppressive force. While he is linked to parental repression – in his alliance with his shrill and embittered mother – Mabel is child-like in her submission to authority, her willingness to please, and her open emotional responses. (Childlike too in her naive dress and the hairclip she sometimes wears.) Contrast the parallel episodes with the kids: the elation Mabel feels when the school bus finally comes in to view; her natural physical and verbal interaction with them (she loses the race home; asks for a back rub; want to know what they think of her); the party she orchestrates, with music and dance and costumes and nakedness. for which she is punished so cruelly. Against this, we have Nick abducting his kids from school the day after he's sent Mabel to the hospital; a muddled bid to assuage his own guilt which involves marching them down the beach and insisting that everyone has fun – eventually pouring beer down their throats to pacify them. It's not that he doesn't love them, he simply doesn't speak their language.

Carney points out that husband and wife are both images of a director:

Mabel an improviser, actively engaging with her co-performers, spon-taneously drawing them out of themselves (not only the kids, but Billy Tidroe, Mr Jensen, and those relatives who welcome her back home); Nick a dictator, marshalling his minions to enact a received, predetermined sem-blance of 'happy families.' Nick bark outs his instructions, hand to mouth as if he's used to wielding a megaphone. Mabel, in contrast, expresses herself physically, in dance, play, and the pronounced gestures and tics which accompany her breakdown.

Nick's great showpiece is the welcoming party he assembles for Mabel's return from the hospital, a farce in which the audience (the friends of the family) are asked to leave before the performance has even begun, scripted with banalities ("Normal conversation," Nick demands. "Weather!"), and which eventually founders on its inherent misconception – and its leading actress's subversive performance. "I wish you would all go home, Nick and I want to go to bed together," she announces to the assembly. And when that fails, she tries direct action: an impromptu dance on the couch does the trick. Like Myrtle in *Opening Night*, Mabel refuses to stick to her appointed role – they both 'lose the plot,' a characteristic many critics have ascribed to Cassavetes himself over the years.

Cassavetes' cinema of disrupture hinges on just this refusal to promote convention over individuality.

"I have five points, Nick."

Mabel

"There's a lot I don't understand," Cassavetes admitted. "I'm totally an intuitive person. I mean, I think about things that human beings would do, but I just am guessing – so I don't really have a preconceived vision of the way a performer should perform. Or, quote, the character, unquote. I don't believe in 'the character.' Once the actor's playing that part, that's the person. And it's up to that person to go in and do anything he can. If it takes the script this way and that, I let it do it. But that's because I really am more an actor than a director. And I appreciate that there might be some secrets in people. And that that might be more interesting than a 'plot.' All people are really private – as a writer and a director, you under-stand that that's the ground rule: people are private."[11]

Cassavetes' narrative strategy is almost always to dispense with expla-nation or explication; he begins scenes (and entire movies) in midflow, and cuts them before they reach a dramatic end-point. Conversely, he'll focus on apparently mundane and dramatically superfluous action with the concentration of an anthropologist (according to an intriguing rumour, one cut of *A Woman Under The Influence* played with the minimalist severity of Chantal Ackerman's 1975 film *Jeanne Dielman, 23 Quai du Commerce, 1080 Bruxelles*). There's a correlation with bebop here. Like Charlie Parker and Miles Davis, Cassavetes could take a standard tune and turn it inside out, find a new stress or an unexpected rhythm. In these ways, the artist can put his audience off balance, and hopefully in a more receptive state. In *A Woman Under The Influence*, for instance, we are invited to expect Nick to come home and discover his wife with Garson; he doesn't, but there is an unresolved tension lurking in the house which makes Nick's misdirected outburst at finding Mr Jensen in his bedroom all the more violent.

Equally, when Nick's mother blurts out to the doctor that last night Mabel had a man in the house (Garson), Cassavetes demands that we make the connections: that Mabel has confessed to Nick; that he in turn has felt the need to tell his mother. And so the betrayal shifts from errant wife to faithless husband, and the shocking realisation that Nick is committing Mabel to an institution out of embarrassment, just as she says.

"You got embarrassed and you made a jerk of yourself, that's all," Mabel pleads, in the aftermath of Nick's fight with Mr Jensen. "I make a jerk of myself every day. I'm not sore at you. I always understood you and you always understood me. And that's just how it was. 'Til death do us part,' Nick, you said it. They can't pull us apart, they can't force us apart."

Unusually, Cassavetes shoots Mabel's close-up here in wide angle, subtly distorting her face as if she'd been cornered by the camera. Caged, desperate, she knows she needs to touch her husband where he's most vulnerable – she needs to remind him that he loves her, that they're together. But Nick shuts her out: 'Mabel, I don't know you.'

Gena Rowlands is naturally a poised and sophisticated actress; the phrase 'lady-like' invariably comes up when friends talk about her. But Mabel has none of that. There's turmoil in every gesture she makes. Under duress, her nervous insecurity fiddles and flinches in involuntary spasms; because she hasn't the language to articulate her desperation it comes out in guttural exclamations, splutters, digital semaphor, airs and affectations, a gurning grimace, or even chop-socky histrionics.

"All I know is this woman couldn't speak," Rowlands explained. "When you can't speak – when you're playing that kind of part and becoming involved in it – then things will start happening with your body. The human spirit will not take it silently. If you cannot express something verbally, it will come out in some other way – and in her it came out in bizarre physical gestures. But I didn't plan it, I didn't plan anything physically for this picture."[12]

Unlike her husband, Rowlands disliked to improvise and would stick closely to the letter of the script. Her technique involved detailed emotional preparation. Cassavetes said that he once stole a look at her copy of the script and felt guilty, as if he'd read her diary: it was full of observations and reflections, notes about her character's feelings towards everyone else in each scene. Highly sensitive to those around her, stricken and beseeching, Mabel was the most draining and demanding part John could have written for his wife.

"You know it's us." Mabel pleads. "You're going with them now? They're on the outside and we're supposed to be on the inside."

More than any character he ever wrote, Mabel is love and only love. And perhaps that is the greatest virtue of this, one of the greatest performances in all of cinema.

Cassavetes: "Gena reads this script and she takes and interprets that woman as someone that is innocent. That's not my interpretation. That's not in the script. You could interpret it as a person that fights it. She interprets it as someone that's innocent. She's crazy, but she's shy, too, really. She's not an outward person really. She's outward because she thinks she's supposed to be. She wants to please somebody. Gena has a lot of consideration for the character and the woman behind the character. She tries never to vulgarize or caricature people she's playing. She really resisted turning Mabel into a 'victim' or a 'case' or a 'feminist.' That was her insight."[13]

"I remember an argument between John and Gena on the set, they got so pissed off with each other you just stood against the wall and waited for it to blow over," Mike Ferris says. "Gena was such a lady, she never swore, but he drove her to it almost: 'If I had a knife, I'd cut your heart out right now!' She wanted some direction and he refused to give it to her. And it built into something John used. He didn't want his wife to get angry at him, but he didn't care. He'd say 'Gena, I refuse to tell you what to do, I'm not going to talk about it. It's got to come out of you, you, you. Not me. I don't know what she'd do! You tell me. Show me. Find out.' He'd walk out. 'Don't ask me again.'

When he was being apologetic and speaking to her he'd talk in half-words. 'Gena, you, d'you. I. Don't you. I.' He would do anything to get a performance out of you, including not tell you anything."

★   ★   ★

Mabel spells it out, all the reasons that Nick needs her, each torturous point wresting her closer to hysteria, the camera sticking back with Nick and Doctor Zepp (Eddie Shaw); the sight of this woman falling apart demanding distance, separation, awe.

"I have five points Nick. I figured it out: One is love. Two is friendship. And three is comfort. Four is. I'm a good mother Nick. And. I belong to you, that's it. Five points."

"That was a night I will never forget," Bo Harwood says. "John got Gena so upset. He really humiliated her and got her mad and yelling at him. The whole crew was breathless. The friction, the tension, the insanity in the air. He was behind the Mitchell camera and Mike Ferris was behind the Arriflex, shooting towards the fireplace where Gena was doing 'I have five points, Nick.' John did these terrible things to her. He would take his eye off the eyepiece and shake his head. 'Ughh. Cut.' And we'd start rolling again. He started making noises off the camera – like a little boy making a fart noise with his mouth. You can see it in one of his shots, you see the background start to drift up, that's John taking his eye off the eyepiece and the camera wasn't balanced. And he makes a noise. She stops, composes herself, starts over again. This went on again and again, where he would interrupt her with these sounds, and finally she said 'How dare you, how dare you think you can conduct everything,' and on like that, and he just let her blow, 'Okay, all right. Okay, you think you can do it again? Then roll!' And the next take I think was a print."

"'I have five points Nick.' Oh God, we shot that over and over, I thought we were all going to die, and we would be buried and over our graves would be written 'I have five points Nick'," Elaine Kagan groans. "Horrible. We had to scrape Gena off the floor."

"When Mabel goes nuts and Doctor Zepp goes over there to calm her down, you see how devastated he is?" Bo Harwood asks. "That's Eddie Shaw, Sam Shaw's brother, and he ran a music publishing company. Eddie was so freaked out after we cut, he was over by the window crying. I went over to him and he could hardly talk. He said 'I thought she was really gone.' So when you see him not knowing what to do, that's what was going on. That was the kind of set it was. And most of us were just a bunch of pups. That's how we thought movies were made."

The scene has similarities with Jess Polanski's declaration of love to the humiliated Ghost Wakefield in *Too Late Blues*: another 'strange,' vulnerable woman offering all she has to a man paralysed by his own shame. In 1961 Cassavetes had talked about a film based on "a girl's suicide, caused by society's inability to educate in terms of love. Nobody in this world seems to be able to love beyond a certain point." Talking about *A Woman Under The Influence* 14 years later, he returned to theme: "the way our world is structured, there is no room for women to have an education, an emotional education," he said.[14] Asked about the main thing that interested him, he answered: "The woman did – the problem of being alone after being promised love." If Ghost's inaction leads to disillusionment for Jess, Nick's takes Mabel into madness.

"I don't believe any man can be told when he makes a jerk of himself," Cassavetes noted. "Now as an actor, Peter [Falk] became very passive when we did the scene with the doctor. Those were peculiar choices that he made. When the doctor came in, he had the freedom to throw him out. But he chose to let him in. Peter also had the freedom not to stand by and let her go crazy. And when he came upon her and tried to stop her, it was too late and he knew it was too late and why did he wait that long? Now in talking with Peter afterwards, Peter said 'She was doing great. I didn't want to stop her.' That was a lie. Peter is a tremendously internal man, and I think he wanted her to be committed. I think he wanted her to go away. I don't think he recognised her worth because to him, at that moment, she was worthless. She wasn't behaving like he would behave, so he didn't want her anymore. That is what I saw."[15]

What follows is worthy of any one of the cycle of 'family horror' movies which were so popular in the early Seventies (*The Exorcist, It's Alive*): Mabel reduced to a hissing monster, repeling the doctor by making the sign of the cross, being pulled off her screaming children and forcibly drugged. Interestingly it's shown from Nick's point of view – Cassavetes even gives him a moment alone downstairs, listening to the rumpus above, then mounting the stairs to witness his very own home horror movie.

"It's a very difficult thing for someone to double-cross somebody," Cassavetes said. "I felt it was necessary for Nick to go upstairs and make up his mind that he would actually do this in the face of the children. It's the hardest thing in the world to put someone you love in an institution."[16]

The sequence is so powerful, it could easily be the climax of the movie. And it probably would have been, had Cassavetes been intent on making feminist melodrama. But this film-maker never held truck with any ideology, and the last hour of *A Woman Under The Influence* clarifies that his subject here isn't just equality but love – as complicated as that.

"John didn't make a picture about women's liberation, he made a picture that he always makes, this problem of love," Peter Falk says. "People have the capacity to love and a need to love. The problem is that envy, greed, weakness, stupidity, irrationality, superstition, whatever the foibles are, get in the way of it. All his stories deal with almost the same thing: love is hard, love is difficult, love is necessary."[17]

Cassavetes doesn't demonise Nick Longhetti; he pays him the compliment of holding him responsible. He shows him back on the job the day after Mabel had been committed, so consumed by guilt that he causes his closest friend Eddie to pitch head over heels down a dangerous slope where they're working. He shows him impetuously stealing away his kids from school so that they can bond, down on the beach. And he shows him in high excitement, six months later, pulling on his best clothes and leading a convoy of well-wishers to throw a surprise welcome home party for his wife. Everything Nick does may be wrong, but his every error is another confused expression of love. And from that, Cassavetes divines hope. Flying in the face of critical opinion, he liked to insist that *A Woman Under The Influence* was his 'most optimistic' film.

It's not hard to see why so many people would disagree with that statement. The last hour of the movie – with Mabel's much-anticipated reappearance – is a steep escalation through misunderstanding, embarrassment, uncomfortable intimacy, grievance and resentment, anguish, an almost Strindbergian inadaquacy and emptiness. To spotlight just a few moments of bleak trauma from the family reunion: the camera zoomed in on Mabel's face and refusing to let go as she blinks back tears, reunited with her kids;

the family, sombre, still and staring like a group portrait, only Mabel is the object of everyone's intense scrutiny, as she comes back to rejoin adult society – and promptly falls flat on her ass;

her dad (Fred Draper) abjectly attempting to fly the coop – "I'm not a spaghetti man" – then his pained embarrassment at his daughter's demonstrative affection;

"So what was it like? Terrible? Good, bad, what?" Nick to his wife;

"That's the end of the jokes. We just talk. Hello, how are you? Normal conversation. Weather. Too hot, too cold" – Nick lays down the law;

"Dad, will you please stand up for me?" And so he stands;

Mabel runs to the bathroom and tries to kill herself.

* * *

But there are moments of relief too, isolated moments when Mabel, the children and even Nick assert themselves in open and liberating ways, equally harrowing some of them, but also inherently cathartic: Nick dragging his wife out of the room and into the shadows to remonstrate with the cowed and inhibited convalescent ("I'm with you. There's nothing you can do wrong. I just want you to be yourself. This is your house. To hell with them.");

Mabel (offscreen) "Tina, you're so fat! My God! Did you see Tina's ass?";

Mabel dances *Swan Lake* on the couch;

"Leave my daughter alone, you!" Mr Mortensen finally stands up for her;

Nick throws out the guests;

the kids instinctively protect their mum, they cling to her, and when Nick yanks them upstairs – twice – they run straight back down to her. In so doing, the children dictate the ending, and a return to normality. Falk/Nick throws up his hands and smiles: "They want to know you're all right. They want you to put them to bed."[18]

And so it goes. A sticky plaster is applied. The table cleared. Lights put out. The bed made. Tender, touching simplicity. Like *Faces*, it's a passive, quiet, domestic ending, but this time there is an underlying feeling that what has been ripped apart may be restored. As Ray Carney observes, it is an ending borrowed from Ozu's masterly *The Flavour Of Green Tea Over Rice* another film about marital discord culmininating in loving reconciliation.[19]

Describing the final act in the synopsis he wrote for the press book, Cassavetes said: "Nick is also changed and no longer willing to sacrifice her for anything or anyone. He fights to get her back, fumbling, shouting, aggravating the situation by his determined ridiculous demands for her instant return to the 'old' Mabel. He openly forces the neurotic, quiet personality of the new Mabel back into the up-and-down personality of the old one."

"In the course of this final sequence Mabel attempts suicide in front of her children only to be slapped down finally into submission, her young and innocent children racing madly and hysterically about the house charging at their father, confused and upset – for these three kids exposed to adult madness desperately fight to maintain a grip on their own realities. When the storm of emotion clears everything appears to be calm – graceful goodnights to the kids, much kissing and apologising. Nothing that has taken place seems to have any importance except that Mabel has been set free. The children still accept their parents and Nick and Mabel have in some way discovered they can accept the difference between commitment and emotional needs. The ritual of preparing for sleep, re-establishing, without conversation, the need to make room for the dilemmas of love."

Filmed over 13 weeks from autumn 1972 into February–March 1973 the turbulent and traumatic emotions engendered by *A Woman Under The Influence* proved a strain. "Once we began shooting, it was hell," Cassavetes rued. "At night we'd collapse, make coffee, then start talking about the work. Yesterday's work, last week's, last month's, next week's, next month's. We'd wake up in the night, and talk some more. It was that kind of total commitment. Sometimes the tension on the set was so great we could taste it. We'd quarrel, and somebody would say, 'No, that scene isn't true, it isn't honest, let's do it again.' We sat around the [Longhetti] house and again talked out every scene until it seemed right, seemed right in this particular environment."[20]

The pressure was particularly hard on Gena Rowlands, who to this day refuses to watch the film. "Gena put so much of herself into the film that as the picture went along the problems became more and more hers. By the time the picture was over she had so thoroughly understood the investigation that she had made, that she became like Mabel, in a sense, after the picture was done. Sometimes, you have to snap your fingers and say, 'No, no, you're not Mabel; you don't have to get excited every time you see that problem. That's been, uh, covered'."[21]

The editing was started by the Englishman who had worked on *Husbands*, Peter Tanner. The collaboration didn't work out. "It was a good picture, but it was far too long," Tanner says. "I really couldn't take these long, long scenes which didn't seem to me to do anything for the film. John thought they did. He said 'If the audience suffer, they suffer, I don't mind.' I said, 'Yes, John, but then you don't get the money at the box-office, if they're suffering all the time'."

"After we'd done one cut, he said, 'Peter, take a week and you recut it as you think, then I'll come and see it.' I cut it down quite a bit, and he came and saw it, and by about reel four he walked out of the theatre, and didn't come back. So it became rather strained between us."[22]

Tanner's assistant, Tom Cornwell, stayed on, and a gifted young editor named Robert Heffernan. But the editing dragged on and on. Cassavetes had been invited to use the editing facilities at the American Film Institute's Greystone Mansions for six months as an artist in residence. Cassavetes wouldn't leave. He brazened it out for nearly a year and a half, cutting and recutting. "It was so much fun," Bo Harwood remembers. "It closed at six or seven at night, but we'd sneak people in at night for screenings. The security guard doubled as our projectionist. I remember we broke into the cigarette machines because we had no money."

Bo or Mike or Seymour would get a phone call at 3am. "Hey, whaddaya doin"? Come over here. You know that scene, I want to show you this thing...'

Al Ruban came in and helped at the mixing stage. He claims to have seen a cut that was even more traumatic than the release version: "I saw an early version that was so much stronger, with two female critics from the *Daily News*. And it was the toughest film I had ever seen. Both those women were sobbing at the end of the film. I told John, 'This is the best film you've ever made. Is it going out like that?' And he said, 'No, it's too tough.' So he toned it down a little bit. It would leave you in a state of shock. I could envisage an audience taking ten or 15 minutes just to leave the theatre, it was that strong."

Interestingly, the only time Cassavetes alluded to cuts he'd made in the film, he told *Positif* that, "There were more scenes of Peter and Gena alone together. I loved what happened between them. There was a very nice scene in the morning, where they talked about their dreams, and another when they walked in the rain. But seeing the film from beginning to end, I realised that maybe unconsciously I'd given the public what they wanted, which undoubtedly corresponded with a certain romantic desire on the part of myself and the actors. But ours isn't a romantic film, since marriage isn't totally a romance, as I see it! The moments when you have the time to be romantic are very short in a marriage. So I gave up those scenes." He added that the first cut ran three hours 50 minutes.[23]

According to Bo Harwood, who stood by Cassavetes' side throughout the two and a half year production, John was turned down by every money source he knew. "The unions were very much against us. Our credit was cut off at the labs. Distributors didn't want to know. We were very much on our own."

Like Peter Tanner studio executives thought it was too long, or too depressing, or just badly made. Fashions had changed: what had seemed exciting and new in *Faces* – the spontaneity, handheld camerawork, and the relentless barrage of emotion – were now considered tokens of indulgence or sloppiness. People could point to glaring continuity errors (when Cassavetes allows himself a truly romantic montage immediately following the spaghetti scene, for example, there are three or four 'mistakes' within a 40-second sequence), as well as to elisions which might be mistaken for mistakes ("What happened to Garson?" they wanted to know).

According to Cassavetes the critic Molly Haskell told him it was "the biggest piece of garbage I've ever seen."

Cassavetes' frustration comes through in numerous interviews he conducted late in 1974: long, rambling, and passionate as ever, but impatient and disillusioned. He sounds burnt out: "I can't take the fight any more. I run out of breath too fast," he told one journalist.[24]

"I feel that my filmic life has come to some kind of an end," he told another.[25]

And to yet another: "I don't think I could ever make a film like this again. I mean the kind of film where you do everything. I've done it four times, and I don't know that I could do it again. I would want to have more ease and relaxation. Some endorsement of my talent and the film I'm making. This way it's too difficult. Is it worth it to kill yourself to make the film?"[26]

He railed against the distributors' greed and cynicism. "Now the big question is: can a picture make 100 million? Who the hell cares? If you're thinking that way, you're not making films, you're making money. If that's what it's come to, let the audience look at pictures of money, put money on the screen, and then rape it, shoot it, defecate on it – because that's basically what everyone is doing."

"They'd make a picture about a revolution in which all the major studio heads were killed if they thought it would make money," he complained. "I don't say I've been a saint in my life, but I couldn't sell my soul out for a thing I just don't believe in. And if that means I'll never make film again, then I'll never make another film again."[27]

"John was also very picky about who was going to distribute the film," Harwood allows. "He cared where the money came from. He didn't like money very much, and if it wasn't from a decent source he would turn it down, it didn't matter if we were starving. We worked on the film for months for nothing. Then in post-production it was $65, $75 a week. And it was probably the best time in my life."[28]

Cassavetes decided to distribute the film himself. Al Ruban cut a deal with Columbia, who owned the Columbia 1&2 duplex on 2nd avenue and 62nd street to hire out one of the screens. Cassavetes then decided to go the whole hog and hire out both. Ruban was persuaded to incorporate Faces Distribution, and when it opened in December 1974, the film just took off: "The picture opened, and the public took to it right away. I had to do very little phoning out looking for theatres," Ruban remembers. "My largest job was answering the telephone."

"The reviews were either really good or really bad," Harwood says. "Women were storming out of it, and John loved that, it meant they felt something." Among the more vocal critics:

Pauline Kael: "It's a didactic illustration of Laing's vision of insanity, with Mabel [as] the scapegoat of a repressive society. She's a symbolic victim, and a marriage victim especially. The actors, no longer given their heads, are merely figures in a diagram."[29]

Stanley Kaufmann: "You can read [the plot] any way you like. The film isn't really 'about' anything. To me this film is utterly without interest or merit."[30]

William S Pechter: "What is that identity of Mabel's with which those roles of wife and mother are supposed to conflict? [. . .] Where the character of Mabel ought to be is a blank space captioned 'Victim'."[31]

John Simon: "It was by no means clear whether and by what the heroine was oppressed, and whether her abject stupidity, indeed her near-idiocy, made her a representative specimen. *A Woman Under The Influence* struck me as muddleheaded, pretentious and interminable, fooling some people because of its factitious social significance."[32]

In her book *From Reverence To Rape*, Molly Haskell describes it as a "harrowingly loony drama starring Gena Rowlands as a housewife driven mad by babytalk." Comparing it to Martin Scorsese's *Alice Doesn't Live Here Any More* and Frank Perry's *The Diary Of A Mad Housewife*, she declared that "In their brief against society's insensitive husbands, *Alice* and *A Woman* both lapse into a shrill, accusatory tone, turning Burstyn and

Rowlands into fashionably helpless symbols of martyrdom that deny the spunk and resourcefulness they radiate as women. Yet," she added, "as I can testify, having lectured with both films around the country, housewives respond intensely to these characters."[33]

These ideological readings (and you have to wonder how *A Streetcar Named Desire* or *Tender Is The Night* would have fared with such critics) invariably caricature Mabel in the role of social signifier, a symbol of wife-as-victim, force Nick into the role of victimiser, and then complain that the characters don't fit the thesis and in any case the symbolism is simplistic. And so it is, but it's a symbolism of their own devising, a thesis they have superimposed on the movie. (And no wonder the film felt long to anyone so far in advance of its conclusions.) As Cassavetes himself realised, he could have made a more successful film had he made it more clearcut: if, for example, it had been Nick who took a lover, not Mabel, it would have been more easily appreciated. What these critics missed is precisely the complication of human interaction, the competition and contradiction of personal relationships, the confusion and compulsion, the give and take, the exhausting experiential flux which makes this film so much more than Kael's 'diagram': like only a handful of movies it cuts to the very heart of who we are and how we behave.

A Woman Under The Influence became Cassavetes' most popular release, and even picked up Academy Award nominations for Gena Rowlands as best actress and Cassavetes as best director. (They lost, to Ellen Burstyn for *Alice Doesn't Live Here Anymore* and Francis Coppola for *The Godfather II*, respectively).

Asked to account for its commercial success, Cassavetes came up with a typically gutsy explanation: "Richard Dreyfuss was on a TV show with Peter Falk and Dreyfuss said 'I saw a movie you were in and I went crazy. I went home and vomitted. It was the most depressing movie I've ever seen.' Peter called me up and said 'Dreyfuss just destroyed our movie. He said it made him vomit.' I told Peter, 'That's all right. That's what I feel about it, too.' Thanks to Dreyfuss, the film became an enormous success: everyone wanted to see the film that made him sick and see if it would happen to them too."[34]

Bo Harwood remembers the day the Oscar nominations were announced. The company had moved into offices on Wilshire Boulevard, above Mann's theatre, where *A Woman* was playing. "Ted Mann owed John money or something, so he gave us the second storey. Fourteen offices. We had three cutting rooms, a conference room, a dark room, an accounting room, a music room, a layout room for Sam Shaw for ads. It was great. We had a TV set in the editing room, and we heard we had got nominations for best actress and director – after all we had been through, it was just too much."

"About five or six o'clock that afternoon I went into John's office, which was a corner office, and if you went out through the window there was the fire escape, just about six feet away from the marquee of the theatre below. John pulled out a bottle of Cognac, a couple of glasses and some blankets, and he put the blankets down on the fire escape so we'd be comfortable, and we looked down and saw people lining up for our movie. He poured me a glass of Cognac, poured himself one, and he looked out over Hollywood and kind of tipped his glass, and he looked at me and said 'Fuck "em".'"

1 Mike Ferris, Author's interview (2000).
2 Judith Crist, *Take 22*.
3 It may even be that Falk owed Columbo to Cassavetes. Even though it was a Columbia movie, *Husbands* had been screened repeatedly at Universal Studios – where John has his offices – for months on end, and it was in this period Universal decided against Bing Crosby and chose Falk instead.
4 The episode in question, 'Étude in Black' was scripted by Steve Bochco, who had recently contributed to *Silent Running* for Ned Tanen, and would go on to create the hit TV shows *Hill St Blues* and *LA Law*, and it was directed by Nicolas Colasanto, best remembered for playing 'coach' in the first series of the TV sitcom *Cheers*. Cassavetes played the lead along with Blythe Danner and Myrna Loy. Jousse claims it was directed by Cassavetes under the Colasanto alias, but as far as I can determine this is inaccurate.
5 Judith McNally, *Filmmakers Newsletter*, January 1975.
6 Bo Harwood, Author's interview (2000).
7 Dasgupta, *Film*.
8 Dasgupta.
9 Loeb, *A Conversation With John Cassavetes*.
10 The invention of the Steadicam, and the example of directors like Woody Allen and Lars Von Trier in *Husbands And Wives* and *Breaking The Waves* has since brought the intensity of handheld work into the mainstream.
11 Quoted in Ray Carney's *Cassavetes On Cassavetes*, Faber, 2001.
12 Crist.
13 Carney, *Cassavetes On Cassavetes*.
14 Loeb.
15 Loeb.
16 Loeb.
17 Falk in *Out Of The Shadows*, directed by Paul Joyce, Lucida Productions.
18 'I found the best approach was to be kind of cold to the kids. I just hoped they would pick up, as an adult would, where the story was going,' the director related. 'As a matter of fact I was really quite thrilled. At the end the kids automatically attacked the father. I never said for them to do that, they just did it – and in an exquisite way. The delicacy with which they approached their own intervention and the taking of sides was something that could never have been told to them.' Cassavetes to Judith McNally, *Filmmakers Newsletter*, January 1975.
19 Carney, *The Films Of John Cassavetes – Pragmaticism*.
20 Carney, *Cassavetes On Cassavetes*.
21 Larry Gross, *Millimeter*.
22 Peter Tanner, Author's interview (2000).
23 Michel Ciment and Michael Henry, 'Interview with John Cassavetes,' *Positif* 180, April 1976.
24 Kathleen Carroll, 'Cassavetes – Hitting 'Em Where They Live,' *Sunday News*, November 1, 1974.
25 Dasgupta.
26 McNally.
27 McNally.
28 A year after release, cast and crew received cheques from Cassavetes and Falk and a letter thanking them for their work. 'It was a ton of money, thousands of dollars,' Ferris remembers. 'Enough that I could start some savings.'
29 Pauline Kael, *The New Yorker*, vol L, No.43 December 9, 1974.

30 Stanley Kaufmann, *The New Republic*, December 28, 1974.
31 William S Pechter, *Commentary*, Vol 59, no 5, May 1975.
32 John Simon, *New York Magazine*, Vol 9, No 9, March 1, 1976.
33 Molly Haskell, *From Reverence To Rape*, University of Chicago Press, second edition, 1987.
34 Brent Lewis, John Cassavetes Recalled, *Films And Filming*, April 1989.

A Hard Line

Gary Oldman

I obviously came late to the films of John Cassavetes. *Shadows* was already in the theatres around the same time I was taking my first few steps.

In the late Eighties, I was living between London and New York. I was channel-surfing one evening and happened upon a Cassavetes season showing on the Sundance network. At first I thought it might be a Sixties documentary – the people were that real. The film was *Faces*. His early vérité signature – an expressive hand-held camera, zooming-in on those screen-bending close-ups kidnapped me. I sat mesmerized, a hostage, in awe.

Cassavetes acted in films to subsidise the writing and directing of his own. This is commonplace today. I'm considering several offers at the moment, all of which have questionable integrity. However, the financial rewards are such that it will push me a little closer to realising my second feature. My denial won't let me call it selling-out. It's called buying creative freedom. If you can stay 40 percent whore in this business you're doing very well.

Cassavetes didn't have to make films. He could have pursued a lucrative acting career and that would have been that. He needed to make films. Film was his passion, his oxygen. He made them at personal sacrifice to his acting career. They received critical disdain, enjoyed marginal commercial success, and I'm sure he never saw a dime from them. He is like any great artist who picked up a paint-brush or modeled a piece of clay. Unfortunately, he chose an expensive paint-box. He hocked, he begged and borrowed, but he did get them on the screen; and more remarkably, he made them with the people he loved and admired. We don't see Robert Redford popping up.

The industry hasn't really changed a great deal in the intervening forty-something years since Cassavetes first rolled his camera. The so-called 'independent cinema' (a movement he arguably fathered) is fast becoming stifled by the same contractual considerations to investment that has oppressed the studios for so long. A gem slips through, but overall, the American mainstream is still churning out the same sentimental, insincere and uninspired nonsense it always has.

I'm no snob. Hollywood had its moment. We have for example, three versions of *Showboat* as a result of a bestseller of 1927. It took its lead from literature and was run by people who knew what they were doing, listening to their instincts and not the demographic.

When Cassavetes came along a hard line was drawn. Suddenly there was film as commerce and film as art. He filled a niche as commentator. Cassavetes understood that when an art form is run by committee, preoccupied with making money, chasing Oscars and wanting to please everybody, it becomes safe, generic, corporate and soulless. I'm convinced he picked up his camera out of a moral imperative to these preoccupations. He challenged the status quo. His talent demanded it. The result was revolutionary. He gave us films of such stark authenticity and pained awkwardness; characters so deep and complex, that he hurled a firecracker in amongst his fellow peers.

I read somewhere that Martin Scorsese, a close friend and student of Cassavetes, has called the films, 'epics, of the human soul.' Scorsese, by his own admission, saw *Citizen Kane* and Cassavetes' *Shadows* and has been 'trying to combine the two ever since.'

Cassavetes was inspirational for me with my own foray into directing. I'm British, so the social realism of Ken Loach, Tony Richardson, Alan Clark and Mike Leigh are present in *Nil By Mouth*. However, I was looking for something different. A palate that was sinister, with the ever present threat of violence, without being too stylized or film-noir-ish. I wanted an atmosphere, a mood, which you can only achieve through lighting, but I didn't want to 'feel' the lighting. I worried it might take away from the film's overall realism.

The cinematographer, Ron Fortunato and I looked at *The Killing Of A Chinese Bookie*. I love the density of the blacks with the occasional explosion of colour in the marquees and neons. The dark velvety reds, orange and blacks of the night club interior vs the scorching white-hot Californian sunlight. Ron and I finally settled on a gray murky palate, inside and out, suggesting no escape. I happen to like the older stocks from the Seventies, so we used no filtration, minimal correction, and of course the 16mm with the long zoom does a lot of the work. This got me closer to the stock they may have used. The night exteriors and the night car interiors were heavily modeled on *Bookie*. We used existing lighting, like the sodium yellow in the street lamps, and exaggerated it slightly.

The scene that was most inspirational is where Cosmo, the film's hero, is given the gun and the location of the Bookie he is to kill. The scene (inside a car) is played conspiratorially, its passengers silhouetted by the sparkle of approaching headlights. We catch a reflection off the gun, the odd profile, but it's so dark that I confused the hero with the bad guys at one point. There's a kind of industry wisdom. The unwritten rule book of what to do and what not to do. If you can't see it, you won't hear it. Cassavetes pushes the envolope, he throws the book away. The most pivotal scene in the film is played in total black. Very daring, very exciting. All of *NBM*'s night car interiors use teeny-tiny Christmas bulbs. That's it.

I think it sad that for many outside of the industry, Cassavetes will be remembered for his roles in *Rosemary's Baby* and *The Dirty Dozen*. For the few, he was so much more than a gifted actor. He was an innovator, a generative force, an artist and poet. It's ironic that one can find every conceivable piece of rubbish ever made on tape and DVD, yet much of Cassavetes, work is unavailable, My own copies of *Husbands* and *Love Streams* were taped from the television. And try finding a book on the man! About five years ago I was browsing the shelves of the National Film Theatre bookstore in London. I asked the sales assistant if she could look up Cassavetes on the store's computer. She had trouble spelling his name; okay, for that, she can be forgiven. But she had never even heard of him. It goes without saying, neither had the computer. One of my favourite Cassavetes quotes is taped just above my desk. It's there as a reminder. It reads: 'to compromise an idea is to soften it, to make an excuse for it, to betray it.' Well, he didn't. And it shows.

Gary Oldman
(Writer-director: Nil By Mouth. Actor: Meantime,
The Firm, Sid And Nancy, Prick Up Your ears,
Bram Stoker's Dracula, True Romance,
Leon, The Contender, Hannibal)

8

The Killing Of A Chinese Bookie

'C'mon, baby: choose a personality!' Cosmo Vitelli to Mr Sophistication

One day in 1975 Cassavetes put down the phone in the new, enlarged office of Faces Distribution Corporation, turned to Al Ruban with a disbelieving chuckle and reported, "Guess what: Jon Peters just offered me $300,000 to direct Barbra Streisand in a remake of *A Star Is Born*."

"And what did you say?" asked an incredulous Ruban.

"I told him I couldn't do it for less than $500,000," snickered John. The phone rang again, and Cassavetes picked it up. "You'll pay me $500, 000? Look, I'm sorry, I just can't do it – and honestly, I don't know why I would want to!" And that was that.[1]

Most of us would have been tempted. Four times now, Cassavetes had gone his own way to make movies truly independent of the system. He had written and directed them, photographed them, sometimes acted in them, funded them himself, edited them and even released them. It had never been easy.

The belated popular success of *A Woman Under The Influence* was a welcome vindication, and the Oscar nominations must have boosted his self-confidence, yet Cassavetes knew how close he came to breaking point. The expense was terrifying, he said. He might have meant it financially, psychologically, or both. While he always had scripts on the go, he wasn't sure which way to turn. *Woman* had been the culmination of certain ideas he had been developing for years: ideas about men and women, emotional stagnation and spontaneity, marriage and love. He had taken these ideas to the peak of tragic expression, and in the process discovered an affirmation of love so pure it was dazzling. Where do you go from there?

Between 1973 and mid-1975, Cassavetes was preoccupied with finishing *A Woman Under The Influence*, getting it on the screen (a job prolonged by its success) and coping with the attention it garnered. Bucking Hollywood wisdom, he booked it into blue collar theatres outside of the cosmopolitan New York and LA art house circuits, and reached the very people he made the movie about. US box-office eventually came to something in the region of $6 million. Even so, "Distributing *Woman* was tough; you're doing something you don't wanna do," Seymour Cassel observes. "You're on the phone all the time, you're checking up on theatres, they're using back-up prints in another theatre and taking money without reporting it. The chains would do that. Many times I went up to northern California with a big black friend of mine and we would go into projection booths and take the print. Every theatre had a backup print. And they would be late paying. These guys owning 70, 80 theatres, forget it."

"We did *The Killing Of A Chinese Bookie* just to get out of the distribution business," Cassavetes said later. "Martin Scorsese and I were talking, and in one night made up this gangster story. Years later, when I didn't know what to make, I thought we'll do that story about this night-club owner who owes a lot of money, and is talked into killing someone."[2]

Cassavetes had a love of gangster films which stretched back to his childhood, when James Cagney had been his favourite actor, and he played cops and robbers with his older brother on the beach. The genre was going through a fresh wave of popularity in the early Seventies, after *Bonnie And Clyde* and *The Godfather*. As a favour to Ben Gazzara (who played the title role) Cassavetes took a cameo in Steve Carver's *Capone*, produced by Roger Corman in 1975. "Gangster films are important – I would like to make one," he told Larry Gross that same year. "I would have to make it sheer entertainment. That's what we expect from that specific genre. I don't know whether I'm capable."[3]

In *The Killing Of A Chinese Bookie* – his eighth movie as director – Cassavetes would show guns for the first time, and with much of the action set in a strip joint there would be considerable nudity – another first for him. Everyone believed it would be a great success. On paper, it looked like Cassavetes had gone Hollywood after all, albeit on his own terms. To save on money for extras, Sam Shaw even invited a number of studio executives to come in and dine in the background of a restaurant scene (the scene involving Seymour Cassel, Val Avery and Timothy Carey). They all readily agreed, and turned up for two nights' running. "John shot it handheld, and passed in front of them so they were never on camera except as silhouettes in the shadows," Shaw recalled. "They were all happy to be in a Cassavetes movies, but they'd never produce one, and John knew it."[4]

Gazzara plays Cosmo Vitelli, owner of a strip club in downtown Los Angeles, the Crazy Horse West. The club is his domain. He chooses the numbers and arranges, writes and directs the routines – kitsch burlesque starring 'Mr Sophistication (Meade Roberts) and His Delovelies' – and he's the announcer.

To celebrate paying off the final instalment on the club (Al Ruban is mischievously cast as the bagman), Cosmo takes three of his girls, including *his girlfriend, Rachel (Azizi Johari), to play poker at a casino run by the mob – the Liberty Bar – but he finishes the night $23,000 in the hole.*

The gangsters (they're mostly played by old Cassavetes' hands: Timothy Carey, Seymour Cassel, John 'Red' Kullers) come to him with a proposition. A certain Chinese mobster is too heavily protected for them to reach. If Cosmo kills him, they will write off his debt. Cosmo puts forward a counter-offer: he'll reduce the debt, but he won't kill anyone. If he can lure the Chinaman out of hiding, perhaps by taking his girls down to Chinatown, the mobsters agree to reduce the debt.

But Cosmo can't go through with it. Instead, he takes the girls to watch a Chinese movie. He'll pay, he says. But it's too late for that. They work him over, and then they put a gun in his hands and tell him to kill the Chinese bookie. Or else.

The assassination goes according to plan, only Cosmo escapes with a bullet in the chest. The gangsters wanted him dead. Their attempts to finish him off backfire, and Cosmo returns to the Crazy Horse West to ensure that the show goes on, even if it's only for this one, last night. [The version under discussion is the 109 minute cut released in 1978; the original 135 minute version – no longer available – reportedly included significantly more material front- and backstage at the club, including a 'Gunfight At The OK Corral' number, a few snippets of which remain, a scene in the dressing room anticipating the pep talk Cosmo gives to his troupers at the end, and more material immediately before and after the visit to the casino. Cassavetes claimed the original edit was rushed, and cut into the negative, so that the second version is not only shorter, but uses some different takes.]

Although Cassavetes liked to gamble, and he was as street-savvy as any New Yorker, his knowledge of real-life gangsters was very limited, and he wasn't much susceptible to their world. "All gangsters are really barbarians," he said. "They make me uneasy, not because they intimidate me, but because I have nothing to say to them . . . everything they hold true is in fact false."[5]

Seymour Cassel remembers a curious story, how he and John were held up at gunpoint by a robber. John protested that he didn't have any money, they'd just been playing softball. "The guy said, 'I know you have money, you're an actor, I've seen you on the television.'

John said, 'Look, I've got 20 bucks, I'm going to get some ice-cream for Se and I. You want to have some ice-cream? Why are you robbing people? Why don't you get a job?'

The guy said he couldn't get a job, and John said 'I'll give you a job!' And he did, on *Chinese Bookie*. The guy's an actor now, and he became a friend. Turn's out, we're having ice-cream, he didn't have any bullets in his gun, but we didn't know that at the time. John even gave him the change from the ice-cream. I couldn't believe it: tipping him for not robbing us! John believed he could convince anybody of anything – and he usually did."

Cassavetes claimed he wrote the screenplay just two weeks before shooting. If so, it was a story he had elaborated many times over to friends and family. It seems that the themes of *Chinese Bookie* emerged from similar preoccupations in *Mikey And Nicky*. This long-delayed collaboration with Falk and Elaine May finally got underway in 1973. It was almost as intense as one of Cassavetes' own films; he loved making it (he even directed some second unit material), and considered Nicky to be perhaps his most fulfilling role – yet it had been an arduous and troubled production, and May too was having trouble getting it distributed. (It was eventually released in 1976.)

Both films are set in the *neo-noir* criminal margins of LA, and both feature borderline legitimate characters whose involvement with the mob occasions betrayal and premeditated murder. Fearing for his life after double-crossing a gangster, and subsequently a bookie associate of his has been murdered, Cassavetes' Nicky calls on the only friend he believes he can trust: Peter Falk's Mikey. But their relationship is fraught with resentment and Mikey brings a hit man in tow. Fundamentally, Mikey and Nicky are liars. Their friendship is a sham. Mikey's help is proffered in bad faith, just as Nicky knew it would be. Obnoxious and self-pitying, he spends the movie needling out the truth, to expose Mikey's duplicity if only for Mikey's benefit.[6]

There is some kinship between Cosmo Vitelli and these men. Cosmo is a private man, a stranger even to himself. But he hides in plain sight, camouflaged in a flamboyant sense of style. He favours tuxedos, ruffled shirts, a pinkie ring. "You're a low-life," he complains to Marty (Ruban). "I do business with you, but you have no style." Dapper and convivial, he takes his strippers with him like an entourage – or bodyguards – in his chauffeur-driven limousine (the chauffeur, Lamar, is played by David Rowlands), even presenting them with colour-coded corsages. He sleeps with the black girl, Rachel, but their relationship is proprietorial and impersonal; "She's my girlfriend but she also works for me," he insists. It's clear from the scene in which he auditions a compliant waitress – the frame actually decapitating the girl as she performs – that his interest is simply physical. Caught by Rachel on the verge of cashing in this particular casting couch transaction, Cosmo protests "I'm a club owner. I deal in girls."

Amy Taubin in *Village Voice* called the film "a male anxiety dream . . . a tit-obsessed castration fantasy," and she isn't wrong. In fact the only woman Cosmo seems to have any deeper emotional rapport with is Rachel's mother, Betty (Virginia Carrington). It's to Betty that he unburdens himself with a bullet in his chest, the double-cross on his mind. It is the only time he speaks intimately, remembering his father and his mother as if to recall a sense of himself he had forgotten. He might as well be talking to the wall for the sympathy he gets: "I don't give a damn about your father. I don't care."

"Well I care!" he snarls, a rare flash of anger breaking through his preternatural composure. His disclosures are banal, their delivery awkward and embarrassed, and the timing is all wrong. The last thing Betty wants is a dead white guy bleeding all over her house.

This, then, is another first for Cassavetes: the man alone. The existential anti-hero. Unlike Harry (Gazzara) in *Husbands*, he has no male friends to see him through a crisis; unlike Nick (Falk) in *A Woman Under The Influence*, he has no family. Where other Cassavetes movies are characterised by a babble of overlapping voices competing to be heard, *Bookie* is a film of long silences. "I've got a golden life. Got the world by the balls!" Cosmo announces early on, after paying off his club; but directed to an unimpressed stranger in a bar, the declaration rings hollow. No sooner has he achieved independence ('You can work for yourself now') than he goes and finds a bigger rope to hang around his neck. It's all he has to hold on to. As Cassavetes wrote in the press book, Cosmo is "an ordinary man who has constructed his life as many American men do. He had defined himself in terms of his work; it is more than a way to make a living, it is his entire existence – paid for in monthly instalments."

Three times in the first half of the movie, Cosmo falls back on his club to define himself: to the customers at the Crazy Horse; to Rachel; and to the gangsters putting the squeeze on him. I am a club-owner therefore I am.

But forget the seedy milieu, the film "is about a conformist," Cassavetes told *Monthly Film Bulletin*. "Somebody who would have been a white-collar worker years ago, and who does all the right things and who is going to be killed for it."[7] The gangsters are businessmen. At the casino, debtors are presented with forms 17 and 220B, as if they were filling out tax returns.

Cosmo is smiling and polite even when he's being strong-armed. Invited to kill a man, Gazzara gives an apologetic smirk. "I don't want to get involved," he says. "I keep my mouth shut. I turn my back." But yeah, he's killed gooks before. In the war. "I'm a club-owner," he protests. "I don't even buy liquor from San Francisco. I deal with merchants, butchers, bakers, milkmen." But the money, he wants. That's the bottom line. If he has to choose between losing the club and murder, well, he'll look for a compromise.[8] To conform is inevitably to compromise. (Nick Cassavetes: "I never saw my father compromise on something he believed in.")

Cosmo likes order and control, keeps a tight rein on his emotions, insists that the revues at the Crazy Horse West run like clockwork. (The Greek word kosmos means 'order' and 'the world'; Vitelli presumably derives from vital, and the Latin vitalis, pertaining to life. Thus: 'ordered life.') But his sense of order is spurious, and even a kind of cowardice. Whether it's at the poker table, or dealing with the gangsters, or just driving down the freeway, his control is repeatedly undone. When he gambles he loses. When he negotiates he's duped. When he drives, his car breaks down. In the film's best joke, he phones the club en route to the assassination to check up on the show to discover it's anarchy without him: "Is it the Paris number? For Chrissake, you been in the place seven years, you don't know the Paris number? Well are there signs on the wall? 'P,' 'A,' 'R'."

The club is a locus of denial; Cosmo's chief means of protection from the frightening and risky nature of life. Cassavetes said with some pride that in this film "I was able to imagine a self-contained world different from the one I live in," the irony being that this is just what Cosmo maintains: a world apart, a world where he is king. In the film's magisterial first shot, we see him sauntering down the front steps of the Crazy Horse West in his white tuxedo, winged shirt open at the collar, the master of all he surveys and a ringer for Rick Blaine in *Casablanca*. Like Rick, he will be forced out of the safety of the neutral zone of the club to engage in life and death decisions.

In reality, the Crazy Horse West was 'Gazzari's' (the sign can be glimpsed in the background when Cosmo goes down the street for breakfast after losing at the casino), a rock venue on Sunset Strip just a few blocks down from the Whisky-A-Go-Go, where they had shot *Faces*. (Mr Gazzari liked the name Crazy Horse West so much he kept it.)

The artificial other-worldliness of the Crazy Horse is signalled in the lurid magenta light which bathes everything and everyone within it, and which contrasts markedly with the exteriors: brilliant, glaring daylight scenes giving way to the pitch nocturne of the movie's second half. Such an expressionist use of colour was another departure for Cassavetes; as usual he preferred not to dwell on stylistic effects in his interviews, but they weren't achieved by accident. Al Ruban confirms that John had asked him to serve as director of photography on the film, but they argued about the look of the club scenes: "He wanted all these magenta filters on the lights, and he wanted that on people's faces too, which I couldn't put up with. I wanted to light their faces properly, so it was real. I shouldn't have argued the point with him because he was the director, and he just did it anyway, but that's why there's no director of photography taking credit on that film. Because a number of people did it. Including John and myself and some others."[9] As for the vividness of the film's colours, Ruban says "We grew up in the age of Technicolor films, when colours were more true and weren't averaged out for television. We always wanted as true and vivid a recreation of colour as possible; John used to rebel against my using filters at all."

At least three of Cosmo's dancers were professional strippers, but the burlesque routines they perform are as anachronistic to the mid-Seventies as the standards which accompany them – most notably 'I Can't Give You

John Cassavetes in 1969 *(courtesy of BFI)*.

The early acting career of John Cassavetes, clockwise from top left: with Mark Rydell and Sal Mineo in *Crime In The Streets* (1956); with Sidney Poitier in *Edge Of The City* (1957); with Robert Taylor in *Saddle The Wind* (1958); and with Angie Dickinson in *The Killers* (1964) *(Ronald Grant Archive, Kobal)*.

Gena Rowlands in her MGM starlet days circa 1957 *(courtesy of BFI)*.

John Cassavetes recording the music for *Shadows* with Shafi Hadi *(Ronald Grant Archive)*.

Filming *Shadows* (1959) in New York's Central Park, left to right: Cassavetes, Tony Ray and Lelia Goldoni
(courtesy of BFI).

A scene from *Too Late Blues* (1961), from the left, Bobby Darin, Cliff Carnell and Seymour Cassel *(courtesy of BFI)*.

Burt Lancaster and Judy Garland in *A Child Is Waiting* (1963) *(Kobal)*.

Gena Rowlands in *Faces* (1968).

Peter Falk, Ben Gazzara and Cassavetes in *Husbands* (1970) (*Kobal*).

Cassavetes with Charles Bronson in *The Dirty Dozen* (1967) *(Ronald Grant Archive)*.

Cassavetes on the set of *Rosemary's Baby* (1968) with Mia Farrow and Roman Polanski *(Camera Press)*.

Cassavetes with Richard Dreyfuss in *Whose Life is It Anyway?* (1981) *(Ronald Grant Archives)*.

Cassavetes with Susan Sarandon in *Tempest* (1982) *(Ronald Grant Archives)*.

Seymour Cassel in *Minnie And Moskowitz* (1971).

Cassavetes directing *Minnie And Moskowitz* with Tim Carey (left) and Seymour Cassel (right) (*Kobal*).

Previously unpublished photographs of Cassavetes directing O. G. Dunn in *A Woman Under The Influence* (1974) taken by Mike Ferris, the film's cinematographer.

Gena Rowlands in *A Woman Under The Influence*, for which she earned her first Oscar nomination.

Meade Roberts in *The Killing Of A Chinese Bookie* (1976).

Cassavetes, Ben Gazzara and Gena Rowlands in *Opening Night* (1977) *(Kobal)*.

Gena Rowlands was again nominated for an Oscar in *Gloria* (1980).

Peter Falk in Cassavetes' stage play *Knives* (1981)
(Joan Almond).

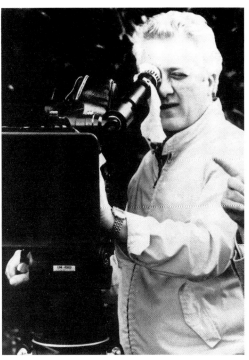

Al Ruban, who worked with Cassavetes as cameraman,
editor, actor and producer from 1959, on the set of
Love Streams (1984) *(Rex)*.

Seymour Cassel, Cassavetes and Gena Rowlands on the set during the last day of filming
Love Streams (Joan Almond).

John and Gena in the early Eighties *(Ronald Grant Archives)*.

Anything But Love,' which dates back at least as far as Howard Hawks' 1939 screwball *Bringing Up Baby*, and which serves as a Dennis Potter-ish counterpoint to the action, which is anything but loving.

The club's parade of scantily-clad female flesh is compered by the paunchy, middle-aged Mr Sophistication, a master of ceremonies with a top hat and cane, albeit a severely degraded one in these circumstances. His tone-deaf renditions and grotesque circus make-up mark him as a freak in his own estimation, and he functions as a sort of grotesque mirror-image or stand-in for Cosmo. According to Ray Carney, the longer 135-minute cut of the film reveals a still of Emil Jannings in Josef von Sternberg's *The Blue Angel* on the dressing room wall: another 'sophisticate' brought low by the seedy allure of a nightclub, and an obvious model for Meade Roberts' role (Roberts, incidentally, was a writer friend of John's who had fallen on hard times). In his final shambolic routine, Mr Sophistication is reduced to a body vest on which he has sketched the cut of a tuxedo: the emperor with no clothes.

'There are people struggling to keep the show alive.'

Cosmo Vitelli

By his own account, Ben Gazzara struggled to come to terms with this apparently uncharacteristic, abstract genre exercise and such an opaque role. Naturally pugnacious, Gazzara spends the movie holding himself in check. "At the beginning, I didn't know what we were doing, I was really lost," he told Doug Headline and Dominique Cazenave. "I called John and said 'What's going on? I'm not having any fun!" He answered: "Me neither. We'll see. Maybe we'll end up enjoying ourselves, or maybe not – maybe we'll suffer." In fact, we quickly began to enjoy once I understood the role. I hadn't done my homework.

"I remember when we shot the scene in the limo, where I'm alone without the girls, and John was on the floor, holding the camera. Between takes, he explained what the film meant to him. "All these people who destroy art, who persecute you, who make you do things and never leave you alone." He began to cry. I thought "My God! It's really a personal thing for him." So, the gangsters were a metaphor, and Cosmo was John, certainly. The club was where Vitelli created beauty, with its girls, the music, the jokes, the spectacle – that was the best part of Cosmo. The gambling, the drink, that was the dark side of the artist. and the gangsters were the system, which was so hard on John."[10]

Al Ruban sees it the same way: "To my mind, it was autobiographical. The club was the world that he created and valued more than anything, much like the films that John made and was so protective of, and the gangsters were the men in the suits, the pressures that come to bear not only to sign you up, but to change you to their will. I think it was something about his life in movie-making that he was able to crystallise and put into this one film."

They're right of course, but it's important not to read the metaphor too literally. For example, while John Cassavetes liked to drink and gamble, there's no indication that he considered this to be a 'dark side,' (nor, according to Ruban, would he bet beyond his means). Ben Gazzara would be the first to agree that he wasn't playing John in the sense of impersonating him. John was restless and extroverted, Cosmo is smug and contained. John was surrounded by family and friends, Cosmo has no-one. John was fearless – a description applied by Martin Scorsese among others – and Cosmo is haunted and afraid.

Perhaps the most crucial distinction to make is between John and Cosmo's radically opposed conceptions of 'art.' As Mr Sophistication's sorry tragi-comic pretensions to cultural *savoir faire* remind us, the strip club is another form of theatre, operating on different levels of reality front-stage and back. On stage, in Cosmo's realm, the girls caricature titillating male fantasies of female sexuality in arch gestures and stilted postures; backstage, under Cassavetes' direction, they're free and at ease with their bodies, they speak naturally, laugh, argue between themselves, apparently oblivious to the presence of the camera. Cosmo's choreography is stale and over-rehearsed, an escapist spectacle in thrall to tired conventions of erotica; Cassavetes' direction is almost the exact opposite, fresh and spontaneous, confrontational, non-spectacular, and thoroughly original.

For all his stoicism and his enduring sense of style, Cosmo's pep talk at the end to a dejected Mr Sophistication has to be understood as a hollow and complacent credo: "The only people who are happy are the people who are comfortable," he claims, with a wince. "Look at me. I'm only happy when I'm angry, when I'm sad, when I can play the fool, when I can be what people want me to be rather than be myself. Understand? That takes work. You work overtime for that. Doesn't matter who you are or what personality you choose. C'mon, baby: choose a personality! Let's go down there, we'll do a great show, we'll smile, we'll cry big glistening tears that pour onto the stage and we'll make their lives a little happier, so they won't have to face themselves, they can pretend to be somebody else."

In other words, the show must go on – and don't worry about the bullet in your chest. Cosmo may not be a great director, but he's a great showman, and a natural escape artist. He pulls off an assassination too tough for the mob and gets away with it (almost); he talks his way out of trouble with Flo (Tim Carey) and turns the tables on the other hoods sent to kill him (Seymour Cassel and Robert Phillips). Again and again in this film he merges with the shadows; indeed this is his principal survival tactic against the gangsters. Cassavetes under-exposes all these nocturnal scenes – it's hardcore *noir* – so that we're squinting to make him out. He's literally undefinable, and that's how he prefers it.

If there's any doubt at the end, as to whether Cosmo will live or die, stepping out of the club onto Sunset Strip just as he did in the opening shot, the ambiguity shrouds the more important truth, that at best he's been existing on a half-life the entire movie, running away from everyone, and most of all from himself.

'Will you please tell me what is going on?'

Rachel

The Killing Of A Chinese Bookie was financed with profits from the release of *A Woman Under The Influence* and some European pre-sales. Supremely confident in the film, and encouraged by their last experience of distribution, Cassavetes and Ruban were eager to retain control of the movie. When the Columbia duplex became available at short notice for an exclusive New York engagement, they edited in double-quick time to take advantage of it.

"Right up to the day it opened I thought it was going to be a great success, I thought our fortunes were made," Al Ruban recounts. As usual, he and John went along to the cinema to check out the lines on the first day. "You could count the number of people going in, one by one," he recalls. "And the ones who came out were so angry! Really angry! And expressive! They would talk to the people in line telling them not to go in!"

After just seven days, they pulled it. *The Killing Of A Chinese Bookie* didn't even last that long in Los Angeles. "I remember how excited we were, because it opened at the Mann National in Westwood," Mike Ferris says. "They used to paint a giant mural on the side of the building, which was a main thoroughfare, so it would be like a 160 foot poster. So we were excited. I was there the day it opened. People hooted and hissed and left. The theatre didn't empty but they didn't like it. It was kind of mean. Ugly. I thought it was a fabulous, mesmerising film."

Cassavetes faced it straight on. "Let's pull it before they can kill us any more," he told Ruban.

Speculating about the reason the film was rejected, Ruban suggests that it was too negative for the time. "It shows you what not to do, it shows a man at a crossroads choosing the wrong way to go. Clearly it forces an audience to say he didn't have to kill that person. Maybe that's why they didn't like it. And I think it makes great demands on the audience. That's one of the things I like most about the picture."

For his part, speaking after re-editing the film in 1978, Cassavetes thought that Cosmo was too much the conformist for the audience. "I remember very distinctly when we were shooting the scene in which he lost all the money, and then he went and shook the hands of the criminals. And Ben Gazzara did it with such skill and sincerity. I kept thinking, if we do this another twenty times, maybe Ben will reach the audience by enjoying it more. I thought the difference between success and failure, in terms of the audience response, would have been had he said, 'Thank you very much!,' instead of 'Thank you, thank you.' I thought that little point would either make the audience go with him as a character or say I want to shy away from him, because he really is polite, he's not putting anyone down, he's not standing up for himself. I think it became a sad film for most people, because that point of reality was something they couldn't swallow. I'd like to make that film about four or five more times," he said. "It had interesting characters. Interesting people."[11]

The reviews were terrible. *Variety* wrote that, "True to form, John Cassavetes challenges a Hollywood cliché: that technology is so advanced even the worst films usually look good. With ease, he proves that an awful film can look even worse." Writing in the *Saturday Review* under the headline 'To Each His Everyman,' Judith Crist derided "a mess as sloppy in concept as it is in execution. As if an artsy-smartsy amateur had attempted a remake of one of those taut little low-budget crime thrillers in which Cassavetes established himself as an actor." Even his most sympathetic critics were disappointed. Proclaiming Cassavetes a genius in *America* magazine, Robert E Lauder admitted *"The Killing Of A Chinese Bookie* is a disaster . . . Cassavetes' most self-indulgent. So erratically edited and so lacking in structure that he may be the only person who can make sense of the film."

Without access to this longer, 135-minute cut, it's impossible to say how justified the vitriol was, but Al Ruban has no hesitation in declaring the original, longer film the superior of the two: "With John's films I always think the longer the better," he told Thierry Jousse. "The emotional line is what's important, not the narrative line. And the only way to really get to know these people is to spend time with them."

Many critics were quick to impute the characters' failure to communicate to a failure on the part of the film-makers. There's a suspicion they were thrown by the film's genre trappings, that by encroaching on Hollywood territory, Cassavetes laid himself open to accusations of pretentiousness and self-indulgence. Granted this wasn't the 'sheer entertainment' the director had talked about with Larry Gross just a year earlier. In the same interview, he had observed that 'things aren't so simple. When you learn that, you stretch away from the simple idea of make-believe and you try to incorporate those simpler ideas into more complex feelings.' Announcing itself as a gangster movie, a *noir-ish* thriller, *The Killing Of A*

Chinese Bookie is actually something very close to an anti-gangster movie, an anti-thriller.

Predicated on temporal anxiety – suspense – the thriller is inherently a manipulative form, a heavily structured, encoded style controlled by an omniscient director; concepts anathema to Cassavetes, who, as we've seen, even felt the standard point-of-view shot was morally insidious. *Bookie* rejects most (if not all) generic tropes. On first viewing, it feels utterly formless, an apparently arbitrary assembly of episodes linked only by some association with Cosmo. Frustratingly, even though he's the central character, Cassavetes keeps cutting away to subsidiary roles: the girls, or the chauffeur, or the hoods, or Mr Sophistication. He omits 'important' narrative or psychological developments: we don't see how Cosmo loses so much at poker, for instance, only its aftermath; we don't realise Cosmo is wounded until some time after the event; and the double-cross which justifies the plot is dispensed with almost off-handedly; unheroically, Cosmo backs away from conflict and retires to the Crazy Horse West.

"Everything I've ever learned about film-making is to have it so well-prepared that it's nailed down, but John was the exact opposite," Mike Ferris notes. "He didn't want to know what was going to happen. He wanted to discover it, and be surprised. He created freedom. When it came to the characters he made you feel that he didn't know anymore than you did – that you were asking questions on the same plane. He was searching. Looking for answers about people."

Strikingly, Cassavetes refuses the crutch of a non-diagetic score: the only music in the film emanates from the club or a taxi driver's radio. (He used to joke about how the British critics got excited about the rough naturalistic sound in *Shadows*, claiming he hadn't been able to afford to tidy it up, but the ambient sound in *Bookie* is a conspicuous artistic choice.) It's only in retrospect, or after repeated viewings, that you realise how structured the film really is; that it takes a linear chronological-narrative line but leaves that underneath (again, like a melody in a jazz improv), switching text with subtext, background atmosphere with foreground action to create a more complex cinematic and social experience.

"I can understand that certain people would like a more conventional form, like the gangster picture. You can read it because it's something you know already," Cassavetes noted. "People prefer that you condense, for life to be condensed in films. They prefer that because they can catch on to the meanings and keep ahead of the movie. But that's boring. I won't make shorthand films. In my films there's a competition with the audience to keep ahead of them. I want to break their patterns. I want to shake them up and get them out of those quick, manufactured truths."[12]

In this context Cassavetes' intuitive indeterminism may preclude suspense, but it produces a deeper and more intriguing tension between form and content which mirrors the struggle between his anti-hero and the forces which surround him. Just as Cosmo commits murder with a look of acute disgust, so Cassavetes fought to resist the blood-letting his own script required. Al Ruban tells the story: "The day we were filming the assassination, we had got to the point in the swimming pool, with this old Chinese fellow [Soto Joe Hugh] who couldn't see and was deadly afraid of water, when we broke for dinner. I remember I stayed up there on the set, and when nobody came back after two hours I got worried, and went looking for them. I found them all in a restaurant down on Sunset, and John didn't want to kill the bookie. He had everybody on the crew and the actors there discussing it. As I came in I heard Benny say, 'But John, it's called *The Killing Of A Chinese Bookie*, how can we not kill him?!' We weren't shooting in continuity, so we had shot things already that took place afterward. So we had a bitter fight. He said, 'What do you wanna do?' I said, 'I wanna go up there and kill this guy. This is getting ridiculous. It's now two and a half hours, and we can't afford this luxury.' Well, he was unhappy and we went around it a couple more times, then he said to Benny, 'Okay, let's go kill the Chinaman.' But it was serious. It was not a lark. He really did not want to kill this man."

In 1978, Cassavetes recut the film to its present 109 minutes. "He told me it was because he felt like it," Ruban shrugs. In the US, Cosmo's unprophetic opening line still fell on deaf ears ('Don't worry Vince, things'll pick up'); the jeers and slow hand claps at the Crazy Horse West still echoed through empty cinema stalls. Even so, in recent years, the movie's reputation has grown immeasurably, especially in Europe, where it has come to be regarded as one of Cassavetes' definitive works. Back home on Woodrow Wilson Drive, Gena Rowlands named the family's latest dog Cosmo. It became her special favourite.

---

1 Source: Al Ruban. Apparently Cassavetes also declined offers to direct 'The Godfather'and 'The Exorcist'.
2 Cassavetes on Cassavetes, *Monthly Film Bulletin*, July 1978
3 Larry Gross, *Millimeter*
4 Headline and Cazenave
5 Louis Marcorelles, JC interview, *Cahiers du Cinema*, June 1978
6 See also Appendix: Acting Out
7 *MFB*, July 1978
8 According to Mike Ferris, they shot 80,00 feet of film on this one scene alone, starting at dusk and filming through 'til dawn. 'Enough for four Corman movies,' he marvels.
9 Mitchell Breit, Mike Ferris and Fred Elmes.
10 Headline and Cazenave
11 *MFB*
12 Quoted in Carney, *The Adventure Of Insecurity.*

'Beyond Pain'

Pedro Almodóvar

I think *Opening Night* is my favourite of Cassavetes' films. It has an aura, a taste which is very explosive. It's very raw, very distraught. Those fights in the movie feel real to me. John Cassavetes and Gena Rowlands were the perfect couple and this movie doesn't work out if not for the tension between them – I think that tension was in their private lives as a theatrical couple. The film is about an actress becoming crazy, which is a plot I like very much; Myrtle Gordon (Gena Rowlands) is an amazing character. Rowlands does one of the best drunk scenes I ever saw. And it's a long scene – very long. It's a commonplace thing for an actor to play drunk, but she did it in a completely original way, without doing anything obvious. I asked for something similar from Cecilia Roth in *All About My Mother*, to go beyond pain, and just relax the face muscles. It's very expressive, and I learned that from that big sequence in *Opening Night*. Myrtle almost falls down, but shows nearly nothing. I think this sequence also explains the work of the director very well. It's very dark to suggest this is representative of our work, but that scene where Ben Gazzara is waiting for her, and she's completely sick, drunk. He's at the end of that long corridor, and she's crashing against the walls. He orders someone to give her coffee in her dressing room. But in that long corridor, where she could break her head, he doesn't want anyone to help her, that she must do by herself. To me that's the figure of the director. Sometimes when you see an actor going through a hard time, you have to leave them to make it on their own. It gives you the idea that the director is cruel, but those are the rules of the game.

Pedro Almodóvar
(Writer/director: *What Have I Done To Deserve This?*,
Law Of Desire, Women On The Verge Of A Nervous Breakdown,
Live Flesh, All About My Mother)

9

Opening Night

'When I was 17 I could do anything. It was so easy. My emotions were so close to the surface. I'm finding it harder and harder to stay in touch.'

Myrtle Gordon (Gena Rowlands)

Cassavetes went straight from *The Killing Of A Chinese Bookie* (shot at the end of 1975) into *Opening Night* (a year later), bringing most of the crew along with him, including producer/director of photography Al Ruban, executive producer Sam Shaw, cameramen Frederick Elmes and Michael Ferris, editor Tom Cornwell, and sound recordist/composer Bo Harwood. This core group was augmented by art director Brian Ryman, who took over a disused theatre in Pasadena and worked out the logistics for the film's interplay between front and backstage lives.

Myrtle Gordon (Gena Rowlands) is a popular and respected stage star 'of a certain age.' She has been engaged by producer David Samuels (Paul Stewart) to play the lead role in a new play by Sarah Goode (Joan Blondell). In The Second Woman Virginia goes through a mid-life crisis: her marriage to a photographer, Marty, is brittle and sterile. On a whim she goes to visit her first husband, a man she married when she was still a teenager. His home is a tumult of kids and uproar; it transpires that her unwillingness to have children ended their marriage.

Myrtle has also sacrificed family and children for the sake of career. To make matters more complicated, an ex-lover, Maurice (John Cassavetes), has been cast to play Marty. The first out-of-town try-out in New Haven goes smoothly enough, but then when a young fan, Nancy (Laura Johnson), is killed after chasing Myrtle's car, the actress begins to question the part she is playing both on-stage and off. She turns to Maurice for solace, but he rejects her advances. She feels victimised and alone. There is no hope in the play. And even if she does her part well, that will ensure she's typecast as the 'older woman' in future. The rehearsals are reduced to a shambles when she rebels against the script. She says she wants to find a way to play the role which would make age irrelevant.

She has visions of Nancy, as if she were her 17-year-old self. Her

*director, Manny Victor (Ben Gazzara) tries to tell her what he thinks she
needs to hear, even sleeping with her, but the performances become ever
more eccentric. As Myrtle's apparitions become wilder and more aggressive, Sarah becomes convinced that their star is in need of a psychiatrirst
or an exorcist, or both. Myrtle visits a spiritualist with Sarah, and rids
herself of Nancy.*

   *Finally, on the day of their New York opening, Myrtle disappears on a
drinking binge. She returns late for the show, barely able to walk. Manny
determines to put her on regardless: he thinks the audience could buy the
character as a drunk, at least in the first act. Gradually sobering through
the performance, Myrtle nevertheless departs from the text to improvise
an ending of giddy comic optimism with Maurice. After the show, she is
embraced by an elated Dorothy Victor (Zohra Lampert), Manny's
estranged wife.*

According to Cassavetes, the budget was $1.5 million. Essentially he
funded it himself from his acting work on Larry Peerce's *Two Minute
Warning* (in which Gena Rowlands also appeared), along with perhaps
$500,000 from the European pre-sales on *Chinese Bookie*, and the
diminishing returns from *A Woman Under The Influence*. But the strain
was beginning to show. According to Zohra Lampert, during one rehearsal
break Cassavetes discussed mortgaging his and Gena's house once again:
Gena cried out softly, "Oh, John, not the house, not the house!"[1] Shooting
lasted three and a half months, from the end of 1976 into the early spring
of '77. Mike Ferris remembers that in the last week of production Cassavetes called him aside, reached his arm around his shoulder, and told him
"Look, I'm going to New York to make a picture, but it's going to be a
union picture. Gena's just tired of me putting the house on the block every
time we make a movie."

* * *

What's immediately striking about *Opening Night* is how different it looks
from Cassavetes' earlier work, and especially from *Chinese Bookie*.
Whether in deference to the milieu or the complexity of the screenplay, or
admonished by his recent critical hammering, Cassavetes abandoned his
'vérité' aesthetic and opted for a much more conventional shooting style:
the framing is more symmetrical and less cluttered, camera movement is
smooth, marking social relationships in unhurried panning shots, and the
montage is much less oblique, often following a standard shot/reverse shot
syntax; Cassavetes cuts scrupulously to the metronome of narrative
development, consequently scenes tend to be shorter, and they dovetail
with what preceeds and succeeds them. In common with most melodramas,

one feels the hand of an omniscient director, shaping events and responses
– he even allows composer Bo Harwood a blast of a thundering and mourn-
ful symphonic score to build up the artfully choreographed sequence which
kicks off the plot, when Myrtle's seventeen-year-old fan is killed in a car
accident.[2]

*   *   *

Al Ruban remembers his surprise when John described what he had in
mind for the very first shot of the movie: to start with Myrtle emerging from
her dressing room, coming into the backstage area for a brief exchange
with the prop man, then continuing to pan across, past flying walls and an
open door so you could see the sun outside, and then revealing the actors
on stage, the audience behind them. "That's fine," Ruban said. "But it's
going to take a little time." Twenty minutes later John was back: "What the
hell is taking so long?"[3]

"We talked about it between ourselves on the set," Mike Ferris remembers. "That we were making a more polished picture. There was more set-
up time. A little more lighting. It was more intricate. But it wasn't
something John would ever discuss."[4]

The formalism (even formality) of *Opening Night* sets it apart. At least
in the first half, it feels cooler, more 'intellectual.' Characters like
Moskowitz and Mabel embodied the qualities of self-invention and spontaneity Cassavetes valued in performers unconsciously, but Myrtle Gordon
is an articulate professional actress. The self-reflexivity inherent in Cassavetes' cinema becomes explicit here, in this drama of an actress who at
great personal cost makes a part her own, and in the process transforms a
poor, 'worthy' play into something risky, vital and authentic – and not incidentally, transforms an intriguing, thoughtful film into something a little
ragged and perplexing.

*   *   *

Opening Night is a strange, ambitious, and ultimately frustrating film, and
also one of Cassavetes' most revealing movies. He had written the first
version of the screenplay nearly ten years before, between finishing *Faces*
and starting on *Husbands*, and like *Husbands*, it is a story about the conflict between responsibility and self-revelation prompted by a recent
death. It was intended, obviously, for Gena Rowlands, and they may have
delayed putting it into production until she was old enough to play it.
(Like Myrtle, Rowlands may have resisted it for perfectly sound career
reasons.) There's no question the script was radically reworked in pre-
production.

Anecdotal evidence has John and Gena going through a rough patch in their marriage at this point. That may or may not be true, but *Opening Night* is littered with splintered middle-aged couples putting out feelers (and immediately retracting them; Myrtle/Virginia proffers her hand one minute, thumbs her nose the next). It barely matters which individual is doing the talking, they speak with one voice:

"My life is getting boring. I'm getting sombre. My own tricks bore me." (Manny)

"I'm dying. You know how I know? Because I'm getting tired. It's always the same: You talk. I sleep." (Dorothy to Manny)

"You're not a woman to me anymore. You're a professional." (Maurice to Myrtle)

"You don't get to me. There is no way for you to get to me. You want to take dope? Go ahead. You want to get drunk? Go ahead. You want to go out with some guy four o'clock in the afternoon, be with some guy? Go ahead. You want to be young again, is that it?" (Marty to Virginia)

"There has to be something more when two people have cared for each other a long time – besides agony." (Myrtle to Maurice)

"I'm getting older – what do we do about that?" (Maurice onstage)

* * *

Aging is the subject of Sarah's play. The title, *The Second Woman*, is a reference to the menopause. Her set is dominated by two huge blow-ups of Marty's photographs of two ancient peasant women (in fact they were shots by Sam Shaw), and her characters engage in arch banter about decrepitude. It doesn't look like a particularly good play, not from the handful of scenes we see, but it's worth pointing out that it's only after the fateful encounter with Nancy that Myrtle develops problems with it. The death of her fan exposes the inadequacy of the work, and a deeper spiritual malaise that the play only compounds.

Cassavetes stages the accident (in front of the Orphean theatre, no less) in such a way as to emphasise how inured the theatre people are. True, they must run the gauntlet of autograph hunters, but once they reach the muffled security of the limousine they're protected from the elements, divorced from the outside world. In an image one might call 'haunting,' we see Nancy's hand pawing at the window, her mouth beseeching, but the rest of her features obscured by the streaming rain and her floppy blue rain hat. Only Myrtle shows the slightest interest in the girl while she's alive (she asks her name, advises her to get out of the rain and to see her tomorrow), and only Myrtle shows more than momentary concern after the accident. "What's the matter with us?" she demands of Maurice in her cavernous,

157

studio-like hotel room. "We lose sight of everything. A girl was killed tonight, and all we can talk about is dinner!"

That Maurice cynically rebuffs her only proves her point. It's as if the rest of them were living a parallel life unconnected with the dead girl. Myrtle alone takes it personally.

This is what makes her a great actress. She lives on her raw nerves. She may be neurotic – she smokes obsessively and steels herself with alcohol – but like Cassavetes, Myrtle refuses to separate the actor from the character; if she isn't Virginia, then nobody is. If Myrtle won't take responsibility for her actions, then no-one else will. When Marty/Maurice slaps Virginia/Myrtle, she rebels, first – in rehearsal – by falling to floor as soon as he raises his hand, then – on stage – by refusing to get back up again; in fact she brings the curtain down by pointing out to the audience "we must never forget it's only a play."

These anarchic, subversive acts open up *The Second Woman* in a way her colleagues don't readily appreciate. The writer, Sarah, complains that it's all there on the page: "Here we are sitting around talking as if she had to manufacture the words. See this: Act one, act two, act three? All you have to do is say the lines clearly and with a degree of feeling, and Virginia will appear." But this reductionist predeterminism (the very antithesis of Cassavetes' customary approach) would be the death of Myrtle. She tries to explain to the writer, "Listen, I don't have a husband, I don't have a family, this is it for me – I get my kicks out of acting." If acting is to be limited to a robotic parroting of prescribed lines, then she has nothing. Myrtle is as alone as Cosmo Vitelli, but where Cosmo only knew how to put on a show for the world – all style, no content – Myrtle acts from the inside out; it's her most intimate self-expression. The worst thing Manny can do is call her (as Maurice already has) a 'professional' – it's a dirty word, and Myrtle reacts as violently as if she'd been called a prostitute.

Cassavetes: "You have to fight sophistication. Sophistication comes to anybody who's been doing his job for a long time. But it's a trap, a kind of death. You have to fight knowing, because once you know something, it's hard to be open and creative; it's a form of passivity – something to guard against."[5]

Myrtle's complete identification with (and conversely, her absolute alienation from) Virginia is mixed up by her reluctance to accept her age. But it's not the numbers which throw her, not the years; "Age isn't interesting," she insists. "Age is depressing, age is dull, age doesn't have anything to do with anything." What offends her more is how time dulls her as an artist, and more than that, as an individual – and how Virginia gives her nothing to fight back with. In the first place, as an actress, the passage of time limits the roles she will be offered. But more fundamentally, it lessens her connection with the world: "When I was 18 I could do anything. My emotions were so close to the surface I could feel everything easily, but now, this is years later, plays later."

Hence the strange bond she forges with the dead girl, Nancy, a connection which becomes more real to her than anything or anybody else. She visits Nancy's family as they mourn, but she doesn't belong there, as Nancy's father (Meade Roberts) harshly points out: "You don't have children do you? If you did, you wouldn't have come."

Seeing the girl staring back at her in her dressing room mirror, she sees a vision of herself as she was at 18: young and sexy and alive, with unlimited prospects ahead of her. Extreme close-ups cut between Gena Rowlands' still beautiful but mature face and the alabaster skin of 18-year-old Laura Johnson.[6] And so Myrtle mourns that loss, the girl she used to be, the lives she might have lived, the children she never had. Or rather, she doesn't bury Nancy, but tries to keep her close, a private resource from which she hopes to draw a performance that will transcend the pettiness and resignation of Sarah's play.

It's a startlingly bold and unexpected imaginative leap, this apparition. Isn't Cassavetes supposed to be a 'realistic' film-maker? "Here's a theatrical story, and suddenly this apparition appears – and I started giggling," Cassavetes related. "Everybody knows I hate that spooky-dooky stuff, and they said, 'Are you going to leave that in?' But this is a figment of her imagination. It's something that's controllable by her; it's something necessitated by her own loneliness and individuality."[7]

In other words, what we're seeing isn't Nancy's ghost, or spirit, but Myrtle's projection. She says as much to the spiritualist (Katherine Cassavetes) Sarah drags her to: "Actresses create characters. I created Nancy because I thought there were certain scenes in the play where I was having trouble visualising my own life," she explains. "At some point in life youth dies and the second woman in us takes over. I believe Nancy is the first woman in my own life."

It sounds sweetly reasonable, and no wonder she walks out of the seance. The mood of Myrtle's first encounter with the apparition is delicate and serene. Like Mizoguchi in *Ugetsu Monogatari* or Robert Wise in *The Curse Of The Cat People*, Cassavetes doesn't convey Nancy's 'other-worldliness' through photographic trickery, but only through the narrative disruption of her physical presence and the spatial dislocation of the editing, shock cuts which become more dramatic with each of her appearances.

And this is where Cassavetes' 'figment' gets close to 'spooky-dooky stuff,' because Myrtle loses control of her muse: Nancy takes to taunting Myrtle with her youth and sexuality, physically attacks her, and most shockingly (invisibly) bangs Myrtle's head against the door frame when she takes refuge with Sarah. On the one hand the actress reassures the writer there's nothing supernatural going on ('it's just me'), on the other she volunteers to go and see another spiritualist (this time played by Lady Rowlands).

In rebelling against the naturalism of the stage ('the choking formality of the theatre,' in Cassavetes' words[8]), Myrtle has opened up a Pandora's box of irrationalities that no author can hope to control: not Myrtle, not Sarah, not even John Cassavetes.

Sarah pronounces her crazy and it's easy to see why, but the craziness Myrtle shares with Mabel Longhetti (and, looking ahead, with Sarah Lawson from *Love Streams*) isn't simply a clinical condition, but a reckless and overwhelming spiritual appetite. These women challenge the consolations of convention, complacency and compromise at every turn, not because they're sick, but because they must. Cassavetes acknowledged that he knew nothing about psychiatry, but then he had no use for diagnosis and treatment: "People society would call crazy, I find them to be individuals not able to blow with the orchestra. Most don't know what to do, just like the rest of us," he said.[9] "I'm half-crazy, and I think everyone is on the verge of madness, we just don't want to admit it," he told *Positif*. Madness, as Cassavetes used the term, is intrinsic to human kind, and indeed may be what is most precious, sensitive and individual about us. It's true that their emotional openness takes Myrtle, Mabel and Sarah to dangerously vulnerable places ("I'm in trouble, I'm not acting," Myrtle admits to Manny the day before they're due to open in New York), but it also gives them a heroic quality mostly lacking in Cassavetes' male characters. Like Gus, Archie and Harry, or indeed like Richard Forst, Myrtle needs to reach back to her youth – but she seeks something more profound than sexual adventure and independence: a creative affirmation of her own life force. An artist, she has a more obvious conduit for social-sanctioned self-expression than the housewife, Mabel, or the divorcee, Sarah, but even so her freedom to act is impinged upon by her allocated role: the aging woman of waning powers.

Naturally that role is inescapable – no matter how hard Myrtle struggles to deny it, or how drunk she gets – yet somehow she discovers a way to play it that she can live with. "Take a chance," she implores Maurice, after 'exorcising' Nancy, "Let's take this play, dump it upside down and see if we can't find something human in it." Still the professional, he tells her they don't pay him enough to make a fool of himself on stage, yet the next night, opening night, he rises to her challenge, leaves the text behind and together they improvise an ending of crazy comic defiance.

At any rate, one may surmise that this is how Cassavetes meant the climax to be seen. As supporting evidence, one can point to Dorothy Victor's elated response to the performance – a 'second woman' herself, she has been established as a mostly silent observer throughout the rehearsals. "I remember I wanted to express my unconditional love for Manny, and my understanding of the immeasurable stress under which Myrtle has been operating," Zohra Lampert says. And then there is a speech which, in the context of Myrtle's drunken return seems almost throwaway (it's spoken by the actor who plays Virginia's first husband in *The Second Woman*, John Toll, and it's virtually his only line 'out of character'[10]), but in retrospect neatly articulates the artistic leap her acting represents: "For all the pressure the whole time in New Haven, even when she went wrong she made me laugh. In some crazy way, with all her craziness and all her nuttiness – *it was more real for me being up than being in it*. In some nutty way it seemed like something real." (My italics.)

The trouble with *Opening Night* is that the ending Maurice and Myrtle improvise at the climax of *The Second Woman* doesn't seem to justify the rhapsodic validation bestowed upon it by the audience, or the symbolic weight Cassavetes attaches to it. One can admire Myrtle's determination in going through with the performance (and the sequence in which she returns to the theatre too drunk to walk is tremendous: Gazzara/Manny pushing away his assistant director Fred Draper when he makes to help her, insisting that she finds the strength within herself)? We may even echo the sentiments of the stagehand, Bobby, who tells her "I've seen a lot of drunks in my day, but I've never seen anybody as drunk as you and still be able to walk. You're fantastic!" But Myrtle/Virginia's revelation – "Marty, we have each other" – can't help but feel flimsy after such a build up.

This lengthy (ten minute) end sequence is filmed entirely from the stalls by two fixed cameras, and without recourse to a single close-up (we do get a handful of brief cutaways to Manny, Sarah and the producer, David). It's another experiment in the dynamics of 'real-time'; but with a distancing effect – we're always aware we're watching a performance, albeit one that appears to be improvised. The view is impeded from time to time by the heads of the people in the row infront, and the audience's laughter and applause breaks into the dialogue. (To shoot the theatre scenes, the production placed ads in a local paper inviting anyone to come along for three or four days filming, to the anger of the extras' union.)

The scene tries to effect a double rapprochement: the reconciliation of a couple which in turn facilitates their reconciliation with getting older. Cassavetes throws in the notion of possession, a metaphor for acting in Myrtle's 'possession' by Nancy, and now a metaphor for ageing: "I am not me, I used to be me," says Myrtle. "We are absolutely different people than we were," agrees Maurice. "We've been invaded," concludes Myrtle. "There is someone posing here as us." It's further complicated by the 'hall-of-mirrors' conceit, so that we're watching Virginia and Marty, Myrtle and

Maurice, Gena and John concurrently. One could say that Virginia and Marty talk through their problems, Myrtle and Maurice act them out, and Gena and John dramatise them.

Perhaps it's too distancing, all this conceptual doubling and daring? True, the presentation is exuberantly comic, and the *coup de grace* is as simple and straightforward as an old athletes 'foot-shake,' yet it's hard to feel this horseplay answers (or merits) the trauma Myrtle has put herself through.[11]

According to Ted Allan, who would co-write *Love Streams* with Cassavetes, John previewed a cut of *Opening Night* which brought the house down, and in the same way as he had with *Husbands*, he took it away and recut it, as if to repudiate the audience's enthusiasm. Harry Mastrogeorge – who had read the original script in order to work with Laura Johnson, and who was on set for a few days of shooting – says that, the way he remembers it, the original version was better than the finished film. "With John, what would happen sometimes, it wasn't improvisation so much, but in the heat of the moment he would change text, and I thought what he had written was better than the film. John would change things arbitrarily, I thought. He was a very impulsive guy. He didn't like working within a framework that someone had set for him. I remember standing there during one of the big scenes on *Opening Night* thinking 'John, you wrote a brilliant script, leave the fucking thing alone,' and he kept screwing around with it. He didn't ask my advice, so I didn't say anything. It was a big question with John, whether he would have been a greater film-maker if he'd been less impulsive, or whether that was what made him great. His attention span would break and sometimes that's wonderful, and sometimes you should leave well enough alone."[12]

If, in the end, it's not a wholly satisfying drama, *Opening Night* is still a film of considerable fascination. One great pleasure, textural rather than textual, is the film's counterpoint of stage and film acting. Much more vividly than most backstage melodramas, *Opening Night* contrasts the expansive, gestural acting of theatre with the more internal, psychological mode of screen acting. Granted, Gena Rowlands is a very physically expressive film actress – yet her work here is as subtle as anything she does in *A Woman Under The Influence* or *Gloria*: catch that quick glance she gives her hand mirror after seeing Nancy's apparition for the first time, a nervy double-check to make sure she is who she thinks she is before opening the door. There's a strong flavour of how draining Myrtle's independent spirit is, both to her and everyone around her: the way she collapses into an embrace. Her life is a high-wire act, and her colleagues are reluctantly compelled to marvel – and to catch her when she falls. Rowlands' is a tremendously brave performance. She allows Cassavetes' camera so close to her skin you can practically count the pores; there's a touch of redness around the nose; lines around the eyes, and this cut up against the 18-year-old beauty of Laura Johnson.

One wonders to what extent the film is a portrait of Gena. There are tantilising correspondences: Rowlands is superstitious; she famously throws herself into her roles; like her husband, she enjoyed a drink; and there have been rumours that she came close to a breakdown after playing Mabel.

Al Ruban is quick to discredit such idle speculation: "Nonsense!" he says. "This is a woman who is so strong and confident in her own abilities and so secure. You would never meet a more even-keeled person. Unless she was mad at you. Then watch out!"

Myrtle's neuroses are common to the profession and certainly Gena and John would have discussed these issues: the constant victimisation of actresses ("If you're an actress it's mandatory you get hit," Manny tells her); the obsession with sexual attraction and the fear of getting old.

And of course men also age. Bo Harwood remembers that while he was rewriting the screenplay during preproduction, John would come into the office every day, and he'd come into the music room and ask Bo to put a microphone on him. Harwood would pick up his guitar and they'd start taping: "It wasn't really song, it was raw, neat poetry, very free, unlearned, unclever poetry. Sometimes it rhymed, sometimes it didn't. He'd bang the keys on the piano – terrible! He was tone deaf, no sense of rhythm whatsoever, and I can't write a note of music, but somehow he could convey an idea to me. And if it meant something, he'd just look and smile at me. Then he'd leave and I'd refine it into a musical structure. I've got about 15 – 20 songs from that period – my own private album of Bo Harwood/John Cassavetes songs. He'd come in as Gena: in that frame of mind of what that woman must be going through with her age, her fears, her loss of friends. All that insecurity. I think it helped him rewrite the script."

Zohra Lampert remembers that there was no audition, "only uninvasive talk." She says there was a finished script from the start, but that it "became multi-coloured in the course of filming, which would indicate changes. The actors always spoke the dialogue John wrote. One did not make up one's lines despite the appearance of spontaneity." Discussing the 4am scene between Dorothy and Manny, with its rueful emotional detachment, and the hints of a long and tumultuous intimacy behind it, Lampert gives a vivid account of how that spontaneity was achieved in filming: "We got to it very late at night. John shot one take of the first half, and when it was over he announced, not without irony: 'All right, that was very professional. Now: I want the two of you to sit there and read the paper for as long as it takes, and then we'll start the scene.' In other words, we had delivered a conventional performance that amounted to little more than reciting the dialogue. So we sat and read the paper, camera rolling, probably for about five minutes. Gradually, when our defences had worn away, he signalled us to begin again. It was exciting to have a go at this good and original material. Ben must have felt the same way – note the little abashed gulp of his when Dorothy confesses Manny bored her. Thus, in spending waste film, John had bought freedom for the actors."[13]

On another occasion, Mike Ferris remembers the director stoking up the atmosphere. They were shooting the stage-play, and the morning had not gone well. "I was in a third of the way up the middle aisle I think, and we had another camera over on the other side. And it was a couple of hours after lunch, nothing was going on. I was talking to one of the teachers of the children, quietly. John walked by, heading for the stage, and as he walked by, he said to me *sotto voce*: 'Just go along with this.' I almost didn't hear him. He got up on the stage, starts talking to the actors, and after five minutes we started our conversation up again. But all of a sudden: Boom! He's yelling at us. Didn't use my name, never would. Didn't use her name. 'Who's that talking? If you're not paying attention you don't belong here – and you can go home right now!' He looked at us for about five beats, then he looked at the other camera. He looked at everybody. Ranting and raving for about two minutes – and he just galvanised that place. 'This whole day has been shit. We'll go home and write new scripts!' A little two-minute performance. And then he stopped as abruptly as he started. He turned around, lit another cigarette and walked off the stage. And as he walked past us he whispered 'Great, thanks' and he was gone."

The part of Sarah Goode was originally envisaged for Bette Davis, perhaps because, as more than one critic has observed, *Opening Night* is a variation on *All About Eve* (with Eve as the figment of Margo Past), but more likely because Davis was Gena Rowlands' teenage idol. It was Paul Stewart, an old friend from *A Child Is Waiting* (and before that, of course, a forboding presence in *Citizen Kane*) who suggested Joan Blondell, who had co-starred with James Cagney in *Public Enemy* as far back in 1931.

As usual, Cassavetes rehearsed the cast by reading through the text repeatedly, with intense discussion about character and motivation, but no staging or performing. On the set, he kept as unobtrusive as possible and allowed the actors free reign (they were equipped with radio mics to facilitate movement). It was all a bit much for Ms Blondell.

One day she took Al Ruban aside and told him "I can't tell when the actors are acting and when they're talking about their home-life. I just can't tell the difference."

"That was scary for her," Ruban notes. "She was used to coming to the set, becoming the character, doing her bit and then going home and being this other person. It didn't seem to her there was a point of departure between the character and the actor, and it was scary to be faced with something new like that late in her career."

Cassavetes: "I could see she was terrified of me, because I was this young upstart director, even though I was approaching 50. Paul Stewart said to me, 'Go talk to Joan, she doesn't know what she's doing, she's upset.' And I'd go over to her – I liked her very much, tremendous open face, very warm person – and I asked if she had a problem. She told me 'No, not at all, I'm having the time of my life,' and you could hear the hysteria in her voice. All through the film she would deny it!"

Then toward the end of the film she said "You're going to be very angry with me, I wrote a piece in the paper and it's not flattering to you; I don't know what to say to you, I don't feel that way at all, it just came out that way and I hope you're not offended."

"I said 'No, I'm not offended'."

"She said, 'You want to read it?'"

"I said, 'Let's wait 'til the film is over. Hold it for me'."

"At the end of the film I read it and I started laughing. The worst thing she said, she said 'I dont know where to go. If I go to the bathroom this bastard has a camera. There's a camera lurking around every camera.'!"[14]

"John wanted you to care about the people, and he thought you had to spend time with them to get to understand them," Ruban says. "He believed that pauses were important. The little hiccups that happen in conversation, the little glances, all these things play a part in the make-up of the character, and to shortcut it to get the dialogue done you're cheating the audience. It becomes artificial stimulation."

"Actors who have had some success, like Joan Blondell, or Peter Falk, they build up schtick, repertoires of little devices that they know play well with an audience, so when they come to a point when they can't think of what to do, a small dilemma in their character's development, they resort to that. John would force them beyond that, so these actors would discover more about themselves and take more chances and have a wonderful time, even suffering, because they invested more than they expected. I think that was the blessing for an actor in a Cassavetes film."

1 Zohra Lampert, letter to the author (2000).

2 Admittedly, Harwood complains that Cassavetes truncated his score by burying it in the mix under the clamour of the autograph hounds: "I was devastated," he says. "John said it built up too much expectation. I said the girl's going to be killed in 40 seconds, what do you mean 'expectation'?."

3 In the event Cassavetes cut the shot in half.

4 Mike Ferris, Author's interview (2000).

5 Quoted in Ray Carney, *The Adventure Of Insecurity.*

6 Cassavetes came across Johnson by accident and was struck by how much she looked like the young Gena: the same patrician features and golden hair. He asked his old New York room-mate Harry Mastrogeorge – by then an acting teacher – to work with her in preparation for the shoot.

7 Cassavetes on Cassavetes, *MFB*, July 1978.

8 Brian Case interview transcript 1984.

9 Case.

10 Toll was cast after accompanying his girlfriend to a casting call.

11 Lisa Katzman provides a more celebratory reading of the film in an excellent piece she wrote for *Film Comment*. Katzman claims Cassavetes was "the method acting director par excellence," and goes on to say: "Only for Cassavetes, for whom the moment is the origin of drama, could have conceived of a dramatic resolution that uses method acting technique as a redemptive force by positioning the tyranny of an obsession with youth not as a sexist problem, but as a metaphysical one, which stems from society's neurotic denial of death and aging. Cassavetes created a dramatic framework to accept the moment as a redemptive force and made it work brilliantly. Myrtle's triumph may constitute a liberation from sexist ideology, but it also transcends gender. The only way to live one's life, onstage and off, she discovers, is in the moment" Lisa Katzman, 'Moment by Moment,' *Film Comment*, vol 25, n3, May/June 89.

12 Al Ruban, incidentally, cannot confirm Ted Allan's recollection: "I don't know what he's refering to. We all talked about the ending of the play, how long it went on, and on – and then the backstage stuff. It just seemed to go on too long. But that was never changed. It was always in the script." He also confirms that the apparently improvised ending to *The Second Woman* was mostly scripted: "Some of it was improvised: the grabbing of the feet, that was improvised. A little bit of the dialogue, picking up on the audience reaction to what was going on, you know, when Gena over-emphasised certain words. It changed slightly, but I wouldn't even call it improvisation."

13 Zohra Lampert, letter to the author.

14 Case.

10

Gloria

'You get older, you get tougher'

Phil Dawn in *Gloria*

If *The Killing Of A Chinese Bookie* was a commercial failure, *Opening Night* barely registered at all. Cassavetes released it on one screen in LA on Christmas Day 1977 in the hope of picking up Academy Award consideration. The reviews, while more respectful than those for *Bookie*, were scarcely encouraging, and no nominations were forthcoming. "Shrill, puzzling, depressing and overlong," *Variety* declared. American distributors didn't want to know, and Faces Distribution reluctantly withdrew the film after eight weeks. Cassavetes remarked wryly that he should have charged $8,000 a ticket – that way he might have recouped his costs.

He would never show it, but he must have been bitterly disappointed at these films' reception. "He knew the work was good," Seymour Cassel opines. "It made him tougher." Distributors were close-minded and the critics were no use; the cultural values he cherished were slipping out of fashion. Earlier in 1977 the failure of Martin Scorsese's *New York, New York* and the massive success of *Close Encounters Of The Third Kind* and *Star Wars* seemed to mark a turning point for Hollywood movie-making. The major studios had either been swallowed up by larger conglomerates, or they had become diversified corporate giants themselves (and in the late Seventies, there was still scarcely an independent sector worthy of the name).

Francis Coppola still entertained ambitions to subvert the system, but the press was already sniping about the hubris of *Apocalypse Now*, and the balance of power was shifting decisively towards his more conservative peers, George Lucas and Steven Spielberg. As for Scorsese, he was falling into a drug tailspin which threatened his career and would almost cost him his life. In his book *Easy Riders, Raging Bulls* Peter Biskind records Cassavetes going up to Scorsese at a Hollywood party and berating him for his drug abuse: "What's the matter with you? Why are you doing this, ruining yourself? You're fucking up your talent. Shape up."[1]

A cocaine blizzard hit Hollywood in the late Seventies which left few untouched. Seymour Cassel was another who went snow-blind, eventually landing up in jail. (Cassel remembers going down to Bogota to make a cocaine movie with Sam Peckinpah – a project which predictably enough never got past the research stage.) "John might do some marijuana," Cassel says. "But he was morally responsible to his parents and his wife and family, he would never do anything to really embarrass them. That was the way he felt."

Gena Rowlands claims that John never got depressed – but he did get angry. That anger was sometimes counter-productive. Al Ruban insists that any offers to distribute *Opening Night* and *The Killing Of A Chinese Bookie* (in either version) in the US were derisory ('The studios never understood John's pictures, they could never project what they would make') but he also allows that personality came into it: "Nobody was going to tell John how to distribute one of his films. Nobody. On *Husbands* he drove Columbia crazy. Fighting over the cities it would open in. Fighting over the advertising budgets. On *Minnie And Moskowitz* we ended up spending our own money to advertise it the way John wanted." Over the years there were offers to distribute *Opening Night* in France, but Cassavetes resisted them. It was as if he wanted to put the film behind him.

He picked up his acting career, taking the money to play arch villain Childress in Brian de Palma's telekinetic thriller *The Fury*, and co-starring with Sophia Loren in the conspiracy intrigue, *Brass Target* (both released in 1978). They were meaty leading roles in poor films, and he gave them his best. "It's a great challenge to put yourself up in bad material. You have to try and make it good for yourself," he told another generation of acting students at the American Academy. "The bad things are as good as the good things . . . [in fact] they're better!"[2]

The English director John Hough worked with him twice, on *Brass Target* and three years later on *Incubus*. He remembers him with great affection and respect: "I think he was a genius, a total maverick. I wanted someone who could bring depth to the part, something different, and with John you never knew what you were going to get. Also I had always been interested in his method of working. I wanted to find out his key to directing actors."

Hough attended some script readings at Cassavetes' home in this period: "Ben Gazzara would be there, Gena Rowlands, Peter Falk, and they'd read through without too much emotion. They'd read through and then talk about the scenes, not really acting them out or blocking them. He was all about getting an experience from the actors, not directing them to play it this way or that way. What he would do is get them to do it over and over again and let them find themselves, experiment themselves. It was really enlightening for me. There was no correct way to play a scene with John."

That looseness made for some difficulties on *Brass Target*. "Rehearsing with him beforehand he would improvise and try things and do it completely different from the way he would do it on the day." In contrast, Sophia Loren memorised her lines word for word, and never deviated from the script. "John had a genuine problem with that. He understood the context of a scene. He would say different lines, whatever felt natural to him, and he would get the salient points across but in a different envelope, as it were. So in rehearsing them both she was always waiting for her cue, and it would never come. It was a major clash, and she was the bigger star, so I told John he had to stick to the script. And take after take after take he tried. He began to really sweat. It was pouring down his face. It was clearly genuine, from the agony on his face, he had a mental block about repeating it word for word. He kept apologising to Sophia and to the crew. I've never seen a guy perspire so much."

Hough found that Cassavetes couldn't change, but nor could Loren. "In the end, we reached a compromise: John would ad-lib, but he would remember the cue line so she could come back with her line."

Was he temperamental? "He had a very, very strong character, and he could be argumentative[3], but not really. He was only difficult through his intelligence. He had so much to offer, and that frightened a lot of people who would prefer to work with puppets. He was not difficult as a person. Worked overtime, Saturdays, Sundays. There were never any star-type tantrums. You work on other movies and if the star's car didn't show up [there would be hell to pay]. If that was John he would get the bus or a taxi, and he wouldn't even mention it. He had no star hang-ups whatsoever. The crew adored him. He was a special talent."[4]

'You can't beat the system' – Gloria Swenson

Gloria began as a screenplay called *One Summer Night*.[5] It was written at the behest of Gena – who wanted to do something with kids – and MGM, who called fortuitously just a day after Gena's request looking for a vehicle for child-star Ricky Schroder, a hit in Franco Zeffirelli's *The Champ*.

"I wrote this story to sell, strictly to sell," Cassavetes told *American Film*.[6] He sent it over to Richard Shepherd at Metro, and he liked it too, but MGM lost Ricky Schroder to Disney before a deal was done, and Cassavetes passed the script over to his agent, Guy McElwaine. Columbia were interested, and made overtures to Barbra Streisand, who turned it down. John pressed them to cast Gena, and asked his friend Peter Bogdanovich if he'd be interested in directing. According to Bogdanovich, John did 'everything he could' to avoid making it himself. His mentor Sam Shaw agreed. *One Summer Night* was a feminist twist on the gangster thriller, but it didn't have the complexity or the potential for exploration of John's own films. In essence it was formula stuff.

McElwaine phoned his client a few weeks later. "I got good news and I got bad news," the agent told him. "Columbia loves the picture and they want Gena to be in it."

"What's the bad news?" Cassavetes asked.

"They want you to direct it."

This was a turnabout: a Hollywood studio insisting John Cassavetes direct a picture for them. And on the back of two commercial disasters! Ironically that may have been Cassavetes' best selling point: a perception that he needed to play ball if he was to stay in the game. Anyone who cared to look at *Opening Night* could see that Cassavetes was capable of working very effectively in a more conventional idiom if he chose to. And then they had the script, which satisfied studio executives for the very reasons it dissatisfied its author.

According to Gena Rowlands, John's chief reservation about his screenplay stemmed from the opening sequence. Unfortunately it was fundamental to the plot, the engine which propelled the whole movie:

It begins with the massacre of a family. Jack (Buck Henry) is an accountant to the mob. The first snatched exchanges between him and his wife, Jeri (Julie Carmen), reveal that they're on the verge of flight from their Bronx apartment. He's been caught recording details of mafia transactions in a black book. They believe he's finked to the FBI and been skimming off the top. He's a marked man, his wife is marked, his kids are marked, and now there's a gangster in the lobby. And here's Jeri's friend Gloria from down the hall, looking to borrow some coffee. "I think I came at a bad time," she observes. "You came at a very bad time," pipes up Jeri's shrill six-year-old son Phil (John Adames).

Jeri begs Gloria to take in her kids, but daughter Joan refuses and locks herself in a back room. Phil is packed off with the incriminating black book. "Be a man," his father tells him. "Always be tough. Don't trust anybody."

In Gloria's apartment the massacre reverberates as dull thunder (an eloquent solution to Cassavetes' qualms about showing such atrocity). Now she's stuck with this kid – and she hates kids. She has her own life to lead. A cat. Friends. What's this boy to her? A neighbour's kid, that's all. She packs a bag and they slip through the police lines, but a newspaper photographer gets a snap of them and it's not long before the media have put two and two together.

They hole up for the night in a friend's vacant flat, but the mobsters are hot on their heels. Gloria confesses that she knows the guys that are after them – they're friends of hers. What's more she has a record, she's not about

170

to hand him over to the cops. She tries to push him away, but the harder she pushes the harder he clings to her – which is when the gangsters catch up with them, squealing to a halt right there on a midtown street. She tries to reason with them, and then she shoots them: one, two, three, four. Dead. She hails a cab and they're off again. "That must have been some accident," wonders the cabbie, driving past four mobsters dead in an upturned car. "We're not interested in accidents," she warns him, the quintessential New York broad. "Ya deaf?"

Buses. Cabs. Hotel rooms. Gloria takes Phil to a cemetery so he can say his goodbyes. He doesn't know what he's doing there. She wants to get them both out of town, maybe to Pittsburgh, but she sees mob guys everywhere. At Penn Station she is forced to disarm half a dozen hoods; it's then that she finds out just who is behind them. Turns out it's an old boyfriend, Tony Tanzini (played by the veteran Italian screenwriter Basilio Franchina). She has a quarrel with the boy, and he runs back to the old neighbourhood to hang out with a friend. She finds him seconds after a couple of wise guys. She follows, shoots one of them dead and they get away once more.

It's unsustainable, this life on the lam. She puts in a call to Tony T and arranges to meet him face-to-face. "If I'm not back in three hours, I'll meet you at the station in Pittsburgh," she tells Phil, stuffing hundred dollar bills down his socks. "Maybe we better make it three and a half," he says.

She sees Tanzini in his uptown pad, surrounded by mafiosi. The show-down has a rueful tenderness. She's brought the book with her, but she knows they have to kill her – she only wants mercy for the boy and a quick exit for herself. He is non-commital, and Gloria forces the pace: "I'm going to get out of here now, if you wanna stop me you can." She gets as far as the elevator, shooting a guard on the way, but as she makes her descent the gangsters are raining bullets down the elevator shaft.

An epilogue finds Phil alone in Pittburgh, making his way to a cemetery where he bids farewell to Gloria and imagines her in heaven with his mother. (A taxicab pulls up and out steps an old woman in a veil. "Aren't you going to kiss your grandmother?" she asks. The voice is unmistakeable. Phil throws himself up into her arms and as they embrace her wig falls to the ground revealing Gloria in all her glory.)

Despite his reservations about the script, Sam Shaw agreed to produce the film. Al Ruban came on board but left after just three days in pre-production: "John told me himself he had no interest in the gangsters. No interest in the violence. I didn't agree with anything he was doing. I thought I was entitled to my opinion, and when everything gets shot down, there's not the same incentive to carry on. I said 'John, I never saw any gangsters order orange juice as they eat spaghetti, you're making cartoon characters of these guys.' And getting Buck Henry to play the father! And I didn't like the kid. John wanted to make a deal for me, and I said I wanted to make my own deal. So I was being a negative influence, and I said 'I'm going home, I can't be of any help,' and he knew it, because right away he said 'Okay'."

"In the early days he had so much charm, he was the greatest rug merchant in the world, capable of selling anything to anyone if he wanted to," Ruban reflects. "As he aged, he turned the charm on more sparingly – he just wanted what he wanted."

The casting issues which Ruban mentions do call into question Cassavetes' commitment to the film. As an accountant to the mob (much the same role that Cassavetes had played in *Mikey And Nicky*) Jack Dawn has to be white; it's a stretch to give him a Puerto Rican wife and kids, and maybe too much of a stretch to put lines like "You're the man. You're the head of the family now" in the mouth of Buck Henry, a rather apologetic, self-effacing actor (*Taking Off*) better known for his comic screenplays (*The Graduate, What's Up, Doc?* and latterly *To Die For*) and for co-directing *Heaven Can Wait* with Warren Beatty. He was cast after he'd mentioned to his agent, one Guy McElwaine, that he'd be interested in appearing in a Cassavetes movie to learn how he worked with actors.

As for John (Juan) Adames, the curly-headed Puerto Rican dynamo who plays Phil, he was cast after an open call auditon. Cassavetes met and talked to hundreds of children (he'd never read actors, only talk to them), and settled on the six-year-old Adames after two or three days.

"Are you sure you really want to do it?" he asked him. "Think about it: it'll be summer, you won't be able to go and play with your friends. Making a movie can be boring. If you're just doing it because someone else thinks you should, but you don't think it's such a great idea, then it's not worth it."

Adames thought for a moment or two. "How many words will I learn on this movie?" he asked.

"Maybe two or three hundred," John told him.

"Three hundred! I go back to school and I know three hundred words more than everybody in my class!" beamed Adames.[7]

Making a movie for Columbia meant working with an entirely new crew. A camera operator, Fred Schuler, stepped up to serve as director of photography: his impressive CV included *Annie Hall* and *Manhattan, Taxi Driver* and *The Last Waltz, Fingers, Network* and *The Deer Hunter*. Comparing Cassavetes and Martin Scorsese's working methods, Schuler says: "Cassavetes had a similar sense that conflict and tension were part of creating; he liked to have almost a sense of panic as part of the atmosphere. Of course, Cassavetes as an actor was more intuitive. Marty plans more."[8]

Columbia also assigned an experienced editor, John McSweeney, who had worked with Nicholas Ray on *Party Girl* and been Oscar-nominated for Lewis Milestone's *Mutiny On The Bounty*.

Cassavetes gave him a hearty welcome: "Hey, McSweeney! I hear you're an Irish son of a bitch! Well, I'm a Greek son of a bitch, so we'll get along fine!"

When the director heard his new editor was from the Bronx, he invited him along on a location recce with Sam Shaw, but their relationship ended abruptly one hot night in June at the very first dailies, when McSweeney – unimpressed by indistinguishable rushes from a night shoot – leaned forward and asked Schuler if there was a reason he hadn't used a key light for the scene. Before the DP could answer Cassavetes flew up the aisle screaming: "Who the fuck are you? The studio spy? That's it! I get it! That's why Columbia was so high about making me take you. You're the studio spy! Listen, you son of a bitch, no one talks to my cameraman but ME! Do you hear me? So you just shut the fuck up! And I'll tell you how I'm going to make sure you shut the fuck up. You're FIRED! Go back to fucking Hollywood! I'll get my own fucking editor. I sure as hell won't have a studio spy on my picture, that's for goddamn sure."[9]

Without further ado McSweeney was released from the picture (Cassavetes was subsequently reprimanded by the Editors' Guild for his behaviour while McSweeney was reassigned on double-pay). It's open to question whether the director's rage was genuine or not – conceivably it was on Fred Schuler's behalf – but the paranoia rings true: buckling down to the exigencies of the studio system for the first time in years, Cassavetes may have felt the need to prove to this alien crew who was boss right from the off.

(Peter Bogdanovich remembers meeting Cassavetes midshoot, railing against his crew: "I hate them!" he said. 'Fucking union crews!'[10])

Despite such an inauspicious beginning, Cassavetes was soon drawn into the imaginative fray of the movie. There's a fine description of the director at work by James Stevenson, covering the shoot for *American Film*: "John Cassavetes is framed in the glass doorway of the hotel lobby, a Marlboro burning down to his fingertips, smoke pouring from his nostrils. He is blocking a scene as [. . .] the actors and crew watch. Cassavetes is grey haired; he has a slight paunch; he wears khakis and worn shoes. He looks less like a big-time director than a guy who has come to paint an apartment. But his attitude is intense; his stance combative. He leans forward, gesturing, talking; his hands splay out; his arms suddenly crisscross; his knees bend; he slumps; stands up; he gestures imploringly; points; jabs with a finger; wheels around; a hand flies out, flinging a thought in a certain direction – abruptly, he stops cold; peers like an owl into Schuler's face to see if the idea is grasped – nod, nod; OK; OK – then pivots; spins away, hands waving. He says to Schuler, 'Freddie – it's all yours, baby!' and he sits down on a railing; smoke churns tumbling from his nose; the cigarette burns closer to his fingers."

Relaxed and congenial after wrapping for the day, Cassavetes told Stevenson that he hadn't imagined a major studio would ask him to direct again: "I'd had my run-ins and I thought it had all been over for a number of years. I'd like to think that everybody's against me, but it's not true. Not everyone. Anyway I don't have a quarrel with studio executives. They're just there to make money. Thank God, they are there. We need them. If you're a writer you want to be published."

'That's it: You start running. Run!'

Gloria

Gloria is an escape movie in more ways than one. It's a film about fugitives, a couple on the run, loosely in the tradition of *They Live By Night* and *You Only Live Once*, but it's also an escapist movie, a dream-movie where one woman and a small boy can withstand the might of the *cosa nostra*, the cops are superfluous, you can flee through the streets of New York in the summertime and still look like a million dollars, and where death has no sting. It's a much purer Hollywood romance than *Minnie And Moskowitz*.

Critics have harped on implausibilities in the narrative framework (Would Gloria have stuck around so long? Would the wise guys have been so dumb not to disarm her when she visits Mr Tanzini?), but they're missing the point: this is a movie, not real life.

Gloria's name, Gloria Swenson, harks back to Gloria Swanson – real name Swenson – and her most famous role, as some larger than life gargoyle of herself in Billy Wilder's movie-movie *Sunset Boulevard*. Our first glimpse of Gloria is a classic profile glamour shot, dragging on her cigarette, through the fisheye of Jack Dawn's apartment peephole. Golden hair swept back, sporting high heels, a silk pajama suit and a svelte raincoat (wardrobe by Emmanuel Ungari), she's half Veronica Lake, half Humphrey Bogart ("Do I look like Humphrey Bogart to you?" Gena demanded of Ben Gazzara in *Opening Night*).

Gloria – more than any other character Cassavetes' wrote – is an archetype: a New York moll, a broad, a tough cookie. Gena Rowlands has said that, unusually for her, in preparing for the role she planned how Gloria should walk – and indeed she strides through the movie, always a step ahead of her pursuers. Her words slide out from the side of her mouth like smoke, but when she's riled her top lip curls an Edward G Robinson snarl: "You punks," she berates the hoods who have got their hands on Phil. "Go ahead, punks." Daring them to take an inch.

Like Norma Desmond she's larger than life, but it's the world's loss, not her's. She's also a satiric riff on the hardnosed New Yorker: instinctively antagonistic to bank tellers, hotel clerks, taxi drivers and sales assistants. Even Phil has to laugh at the way she sends a waitress packing: "Take a walk!" Gloria's way of dealing with the mob – shoot and run – is only an extension of how she treats everyone else.

Like a character from a classic Thirties gangster movie she's graduated from the school of hard knocks. You can see the adrenaline pump through her when she's in a tight spot. "I tried very hard not to make her appear to be a hooker," Rowlands said – and you can imagine (with a shudder) how easily Gloria might have become one of Streisand's string of tarts. "My own background for her was something like Virginia Hill[11], someone who carries illegal money . . . who won't talk when she's caught . . . a working part of the mob."[12]

She's a gangster's moll, and more than a moll. Gloria's self-assertion, her determination and her violence see to that. But she's not a *femme fatale* either. Her clothing runs from elegant tailored silk skirts and pink jackets to luxurious kimonos – and she looks great – but Gloria's vamping days are behind her. "I'm overweight and I'm outtashape," she tells Phil (translation: she's no longer young). It's part of the pathos of the character that when we meet her she's settled for a place on her own, a cat and a nice fat safety deposit box. Her boyfriends may have traded her for younger models, but she's got all she wants out of life, or so she imagines. As Cassavetes liked to say about his audience, you have to give them what they need, not what they think they like. In Gloria's case, what she needs is to lose or jeopardise everything she likes: her nice, comfortable life, her friends, her money and her cat.

The violent rupture of the first few minutes jerks Gloria out of her complacency and forces her to take a moral stand against the very structures which have supported her – the *cosa nostra* as a figure for patriarchy. The stand-out scene is the first showdown between Gloria and the gangsters out on the street. It comes immediately after her confession to Phil that she is connected to the mob ("The guys that killed your family – they're friends of mine") and urged him to run off on his own (which he refuses to do).

It's at this moment of irresolution that a car pulls up with a squeal of brakes, and the mob guys tell Gloria they need the kid, and they're not about to leave without him.

So she shoots them.

It's a stunning scene, a shock from any film-maker but especially from this one. A shock because Gloria is a woman; because she knows these guys; because she draws – she shoots – even before they've articulated their threat. "We'll take care of the boy," they had said. She shoots cleanly, rapidly, and so effectively the wise guys' car is upended. It's all over in a flash – as incisive a declaration of independence as you could ask for.

Thus Gloria embodies the contradictions inherent in any idealised conception of female identity. She can be seen both as a post-menopausal feminist icon, symbolically castrating the men who come after her, and as a reluctant madonna, a son foisted upon her. On the one hand you've got Tony Tanzini's conservative analysis, "Every woman is a mother," and on the other Gloria's wise-gal protestation: "I'm one of those 'sensations.' I was always a broad – can't stand the sight of milk."

Rather than seek to resolve the contradiction, Cassavetes embraces the paradox. Both sentiments may be equally true and false. When she turns the tables on the gangsters, Gloria revels in her strength – "Sissies! You let a woman beat you!" – but at the same time, her every action is to protect this boy, to the incredulity of the men who know her. "His mother was a friend of mine," she explains to one of them. "So?"

Cassavetes: "There's a lot of pain connected with raising children in today's world. It's considered a big holdback. So a lot of women have developed a distrust of children. I wanted to tell women that they don't have to like children – but there's still something deep in them that relates to children, and this separates them from men in a good way."[13]

Crucially, Gloria doesn't compromise her independence to be with Phil, she flaunts it. She may sacrifice her cat and her home comforts, but in return she's thrown back on her wits, her resilience, sensitivity and strength of character. You have to lose yourself in order to find yourself: Gloria emerges as one of Cassavetes' virtuoso improvisers. "Gloria was an amazing power trip," Gena Rowlands noted. "Taking on the whole mafia in four inch heels wth a child slung over your shoulder – it was a lot of fun."[14]

The relationship between Gloria and Phil is closer to the screwball antipathy of Minnie and Seymour than maternal *tendresse*. Empowered by his father's final words, Phil is all bluff and bluster, a shrill pintsized travesty of machismo in his disco blue bell-bottoms, white socks and voluble shirt: "I am the man! I am the man! You are not the man – I am the man!."

"He don't know the score," Phil explains to Gloria after a snooty desk clerk has refused them a room. "He see's a dame like you and a guy like me, he don't know." He even makes an unlikely seduction attempt ("Blinking lights – do they remind you of anything?") which is given short shrift by Gloria, who clarifies matters by curtly shoving him off the bed.

The macho six year old and the hardboiled dame: what's interesting is how the age disparity balances out. For all that he's evidently out of his depth, Phil never gives an inch. He's every bit as stubborn as Gloria. He goes, if not head-to-head with her, then at least toe-to-toe. They bicker constantly, but they're good for each other. They draw each other out. And again, you can sense Cassavetes' spirit in the character. "The kid is neither sympathetic nor nonsympathetic. He's just a kid," Cassavetes said. "He reminds me of me, constantly in shock, reacting to this unfathomable environment . . . always full of excitement and wonderment."[15]

Against Phil's wonder and emotion, Gloria tries to maintain control. In their bed scene, Phil probes her emotional life: does she like him? Does she love him? Does she get scared? Does she have dreams? Has she ever been in love? She deflects these questions with wisecracks, or she demurs, or she refuses to answer altogether. "I didn't know when you get older you get tougher," he muses. What Cassavetes cherishes in Phil is his youth; the softness behind his bluster. His ability to get under Gloria's skin makes the film a very pure love story (later she confesses to Tanzini that Phil is "one of the greatest guys I ever slept with").

"These characters go on the basis that there are certain emotions and rules that go beyond words and assurances," Cassavetes said. "They just know. I like that part of the movie. When they're thrown together, they don't pretend to care about each other. So at the end, when they do care about each other, it's because of their personal trust and regard. And that's a beautiful thing to see."[16]

One thinks of Cassavetes as a New York film-maker, and in sensibility perhaps he was, but *Gloria* was his first thoroughly New York movie since *Shadows*. You can see how he savours his return to the city: in contrast to the stasis and interiority of so much of his work, this is a film in perpetual motion, expansive, and largely played out in public spaces. Significantly, these are also the spaces of the director's childhood: the Yankee stadium, the Grand Concourse, Riverside Drive, downtown Bronx and (eventually) uptown Manhattan. When he lived here he was Phil's age, watching Cagney movies, playing cops and robbers with his brother Nick, criss-crossing the neighbourhood as the rent came due.

The first images we see under the opening credits are paintings of New York by Romare Bearden in childlike primary colours, a slapdash graffiti sprawl. This isn't the claustrophobic expressionist city of *film noir* nightmare; it's hot, bright, and busily impersonal. Fred Schuler uses long lenses for the many street scenes, natural light with an occasional blue filter. For the first time, in the escape from the station restaurant, Cassavetes has recourse to a Steadicam. It's a vividly urban movie, made under the press of commuters in transit. Taking a cue from Phil, Bill Conti's Latin-flavoured score accentuates the city's multi-ethnic verve with tremulous flamenco guitar and plangent saxophone solos. Inside the stairwells paint is peeling, plaster is coming away, but the seediness is a given, a fact of life; this is a very matter-of-fact movie. Even the gangsters are just doing a job. This is the way the world works. Theirs is the system Gloria decides you can't beat: a callous system which operates on paranoia and violence. "I'm a policy, I'm not Gloria anymore, I know that," she tells Tanzini.

Nonetheless, the film is an escapade. A fugue. A flight from reality. John Cassavetes turned 50 in 1979. His father died in April, at 89 years old. *Gloria* begins with the death of a father and ends with a dappled, sun-kissed scene in a cemetery. It's the most blatantly romantic ending of Cassavetes' career. By rights we know that Gloria died in Tanzini's slow elevator. Yet here she is, under a veil and a grey wig, shaking them off to reveal her golden hair (shrugging off old age) as Phil jumps into her arms. With its slow motion and swelling chords, it's a woozily rhapsodic and dreamy ending.[17]

To dream is to deny death: it's a theme reprised throughout the film. Trying to comfort Phil after the assassination of his family, Gloria instructs him, "It's like a dream. You go to sleep sometimes and you get killed in a nightmare. You always wake up again and you're somebody else, right?" And again, the first time they visit a cemetery together: "Dead people: it's like, you ever see a ship sail? Well, it's like those dreams we were talking about." Of course in the bed scene with Phil she denies that she dreams, but he doesn't believe it: "Whaddayado? Just close your eyes and black?"

Through her courage and compassion, perhaps Gloria has earned the right to dream a happy ever after. "You can't beat the system," she told Phil. "Gloria, we gotta try," he replied. "You can't just keep shooting everybody that goes knockin' on your door.'

Cassavetes' most conventional movie both in form and content, *Gloria* was only a minor success in commercial terms, but proved very popular with critics both in America and internationally (the film won the Golden Lion at the Venice Film Festival in 1981). While he couldn't entirely disown the film, Cassavetes tended to be dismissive of the acclaim. "Without Gena, we wouldn't have had a movie," he'd say. Still, he liked the characters well enough to write a sequel to it, picking up on Gloria and Phil, still running from the mob 12 years on (the script has never been produced).[18]

"It's an adult fairy tale," Cassavetes summed up. "I never pretended it was anything else but fiction. I always thought I understood [it]. And I was bored because I knew the answer to that picture the minute we began. And that's why I could never be wildly enthusiastic about the picture – because it's so simple."

178

✶ ✶ ✶

Perhaps there was a residual suspicion that he had, after all, made a movie for 'the System.' It's revealing that a script he wrote at that time centred on just this question of artistic integrity and commercial compromise.

Mood Indigo had a strange inception. Richard Dreyfuss came home one evening to find a message from Cassavetes on his answer phone. When he called back, John seemed a little embarrassed, but he invited Dreyfuss over to 'do a thing' at the weekend. Dreyfuss takes up the story: "So I go Sunday night, Gena answers the door, takes me into the living room and John comes out and we do this thing called *Moon Indigo*. It's a great piece about a New York cabbie who writes a play called *Mood Indigo* and is taken to the Beverly Hills Hotel to do the screenplay, where the secretary warns him what Hollywood people are like. It was funny and biting and unique and unbalanced and wonderful. We read it, and John's laughing his ass off, and we finish, and I look up and everyone's trying to stifle their laughter. So I get embarrassed, and take John aside and say 'What's going on?'"

"A week earlier, George Segal had quit *10*. Blake Edwards asked John, 'Do you know Richard Dreyfuss's phone number?' John says, 'No problem, I'll have him call you.' He calls, I'm out, he leaves a message. But by the next day Dudley Moore's doing the picture. I call John back and he goes, 'Aaaaah.' He's a little embarrassed. He doesn't know how to say that Dudley Moore has the part I know nothing about."

"So he says, 'Ya wanna do a thing?' There is no thing. He had to conceive of and write the entire thing. When Gena met me at the door, John was dictating the last three pages."[19]

✶ ✶ ✶

Mood Indigo may have been knocked up in a rush, but it wasn't just some throwaway piece. Going into 1980, Cassavetes developed ambitious plans for staging his scripts as plays as a means of fine-tuning the work – a project which may have come out of conversations with Francis Coppola, who began working along similar lines. With film budgets escalating beyond his means, Cassavetes also needed to attract outside finance. Thus the initiative wasn't so far removed from the original impulse behind Cassavetes' acting workshop at Variety Arts in the late Fifties, when he hoped to use the space to showcase his friends to producers and casting directors.

His first production, staged in November 1980, was called *East/West Game*, the title pointing to conflicting New York and Los Angeles sensibilities. It was evidently based on *Mood Indigo*. John's son Nick played an off-Broadway playwright resisting pressure from Hollywood to sell-out – to the dismay of everyone, even his own secretary.

Ironically, when John Cassavetes took on a new secretary to write his scripts in 1981, she would have precisely the same reaction: "I thought he was very jaded. Mistrusting. We would have fights about it," Helen Caldwell reports. "A studio head would call up and be very sweet with him, and John would tell him to go to hell because they wouldn't give him full control. He was adamant about it: he wanted to do it his way or not at all. I'd go, 'John, how do you know he's going to rip you off, if you're accusing him of something before he's actually done it?' I thought he was shooting himself in the foot." She laughs. "Now that I've been in the business for 20 years, John was absolutely spot-on right. I was the neophyte who didn't have a clue. He knew absolutely what he was talking about."[20]

1 Peter Biskind, *Easy Riders, Raging Bulls*, Bloomsbury, 1998. Biskind also throws in the snide observation that Cassavetes was 'a notorious drunk.'
2 AADA seminar 1970/74.
3 See Appendix: Acting Out on *Incubus*.
4 John Hough, Author's interview (2000).
5 According to Peter Bogdanovich, it was originally *One Winter Night.*.
6 James Stevenson, 'JC Film's Bad Boy,' *American Film*, v5 n4 Jan/Feb 1980
7 The story comes from Gena Rowlands' public Q&A session with Judith Crist in *Take 22*.
8 Schuler quoted in Mary Pat Kellyand's Martin Scorsese biography.
9 This account from Meg McSweeney, John McSweeney's daughter (letter to author).
10 Peter Bogdanovich, Author's interview (2000).
11 Bugsy Siegel's moll, played by Annette Bening in *Bugsy*.
12 Crist, *Take 22*.
13 Quoted in Ray Carney's *Cassavetes on Cassavetes*, Faber, 2001.
14 Gena Rowlands talking to students at the American Academy of Dramatic Arts, 1996.
15 Carney, *Cassavetes on Cassavetes*.
16 Carney, *Cassavetes on Cassavetes*.
17 In his first cut of the film Cassavetes signalled its artificiality even more obviously by printing this sequence in black and white.
18 In 1999 Sidney Lumet remade *Gloria* under the same name, with Sharon Stone in the lead, and it's not too fanciful to see the original's influence in such different movies as *Leon*, *Central Station*, the Taiwanese film *Soul* and even *Thelma And Louise*.
19 Richard Dreyfuss, *Film Comment* v25, n3 May/June 1989.
20 Helen Caldwell, Author's interview.

Life Studies

Peter Bogdanovich

John Cassavetes was unquestionably the most dazzling maverick American picture-maker since Orson Welles – and the most subtly influential. Cassavetes films have an amazing sense of reality, and a poetic view of humanity worthy of an American Renoir.

When he wrote, John dictated his stuff, which is quite rare, although Preston Sturges did it too. They couldn't be more different, and John loved Sturges work. Cassavetes' dialog captured the cadence of regular people talking, and he inspired amazing naturalism from his actors. I once asked Peter Falk if the films were really improvised. He said, "Who the hell can improvise dialog that good?" (John had told me once that Peter's idea of improvisation was, 'Hello' and 'Yes.')

I think the improvisation myth (only his first film *Shadows* was actually improvised) clung to him because of the deceptively haphazard construction of the pictures themselves. They seem not to be constructed at all, but rather to have grown out of a daily free-floating inspiration. John had an extraordinary ability to catch an uninhibited freshness; a genius for making what might be called 'Life Studies.'

I've come to understand the pictures better over the years. When I first saw *Husbands* I thought it was rough in construction, but years later I saw it again and realised it was very well structured indeed, very tight. I told this to John and he said, "Yeah, I thought it was pretty well constructed" – meaning I'd finally caught up with him. All his films were far ahead of their time. Gena Rowlands told me she used to say to John, "Couldn't you be with the times just once? Always ahead, John, always ahead."

The first time I met John Cassavetes was in Don Siegel's office, very briefly in 1968; but we didn't get to know each other until three or four years after I made *What's Up, Doc?*. He came to an early screening we had in New York, and I remember him laughing so hard. It was a small screening, and we needed his laughter. At one point early on, between laughs, he actually said out loud, "I can't believe he's doing this!" I loved that: it remained my favorite review of the movie.

We saw each other quite a bit over the years. I remember I brought him and Orson Welles together in my living room. I think John was a little intimidated, but he covered that by talking a lot. It was funny: mainly, John

181

talked and Orson listened. He told him the whole story of *The Killing Of A Chinese Bookie* and Orson said, "That's very interesting John."

For *Opening Night*, John wanted me to come down and be an extra in the last scene, which I did. Later, I asked if I could help him shoot anything, because he was running late and spending his own money. He said, "Yeah," so I directed three little shots for him of Gena and Joan Blondell pulling up in a car at an underground garage. He was thrilled, he called and said, "I can't believe you did it so fast!" I said, "John, it wasn't anything much" . . . He said, jokingly, "It would have taken me the whole day."

It was on *Opening Night* that I met Ben Gazzara and, as a result, cast him as the lead in *Saint Jack*. During lunch that day, Benny was acting the host – even though John was paying for everything. He said, "C'mon, anything you want to eat – John's paying!" And he reminded me of the character of Jack Flowers in *Saint Jack*.

At one point in 1977 or '78, John and I were going to do a screenplay of his called *Dancing*. It was a damn good story about two sailors and two girls with Peter Falk and John, Raquel Welch and Cybill Shepherd. For some reason I didn't want to direct it, but I should have. (I was wrong in a lot of my decisions.) I brought Ivan Passer on to direct it, but Ivan and John didn't really get along.

John tried to get me to direct *Gloria* too, which he had written as a script to sell. He thought it was my kind of picture: a melodrama. Years later, Gena told me that John had a real dread of doing the opening, the murder of the whole family – which is ironic, because I couldn't face that myself.

Love Streams means a lot to me. I had seen the play as John directed it on a tiny stage in Hollywood, and it was one of the best things I had ever seen in the theatre. Jon Voight was brilliant in it, but he ended up not doing the movie because he said he wanted to direct it, so John told him some version of "Forget about it"!

The film is very sad, and John and Gena achieve a familial intimacy which is very rare in movies. The brother walks away from emotional problems until it's too late – while the sister walks directly into them – even though it may already be too late. She feels too much. He feels too little. It's the most uncompromisingly tragic view of the fall of the modern family, with the intensity of an O'Neill drama, or a Dostoevsky novel, and it's certainly the darkest vision in Cassavetes' work of a society which has lost its bearings, is out of control.

But it has a more personal meaning for me too. In 1980, my fiancee, Dorothy Stratten was murdered, and John was one of the few people who called me to commiserate – but that's not all he did. I had told him that I wasn't going to make movies anymore, and I didn't go out much for a couple of years. Then one day I got a call from John. He said he needed me to come over and help him shoot a scene in *Love Streams*. He said, "I'm shooting at my house and I want you to come over and direct this scene tomorrow."

I said, "I can't do that, John. You've acted and directed yourself before – you don't need me."

He said, "You mean to tell me you won't do me this one favor?"

"Oh, c'mon, John, what do you need me for?"

"It's a difficult scene with Diahnne Abbott, for Christ's sake. You mean to tell me you won't come over and direct one fucking scene? It's very important, I really need your help."

So I went over the next day, and sure enough everyone was there, and being very nice to me. And they joked around: "Peter's here, now well get this picture done quickly."

I remember giving John no direction, and suggesting to Diahnne that she give him a flower, which John liked, so we did that. It was just a couple of shots at the door. He thanked me. This was the first time I had been shooting anything since Dorothy died, and I realised later on that that's why he had done it, to get me out of the house.

It was so generous. And he thanked me in the credits at the end, but it was me who should have thanked him. In fact, I called to thank him, and he said, "Whaddaya talking about, I tried to get your name on the same card as co-director but the Directors Guild wouldn't let me!" That was John.

Peter Bogdanovich
(Writer/director: *Targets, The Last Picture Show,*
What's Up Doc?, Saint Jack, They All Laughed,
The Mask, Texasville)

11

Love Streams

'I got the horses in; I couldn't get the goat. The goat is impossible!'
Robert Harmon (John Cassavetes)

John Cassavetes knew he was dying when he started shooting *Love Streams* in 1983. In fact he had been told that he might have only six months to live if he kept on drinking. He stopped – for a while – and would live another six years, putting his name to one more film, the aptly-titled *Big Trouble*, and writing numerous screenplays.

Yet *Love Streams* is the valedictory work. It's a film which seems to draw on all Cassavetes' strengths, not least his refusal to go gently into that good night. You could call the film a summation, but only with the immediate rider that, true to form, it resists the temptation to conclude anything. It's a beautiful, obstreperous, funny, crackpot, bewildering, bleak and unutterably moving film.

Robert Harmon (John Cassavetes) is a successful novelist living in debauched detachment from the world. Although he has at least one ex-wife and a son, he hasn't seen the boy since the birth; he has forbidden his ex from calling him and doesn't respond to her letters. In return, she receives cheques regularly.

This is how Robert prefers to arrange his affairs. He lives in a big house in Beverly Hills (in fact it's the Cassavetes' home, pressed into service one last time), and he's filled it with a harem of young women. They're sexual play-things, research material for his books, and a substitute family – and because he buys their time, they're virtually interchangeable, he can dismiss them at will, no strings attached.

Sarah Lawson (Gena Rowlands) is also separated from her husband and child, but in her case with almost unbearable sorrow. Sarah has a history of mental instability. At the child custody proceedings, she explains that in fact it's her philandering husband, Jack (Seymour Cassel), who is the crazy one. "I'm a very happy person", she informs the judge. She likes to take her daughter Debbie (Risa Blewitt) and visit relatives when they're sick or bereaved, just to give them comfort and cheer. When Debbie

184

announces she wants to live with her father, Sarah calmly walks out of the proceeding and lies down on the floor in the middle of the busy municipal justice building.

Her psychiatrist (David Rowlands) tells her that her love is too strong for her family. "If you don't get some balance in your life, something creative, some sex – I don't care with whom – then you're going to have to go back to the bughouse where you don't belong."

Robert's life revolves precisely around sex and creativity. To research his latest book (on 'night life') he ventures into a gay club, but remains aloof from the clientele, focussing instead on the beautiful chanteuse, Susan (Diahnne Abbott). She sees right through his drunken seduction attempt, but he forces his way into her car and insists on driving her home. When they get there he falls down the front steps, cutting his head and spraining his hand. He wakes up the next morning, thanks Susan and her mother Margarita (Margaret Abbott) for cleaning him up, and effects a gracious retreat. But when Susan comes calling a day or two later, he doesn't invite her in. He's interested in sex, not a relationship.

Another woman comes to call: this time it's his ex-wife, Agnes (Michele Conway) with their son Albie (Jakob Shaw). She wants to leave the boy with his father overnight. Robert agrees unenthusiastically. When he sees how his father lives Albie runs away, and Robert has to pay off his harem and send them on their way to placate his son.

Robert tells him that he doesn't like men ('they're kinda boring') or women either, only kids and older people: "They have the secret. They don't need anything." He pours Albie a beer for breakfast, and the kid is on the verge of smoking a cigarette when two taxis pull up in the drive. The first one carries Sarah. The second is her luggage from an aborted trip to Europe.

Robert greets her with a warmth we haven't seen from him before, ushers her inside and gives her his car keys, then announces he's taking Albie on a trip to Las Vegas, there and then.

The trip is a disaster. Albie is confined to a hotel room while his dad searches out a couple of hookers for the night. When he returns a distraught Albie to his mother, Robert gets a well-earned sock in the jaw. He goes home, dances with Sarah, but when she mentions Susan phoned he takes off for her house, no matter that she's out and he'll have to make do with Magarita.

Sarah, meanwhile, bucks Robert's paternalistic admonition to go to bed and after phoning Jack (who rebuffs her again) heads for the nearest bowling alley. "This is my first time and I'm looking for the sex," she tells the attendant. Getting her fingers stuck in a bowling ball, she successfully attracts the attention of Ken (John Roselius).

185

Robert is dancing with Margarita when Susan comes home with her date. She is surprised to find her mother dressed up in a blanket, with flowers in her hair and champagne on the side – and again, Robert is sent home alone.

When Sarah comes back, kissing Ken in the driveway, she and Robert have a heart-to-heart, and for the first time it becomes clear that they are brother and sister. "What is creativity?" she asks him. "Would love be considered an art?" Sarah is determined to follow her shrink's advice and find 'balance'; what's more, she is determined to do the same for her brother by finding him something to love. "I'm going to buy you a baby," she tells him.

The next day she returns from an animal sanctuary with two miniature horses, a goat, some parrots, some chickens, a duck and Jim the dog. Robert is at a loss for words and even Sarah admits it looks a bit crazy. She collapses, and fantasises about trying to make Jack and Debbie laugh with all manner of pranks and gags. Despite her efforts, they remain stone-faced.

A ferocious storm breaks out, and Robert valiantly tries to bring the animals in to shelter in the house. In the midst of it, he checks in on Sarah. She has another, even more elaborate fantasy: imagining Jack, Debbie and herself on a stage singing opera, with ballerinas and an orchestra. As the three of them embrace she wakes up to find Jim the dog licking her face. She tells Robert that she has reached an understanding with her family and she must leave now. He sits alone in his room while she packs her things to leave with Ken and the storm rages outside. "Who the fuck are you?" Robert asks a strange bearded man sitting silently alongside the dog. He only smiles.

As Sarah drives off, Robert plays a song on the jukebox, turns and waves goodbye.[1]

Cassavetes met the Canadian writer Ted Allan in Ireland in 1960 when, having extricated himself from the hit TV series *Johnny Staccato*, John warned his agent he had better get him out of town, and fast. Two first-class plane tickets were duly produced, and a role in a film called *Middle Of Nowhere*.[2] Gena wanted none of it, so John flew out to New York alone, met his old pals Al Ruban, Seymour Cassel and Mo McEndree (felicitously on St Patrick's Day), and offered the spare ticket first to Mo, who turned it down, then to Seymour, who knew a good thing when he saw one. The next morning they nursed their hangovers on the plane, and somewhere over the Atlantic realised neither of them had a copy of the script. Cassel remembers "When we arrived we went straight into a meeting with Don Chaffey, the director, and Ted Allan, the writer, and told them what should be changed. And they ended up giving me a small part too."

Ted Allan remembered it the same way: "John would suggest this change and that change and the director would say 'Very good idea.' 'If you do that,' I responded, 'it changes the entire story.' John kept coming back with 'Not if you ...' Only later did he tell me he'd never read the script. 'Is it any good?' he asked. That's how we met."[3]

Fourteen years Cassavetes' senior, Allan enjoyed a relatively successful career as a playwright and novelist, living in Ireland and London for a number of years. He collaborated on the famous Theatre Workshop production of *Oh! What A Lovely War*, but most often wrote about his family, and especially his childhood relationship with his father (his most famous work was *Lies My Father Told Me*, filmed in 1975 by Jan Kadar).

His play *My Sister's Keeper* was produced in London in 1970, an autobiographical two-hander about siblings: Allan and his sister. When Cassavetes first read it, he thought it was 'wonderful', but told Allan that he didn't like the man: "He just sits there and listens to this woman raving".[4]

In 1980 they had a reading of the play at John's house, with Ben Gazzara and Gena Rowlands. "John fell in love with the play," Allan said.[5]

Casavetes suggested opening it out, bringing in the other characters mentioned in the siblings' conversations. It inspired Allan to go back and write a new version entirely, *Love Streams*, and a companion piece, *The Third Day Comes*, which shows how these same characters were indelibly shaped by their father's childhood abuse – and which Cassavetes also hoped to film, perhaps starring his son Nick and daughter Xan.

In the spring of 1981 Cassavetes renovated the Hollywood Avenue Playhouse and renamed it the Center Theater. In May he unveiled *Three Plays Of Love And Hate*, an eight-week revolving repertory programme comprising *Love Streams*, starring Jon Voight, Gena Rowlands, Diahnne and Margaret Abbott; *The Third Day Comes*, with Nick Cassavetes, Michael McGuire and Gena Rowlands; and a satirical Pirandellian whodunnit called *Knives*, starring Peter Falk, and this time written by Cassavetes himself.[6]

"Ted writes mainly about frustrations and revolutions within people, so we get along very well," Cassavetes said.[7]

He and Allan shared a taste for the domestic tragedies of Chekov, Ibsen and Tennessee Williams, though in other respects they saw things quite differently (the Canadian complained that Cassavetes didn't appreciate Shakespeare but loved everything by Samuel Beckett). Between 1980 and 1983 they reworked the material many times. Allan reckoned there were eight distinct versions of the screenplay. Helen Caldwell began taking shorthand for Cassavetes after Ted Allan came upon a handwritten notice she'd left in a copy shop somewhere. ("I undercut the going-rate by a quarter – Ted was always on the look-out for a bargain," she notes.) She

187

worked with the two men both individually or together at John's house; eventually, Allan went off and started on another project leaving John to finish the script to his own satisfaction. "I think John struggled with rewriting someone else's material," Caldwell says. "But they were very close. I never saw them argue."

Love Streams the play differed from the film in a number of respects. According to Cassavetes the tone was more overtly comic, not least because of Jon Voight: "He has a wonderful sense of the ridiculous," Cassavetes noted. "His basic instincts are absolutely humorous."[8]

Not surprisingly, given his poor health, Cassavetes' own performance was more sombre – and he voiced some dissatisfaction with it. "It was perfectly all right for Voight to be a ladies' man, but I felt too old and inadequate," he wrote.[9]

As he also recognised, the blonde Anglo-Saxon Voight simply looked the more likely candidate to play Gena Rowlands' brother. "I was so angry with Jon when he decided not to do the movie," he told Richard Combs. "We were two weeks away from shooting, and there was no way I was going to let the whole production fall apart, so I did it, but reluctantly."[10]

The play had been set in London; that was switched to LA without much bother (although the film's poverty row backlot renditions of Sarah's trips to France and Britain arguably enhance the movie's eccentric charm). Allan and John did disagree over when to reveal the relationship between the siblings – right upfront in the play, a mystery until well into the movie – and Cassavetes cut out both the incest which occured between them and all the psychological backstory Allan had crafted: "The parents didn't speak. The father was absent most of the time. You had the curious impression that Robert and Sarah were inflicting the same thing on their own children that they had suffered," Allan said. "John didn't want to make things easy for the viewer; his attitude was they'll come back a second time to make sense of it."

The psychology – if not the incest – was autobiographical: Allan had been badly beaten by his father, and never forgave him, and his sister had mental problems (apparently when she saw the movie, she told her brother that "Gena played me very well").[11]

Cassavetes had neither a sister, nor an unhappy childhood; what's more, he had a long and loving marriage, and a fantastic relationship with his kids – so what compelled him to film Ted Allan's story? "I was attracted to Ted through his enormous obsession with family and loss and pain," he explained. "I'm not a young man and I treasure the memory of my mother and father.[12] They offer me a great deal of incentive for living, because of the way they conducted the family and orchestrated our lives."

He went on: "I haven't yet been able to deal with my own family in my work. It's just too close, and I'm confused enough by life in general. The connections are so complicated. Long after I was dead I'd have to have some script, or scroll, to be working on up there, or down there, or wherever."[13]

Love Streams offered a form of imaginative out-of-body autobiography; an exploration of the artist's alter-ego. "As soon as John invested himself in the writing, he brought his life, his dreams, his problems to what had been my autobiography," Allan said. "By the time we started shooting, *Love Streams* had gone through one fundamental change: the development of the character of the brother. I went along with John in that direction because his agenda interested me."

Intriguingly, Robert Harmon is a writer who feeds off other people's lives. His *modus operandi*, as we discover in a long vérité-style scene in the first minutes of the film, is to demand his girls offer up their secrets. "Do you sell?" he asks 18-year-old Joanie. "Drugs? Love? Poetry? Anything?" She doesn't understand what he wants from her. "What's a good time?" he goes on. "The best time you ever had?"

It could be a seduction, except that the tone is impatient, badgering, and it's carried out in front of the rest of Robert's giggling and bewildered girls, and with a tape recorder under Joanie's nose. (It could be a film-maker auditioning actresses, come to that.) In very different circumstances, drinking Champagne with Susan after her show at the club, Harmon uses some of the same lines, and this time it is a chat-up. Sensing that he has no interest in her beyond his own agenda, she walks away. But she also takes pity on him. When he stumbles, drunk, and cuts himself, she takes him in and looks after him just as she would her own son.

Harmon is a refined take on Cosmo Vitelli: like Cosmo, he affects a certain style, sports a tuxedo, and presents an attractive, easy-going charm. "Everybody likes Robert," Sarah assures Albie. And like Cosmo, Robert is an artist dealing in girls (they both come with their own personal harem); all his books are about women and sex, we're told. "Maybe you could write about love?" his sister asks him, plaintively.

From the outside, Robert would appear to be well in control of his life; he has all the trappings of success: fame and money and respect, a hedonistic lifestyle and a big house in California. This is what Archie, Gus and Harry in *Husbands* dream of. But Harmon's success is a trap. He controls life only by keeping it at arm's length and sealing himself off from emotional commitments of any kind.

Harmon has a credo: "Life is a series of suicides, divorces, promises broken, children wrecked." With him, it becomes something of a self-fulfilling prophecy. "Robert, you disgust me!" The very first line in the film – before we've even settled into our seats – suggests one way of viewing the character.[14]

Throughout the shoot, Cassavetes repeatedly solicited his collaborators' reaction to his character – not just the other actors' thoughts, but anyone and everyone's. If most people disliked him, he certainly didn't go out of his way to soften the character; what mattered was that they shared an investment in him, good or bad. He'd say, "I understand everybody in the movie except my own character – and I don't want to understand him!" To Michael Ventura, who made *I'm Almost Not Crazy*, a wonderful documentary record of the production, he said: "I like him (Robert). He doesn't know what he's doing – like me. He has feelings, but he doesn't know how to express them."

In *Love Streams* the time-scale isn't entirely clear, but some weeks pass during the first act, and just two or three days thereafter, during which Robert is afforded a number of opportunities to venture out of his sanctuary and risk meaningful engagement.

His first chance comes with the unexpected arrival of Susan on his doorstep. and he won't even let her come inside the doorway.[15]

Almost immediately (45 minutes into the film) he receives another unannounced visitor, this time it's his ex-wife Agnes with their eight-year-old son Albie, who has never met his father before.

Robert doesn't allow Agnes in either, but grudgingly admits entrance to the boy. That he subsequently pays off his girls and sends them on their way to make Albie feel less uncomfortable at least hints that Harmon is not beyond hope – but at the same time the ease with which he accomplishes this exodus is further evidence of his powers of dissociation.

His own speedy flight to Las Vegas with Albie as soon as Sarah shows up might be more of the same, the warmth of their reunion notwithstanding. But it's in Vegas that we witness Robert's most grievous and shocking abstention both from parental responsibility and emotional intimacy. Depositing his son in a hotel room, he goes out on the town all night, returning in the morning, drunk, in the company of two hookers. (Where women are concerned Robert seems to find safety in numbers.) His behaviour is pointedly contrasted with the sympathetic chambermaid who takes it upon herself to order Albie food from room service.

Confronted by the boy's tears , Robert reacts as if Albie has welched on a deal, but as he falls to his knees and embraces his son his anger becomes indistinguishable from shame and contrition; he's obviously still capable of love, even if he does his best to deny it.

Typical of Cassavetes that a moment of compassion such as this should be succeeded by a swift smack in the jaw. Similarly, in one of the film's most beautiful passages, Robert returns home, puts on a record (Mildred Bailey's torch-song 'Where Are You?') and is joined in a slow dance of tacit sorrow and sympathy by his sister – their bodies illumined in the darkened house only by the warm neon glow of Robert's jukebox. But the spell is irrevocably broken as soon as Sarah mentions that Susan called. And lest we imagine that Robert's eagerness to return that call even before the song has played out bespeaks a change of heart towards Susan, his readiness to make do with her mother when she answers suggests that any woman would do. Anything to distract him from the trouble of talking honestly to his sister. "Can we walk and talk?" he asks, brusquely, putting Sarah to bed at 9pm as if she were a child – as if she were Albie, in fact, and he was re-enacting last night's error having learned precisely nothing from his experience.

This is what (almost) all Cassavetes' men do: they pour themselves into their work (Nick in *A Woman Under The Influence*; Cosmo in *The Killing Of A Chinese Bookie*, even Hugh in *Shadows*), or their 'art' (Ghost Wakefield in *Too Late Blues*; Maurice and Manny in *Opening Night*), or drunken escape (the husbands in *Husbands*), and they run away from pain, embarrassment, intimacy, love. The notable exceptions are Seymour Cassel's characters in *Minnie And Moskowitz* and *Faces* – and even he runs away in the end.

"I'm very interested in the theme of family life and street life being part and parcel of one another," Cassavetes told Brian Case. "By 'street life' I mean single life, night life, people in solitude looking, with no responsibility or pain. Loneliness; not wanting to be alone; not wanting to be older; not wanting to give up your lack of responsibility. That really haunts me, because young people I think are in many ways brighter [than the old]. They postpone these things in order to find some beauty, which becomes more difficult as you get older. You can't go back to it. I feel it's an endless subject. Combine it with 'family life', you have night themes and day themes. It's very beautiful to me."

"Robert Harmon has no concept of kids," he said. "He doesn't know to deal with somebody who loves him. He goes out with a bunch of dames, and gets drunk, and makes bargains with the boy as if he's buying off one of his girls. I don't think he's cruel, he's just ignorant."[16]

The women: Cassavetes' women proffer all those things – pain, embarrassment, intimacy, love – sometimes selfishly, sometimes selflessly, but invariably with a courage which challenges the men.[17]

To the degree that these definitions superficially subscribe to conventional notions of femininity, modern feminists may voice reservations about the films, but it should be clear from the very first films (Lelia in *Shadows*; Jess in *Too Late Blues*; Jean in *A Child Is Waiting*) how closely Cassavetes identified with his female characters; they are the adventurers. *Faces*, *Husbands*, *Minnie And Moskowitz*, *A Woman Under The Influence* and *The Killing Of A Chinese Bookie* constitute a critique of repressive, socially conditioned gender roles which can properly be called 'feminist'; while *Opening Night* and *Gloria* allow their emancipated – or at least independently-minded – female protagonists to take centre stage (never an easy place to be in Cassavetes' dramas).

As any American film-maker who lived through the Seventies would have to be, Casssavetes was conversant with feminist debate, and spoke out against the paucity of roles for women in the movies. He told Michael Ventura that Gena "speaks for what she feels women would like to have said. She's very concerned about it. She says 'I don't want to play a victim – I've done that'."

This oblique reference to *A Woman Under The Influence* is pertinent. Sarah Lawson in *Love Streams* is the flip side of Robert Harmon's callous cynicism, but she's also a spiritual sister to Rowlands' most famous role, Mabel Longhetti.

Like Mabel, Sarah is an avatar of love, and she has been institutionalised because of it. Like a modern day saint, she visits the sick and the needy; like Saint Francis of Assisi her love reaches out to all creatures great and small. Hers is the philosophy which gives the movie its name – "Love is a stream. It's continuous. It doesn't stop." – and Sarah's love, more than his own son's, comes closest to redeeming Robert Harmon.

Yet her scenes are in more of a comic register than Mabel's – a mark of how Cassavetes has changed. He's a little less in love with love, you might say. Rowlands makes Sarah just a beat off: hair not so much combed as raked, (she has a girlish braid around the back); facial tics a little broad; and verbally over-anxious. She's too much, this woman, with her second taxi full of luggage and her menagerie of love.

Kooky, granted, but you can feel Cassavetes enjoying this character's excess. She's much more self-possessed than Mabel – it's Sarah who divorces Jack, for example, unthinkable for Nick's wife. She may not enjoy Europe, but at least she gets herself there. She even accomplishes a pick-up at the bowling alley with clumsy aplomb. As she tells her ex-husband on the phone, "I'm almost not crazy now".

Twice in the film she lies out flat on the floor in response to rejection. The first time when the divorce court judge refuses to admit love as a relevant topic in a court of law; then when Robert resists the gifts she brings him. It's a gesture Myrtle Gordon makes on-stage during rehearsal of the smacking scene in *Opening Night*, and in effect it's much the same as Mabel's impromptu dance of the dying swan on the Longhetti's sofa. These are acts of passive resistance and imaginative non-compliance at least as much as they're mental 'episodes'.

Her shrink may be a figure of gentle mockery, with his creative prescription to "get some sex – I don't care with whom", but his diagnosis is more or less correct: Sarah does require balance, her love is too much for her family, she must not end up in the bug house where she does not belong. The psychiatrist may even be right when he tells her that "love stops": "That was the biggest discovery I ever made," Cassavetes told his cousin and art director Phedon Papamichael during one of their many on-set Socratic debates. "Love stops. Just like a clock. Or anything. Then you wind it and it goes again. Because if it stops forever, then you die."[18]

The film's centrepiece is the long-delayed heart-to-heart between Sarah and Robert. It occurs after the siblings' parallel 'dates': Robert's semi-parodic formal romantic evening with Margarita (music and champagne; he in his tux; she dolled up in bed sheets and flowers), an affectionate but rather pathetic charade; and Sarah's comically haphazard impromptu score in the bowling alley, an altogether more liberating experience.

The scene is set in Robert's kitchen, but it is shot predominantly from the hallway, affording a medium profile shot of Sarah as she makes coffee, then turns and sits down at the kitchen table. The ever-elusive Robert, meanwhile, is almost entirely off-camera, screened by the wall (there's one extremely short cutaway to a different angle, a long shot of the pair of them). At one point he leans forward and grasps his sister's hand, but even then we can only see his forearm. This conspicuous visual reticence mirrors the effect of the dialogue: Sarah is opening up to him, but Robert's not all there for her yet.

✻　✻　✻

Sarah: What is creativity, Robert? I don't mean, you know ... I know you're a writer and you're creative. People paint. I don't paint. Would you consider cooking an art?
　Robert: Cooking?
　Sarah: Yeah. I'm trying to find something, something that just I can do. I don't mean I'm the only person in the world that can do it, but something special, like cooking or –
　Robert: Writing? Write poetry.
　Sarah: Nah. Poetry. I love it but it's just so depressing. I get so low, and I don't think that's healthy. I don't even know what I'm talking about. Would love be considered an art?
　Robert: Well, some people think so.
　Sarah: [sitting] Well, you're a writer. You always write those books about sex. Maybe you could write one about love. I could help you with that.
　Robert: We'll see how that turns out.
　Sarah: I love you.
　Robert: I love you.
　Sarah: You know, I'm going to do this damn thing. I really am. I'm going

to find balance. and I think you should do it too. You know, I'm going to do something for you: I'm going to buy you a baby. Really! You need something you can love. It could be some little animal you could take care of.
  Robert: [checking her] Please don't.
  Sarah: Then you'd be balanced, I'd be balanced.
  Robert: Please!
  Sarah: [softly] Then I can go back to being obsessive about my family. [After a pause she resumes just as Robert begins to say something.] You know what dad always said?
  Robert: What did dad always say?
  Sarah: "For every problem there is an answer". [She gets up.] I'm not going to have coffee. I'm going to go right to bed and get up at dawn.

It's a tender, loving exchange between mature adults – and the first explicit indication that they are siblings (though Robert cautioned Albie not to jump to conclusions about his love for Sarah). If Robert can be said to represent intellectualism here, the brain to Sarah's heart (she's soliciting his opinion as a man of letters) his cultivated sophistication is infinitely less expressive than her finely-tuned emotional sensitivity. She's thinking about creativity in ways he hasn't imagined. Like Cassavetes, she seeks to break down the barrier between life and art – and Robert still has blinkers on: women can express their creativity in poetry, not cooking. It's not that Sarah knows the answer, but at least she acknowledges what Robert shies away from: that in their different ways, they're both suffering from the same problem, the difficulty of giving and accepting love.
  Just how hard love can be is illustrated immediately after this conversation, when – like a guilty conscience ringing in Sarah's head – her daughter calls and accuses her of betraying Jack. It becomes a three-way, then a four-way argument, bringing in Jack and Robert, and ending in raised voices and tears, with Robert (true to form) announcing "Love is dead. Love is a fantasy little girls have," and Sarah angrily assuring him that she and Jack have "shared moments of the heart" Robert knows nothing about.
  "For every problem there is an answer." It's a line redolent of American can-do optimism Cassavetes took from his own father, and that pivotal moment in 1947 when it became clear that John wasn't cut out to study business like his old man. For Cassavetes, then, the answer came in the form of acting.
  For Sarah, now, the advice is a spur to go ahead with her plan to buy her brother a pet: a cat or a dog, maybe a couple of parakeets, some chicks, a duck, two miniature horses and a goat. "The goat gives milk, so that's not a waste," she rationalises.

It's such a gloriously nutty and excessive gesture, this many-hooved, -clawed, -pawed gift, it tilts the movie not only into farce – miniature horses stomping past the self-same drinks cabinet where John Marley announced his decision to divorce Lynn Carlin in *Faces* – but into another realm entirely. "When [Robert and Sarah's] very different concepts of the absolute come and contradict each other, the life of the film acquires the truth of a dream," Cassavetes wrote. "It's almost as if Robert and Sarah dream each other, trapped in the same dream from which they can't awake, because in fact their dreams and their lives are one and the same."[19]

Repudiated again, this time by her brother (understandably unimpressed by his new house guests) Sarah collapses. During her blackout we witness two dreams. In the first (which Gena Rowlands improvised) Sarah seats Jack and Debbie beside the swimming pool and makes a bet that she can make them laugh within a minute. Jack bets a dollar, Sarah bets love. She has a table with a timer and half-a-dozen joke shop novelties: chattering teeth, a flower that squirts water and so on. She runs through all of them giggling merrily but her family watch her stony-faced. As the time runs out Sarah executes a spectacular backflip into the pool, fully clothed, which is when she wakes up.

Meanwhile Robert is struggling manfully against the elements. A tempest of Shakespearean proportions is buffetting the house[20], and Robert, dressed in a macintosh and a wide-brimmed straw hat, is doing his best to get the animals into the safety of the house. "I got the horses in. I couldn't get the goat. The goat is impossible!" he tells his sister. He tells her something else too: how if a beautiful woman doesn't volunteer her secret to him, he feels their relationship will always be incomplete. Traced in a graceful arcing close-up, Sarah says nothing, but lies back and closes her eyes.

The second dream is even more elaborate than the first: an opera played out in the spotlight of an otherwise darkened stage, sung by herself, Jack and Debbie with orchestral accompaniment. "In love I'm not sure of me," she sings. "In that I'm not sure of you / I'm not sure of love / I'm not sure of me / Of you." A tracking shot follows a gaggle of pre-teen ballerinas on tiptoe. They resemble bridesmaids at a wedding. "The only one / You promised me I would be the only one," sings Sarah, the refrain echoed by Debbie and Jack: "You promised me I would be the only one". This time the dream ends in an embrace, a family hug – and Sarah wakes – elated – to find Jim the dog licking her face.

Sarah draws strength from this dream. She's tells a sceptical Robert she has come to a new understanding with her family. What that might be is open to question, but the feeling is strong enough to convince her she must leave this house, whether to go back to Jack or to set up with Ken from the bowling alley isn't entirely clear (Ken comes to pick her up). What is clear is that she is ready to face the stormy outside world and put some of her baggage behind her.

That leaves Robert alone with Jim the dog, the other animals and an enigmatic bearded, bare-chested fellow who pops up in the corner of his study, smiling. "Who the fuck are you?" Robert demands, with a wheezy but long and heartfelt cackle.

So, not to put to fine a point on it: who the fuck is he? He's not there, then he's there, and then he's not there, which makes him a figment, perhaps a symbol of . . . what exactly? Thierry Jousse hazards Noah, not very confidently. Carney lets the question hang. In interviews at the time, Cassavetes suggested he might be the dog, which is less flippant than it might sound. The dog has been repeatedly anthropomorphised: he's bears a man's name, Jim; he was bought as a companion for Robert, a 'baby'; and he was explicitly likened to a man by the woman at the pet shelter, Mrs Kiner (played by the Cassavetes' personal secretary, Doe Avedon): "To look at him there's not much in his favour, but he is a great dog for a man. He is so much like a man – and you admire, and you praise, and the dog opens up and he's a warm, wonderful and fine human being."

What's more the actor who plays this enigmatic fellow is Neil Bell. Which may be significant, because Neil Bell also appeared in the stage version of *Love Streams*, where he played the dog.

Bo Harwood tells the story: "Neil Bell was a mime artist and an acrobat. They ran up a dog suit for him, and it was funny, he was really believable as a dog. The way he would rub up against people, or run after a ball, it was the most amazing thing you've ever seen. John said, 'Take off the dog suit!' And he was so good, the audience still bought him as the dog".

"Now jump to 1983, and the movie, which is quite different. And John talked Al into hiring Neil Bell as the dog. Al said, 'How is this guy going to be the dog?' John said, 'I dunno'. But he kept him on salary the whole production, and it was the last night of shooting (except for the operetta, which we did a week and a half later). We had the rain machine outside, the animals in the house, everybody was crazy, it was out of hand, but John always managed to keep it right on the line. All of a sudden, John starts laughing. He says 'I know how I'm going to use Neil'; and he comes up with the scene you see in the movie."[21]

So the bearded man is Jim the dog.

Which is to say? Bo Harwood: "What it means I don't know, but John loved the insanity of it all, and that's the beat before the movie ends. He just loved it. I don't know, honestly. Except maybe, Fuck em!"

As Tom Milne complained in his review for *Monthly Film Bulletin*, "How is one to guess?" And the answer to that must be, one isn't. Or rather: guess away, because there is no 'definitive' way of knowing, the mystery is unfathomable. A problem without an answer, at the last.

These visions and dream sequences (an earlier, much briefer black comic fantasy sequence has Sarah running down Jack and Debbie in a car) didn't occur in the play – "they're entirely John's idea", Ted Allan said.

It's an extraordinary way for Cassavetes to bow out. A child of neo-realism and cinema vérité, long championed as the antithesis of Hollywood fantasy, throwing a surreal spanner in the works.

In part, one suspects, it's a joke: the last laugh goes to Cassavetes – and how it echoes through the night! But it's a lonely joke too, as the last laugh tends to be. Robert Harmon has never been as alone as when his sister moves on, leaving him behind with this strange imposter for company. In long shot, through the window, we watch the last frames of John Cassavetes on camera: he walks up to the jukebox, calls up a song, sways a little, turns toward us and waves a tentative farewell.

"I didn't know what to do," the song goes. "So I'm leaving it up to you."

It feels like an honest ambiguity: Sarah going forth, not cured but believing in herself; Robert stuck in a rut, not cured but having to doubt himself. Which may be a beginning.

"We're making a picture about inner-life – and nobody really believes it can be put on the screen. Including me," Cassavetes had admitted to Michael Ventura. "I don't believe it either, but screw 'em!"[22]

Years later, after Cassavetes' death, Ventura would recall another conversation between the film-maker and Phedon Papamichael on the set of *Love Streams*. "I know what love is," John had said. "Love is the ability of not knowing."[23]

Perhaps that is what Robert Harmon – with his hunger for secrets – still has to learn.

1 *Love Streams* was backed by Cannon, the upstart film production mini-major run by the Israeilis Menahem Golan and Yoram Globus, who were attempting to garner prestige at this time, backing projects by Jean-Luc Godard, Paul Schrader and Andrei Konchalovsky among others. According to Al Ruban they never interfered with the creative decisions. "We told Menahem and Yoram we would take the film to the Berlin Film Festival, and if we won the Golden Bear we'd give it to them. Which we did."
2 Released in the US two years later as *The Webster Boy*.
3 *Film Comment*, vol 25, n3 May/June 1989.
4 JC interviewed by Richard Combs, *MFB*, v51 n603, April 1984
5 Unless otherwise stated, all quotes from Ted Allan derive from an interview by Gerald Peary, 'Complot de famille', published in *Positif*, n 287, January 1985.
6 See Appendix: Stage Works for more on this extraordinary project
7 Brian Case interview transcript, 1984.
8 Combs, *MFB*.
9 John Cassavetes, How Love and Life Mingle on Film, *New York Times*, August 19, 1984.

10 Combs, MFB.
11 The French critic Bernard Eisenschitz saw both the film and the original play. In his estimation "the film is much more 'theatrical', has more subplots and anecdotal riches than the play, which was more thin and stylised nor were there any fantasy sequences in the play." Quoted in Thierry Jousse.
12 Cassavetes' mother Katherine died in April 1983.
13 Combs, *MFB*.
14 Cassavetes moved this scene to the front during post-production, hence the continuity error with his head wound and bandaged hand evident days before his fall at Susan's house. Helen Caldwell was in charge of continuity: "At the screening I was horrified: he starts the film with this horrible gash in his head, then it totally disappears, then halfway through he falls down the stairs. John didn't care: that was where the scene belonged. I thought no-one would hire me ever again".
15 This scene was shot by Peter Bogdanovich at Cassavetes' insistence – see pp. 181–183.
16 Combs, MFB.
17 Again, *Minnie And Moskowitz* could be said to reverse these gender roles, and so too "She's So Lovely" if we admit it into the canon.
18 Michael Ventura, 'State of Grace', *Sight and Sound*, v1 n7, November 1991.
19 *John Cassavetes*, Autoportraits, Cahiers du Cinema.
20 In 1981 Cassavetes and Rowlands starred in Paul Mazursky's updated adaptation of *The Tempest*. See Appendix: Acting Out.
21 Bo Harwood, Author's interview (2000).
22 *I'm Almost Not Crazy* documentary, directed by Michael Ventura for Cannon.
23 Ventura, *Sight and Sound.*

Cassavetes, Posthumously

Olivier Assayas

Just to put things in perspective, this piece was written in 1995 in a very specific context. Most of Cassavetes' back catalogue had been reissued in France with heavy promotion – actually Gérard Depardieu had bought the rights. Almost every single title was running simultaneously in theaters all over town. All of a sudden, a few years after his death, Cassavetes was everywhere, overnight he became the epitome of hip. He became the ultimate model for every single young French aspiring filmmaker. Something, of course he had never been in his lifetime. Before that, only a handful of fans were aware of his work and of their importance. One of them was Denis Lenoir, the cameraman for my films – he shot two of my later shorts and all of my features until *Cold Water* – actually he co-authored the first book in French on his films. Obviously Cassavetes had been a huge influence on our work since the beginning.

I suppose the piece I wrote reflects on this situation.

When is the right time to write about a film maker? Or else what is there to say about Cassavetes these days, who is everywhere, being taken up by the intrinsic simple-mindedness of cinephilia, its entourage of fetishism and automatic approbation. The handful of genuine sentiments that this auteur's work evokes – would it not have been better to set them down in black and white when he was alive and in semi-obscurity; after all, it's not as if the opportunities were lacking.

One of Cassavetes' strengths, which he had in common with many great artists, was his stubborn phobia about being acknowledged by any form of right-on thinking, no matter where it came from.

Recognized amongst New York avant-garde circles from the time of *Shadows*, Cassavetes promptly betrayed them by going and setting up on the west coast and signing a Hollywood contract (which he was to regret): a major fault then, for which he was never forgiven. And if even now his films are not rated as highly in the United States as they are in Paris, this has to be seen as the origin of it. A price exacted through rejection.

Moreover, whilst he had always been assured of some support in France, albeit from a minority, but a solid and faithful one, it did not prevent him from blocking the showing of *Opening Night* in Paris during his lifetime.

At the very beginning of the Eighties, a few of us writing for the *Cahiers du Cinéma* were in Los Angeles working on a special edition, 'Made in USA'. Cassavetes had to have a decisive place in it (this wasn't so obvious at the time). There was nothing we could do, there was no way of contacting him directly. Was it out of faithfulness to *Positif*, which had acknowledged his work earlier and more clearly than *Cahiers*? Was it because by then he was already ill? Whatever the reason, the best we could do was to send him some questions: straight away a secretary gave us his answers over the telephone; they rarely took up more than a sentence and were largely off the cuff, flippant.

Cassavetes couldn't care less and he was probably right not to. In any case the reasons were legitimate: they were his own.

How would he have responded to his films being posthumously, perfunctorily worshipped as they are in France today and have been for some time? How would Cioran have responded to the media parading his picture and his ideas everywhere in those few years before his death, when, immured in illness and loss of lucidity, he was unable to do anything to prevent it?

None of this matters but it's important if we want to understand something today. Of course it doesn't go away completely, there are distant echoes which resonate still, but the films are the main thing. It shouldn't be too difficult to say a few words about them. What would the problem be?

The problem is that the first thing you feel like doing is tearing at the straight jacket, removing the veil of ready-made ideas obscuring not the films so much but the very nature of Cassavetes' talent. To try and read the works pure again, back in true perspective – works that majority taste in its massive appropriation have diminished, simplified, reduced to a few archetypal mechanisms: after all, these are just the misunderstandings that come with success, nothing more.

Yet none of that ever bothered me in the past. Now I would like to disregard the backdrop. Sixties America, that aesthetic which has plagued us, the cut of the clothes, the cars, the hair, the dark glasses, the white man's jazz. Everything that makes me grind my teeth but which doesn't really matter.

I want to ignore all the tricks, the phoney alcohol-induced cordiality, the warm glow of male friendship that I don't see and I don't feel, that mad hysterical laughter: all that overblown triviality where the cinema (of the auteur) audience, increasingly petit-bourgeois, increasingly polite, increasingly sheltered, increasingly tasteful, finds the image of a life it can never pin down, as if that were its punishment for being so mild and timid itself. Chaotic, shameless, the very world it would like to gain access to. The kind of life it is so ashamed of not living, which it desperately tries to make up for by acknowledging that it was only lived by others, by another – anyone as long as it can't be verified and is stripped as far as possible of the means of speech, incapable of answering back. A kind of reality for which Cassavetes' characters – who were truthful in their time, although that didn't seem so important then – would provide an absolute, all the more acceptable for belonging to a world gone, desirable precisely because it is gone by.

And then I want to get over my discomfort in the face of the self-satisfaction of certain types of actors, those endless phoney improvisation exercises reeking of the theatre workshop. Those effects, calculated in the extreme, studied, repeated. That perpetual externalisation of feelings, feelings which dissolve as soon as they reach the surface.

Yet I also recognise how loath I am to put these qualms – which I experience as a gut reaction – down on paper and how much a voice from within, firm, distinct, reminds me of the spontaneous admiration that I have always had for his work. After all, those things are merely superficial. Cassavetes, unburdened of all the mannerisms, lives on, substantially intact and holding his ground, one of the pioneers of contemporary cinema.

Firstly because of his talent as a dramatist. Few film makers in the history of American cinema have written as well as he did, if any. At least none who could lay claim to a body of work so rich, so complex, so nurtured and pure. His texts are impressive, the roles that he wrote for Gena Rowlands, Peter Falk, Ben Gazzara and himself stand out for their own sake, apart from the images, by the force of the words, by the power of his portraiture. And to say that is in no way to minimise his virtuosity from the point of view of form, his perpetual inventiveness, the modernity, the raw energy that enlivens each of his films. Today, when we so much fail to grasp that being an auteur means first having a style, it's good to remember that Cassavetes was also a wonderful inventor of forms. The inventor of his own medium: the path he chose was that of style.

Like Warhol – that great underrated film maker – for the USA, Cassavetes was a sort of New Wave all on his own, an isolated impressionist. In the face of the all-powerful film industry, he stood in opposition, representing the cinema of the auteur – the very nature of which, it cannot be stressed enough, is to function independently, as a craft industry – constructing his own economy, his own system, his own team and inventing for his own purposes his own troupe, as, in similar ways, did Bergman in Sweden, Fassbinder in Germany and of course the New Wave in France.

Certainly Warhol was more fundamentally radical than Cassavetes, taking cinema right back to zero, making films as if he had to reinvent cinema from scratch, little by little. Cassavetes too felt the need to reinvent, but he approached it from a different angle; his approach did not entail challenging the medium – it wasn't Godardian, say, for the sake of ease – but was more an attempt to re-establish the rudiments of the process of the production of films. Cassavetes has a lot in common with traditional cinema: his interest in characters, in feelings, situations and narrative.

But confronting an industry which functions on the basis of 'economic logic', conventional dramatic values and the star system with its pitiful hierarchy, he presupposes that the relationship to money is fundamentally tainted, that the chief organic relationship from which cinema develops must not be one which unites a scenario with a source of finance, but one which directly unites the writing, the film maker's primary impulse, with the people who are going to interpret it, and beyond, with everyone in the whole team. Essentially, Cassavetes reinstates the earlier model of a playwright and his troupe. Suggesting that this example, which is dotted throughout the history of cinema, ever unique, ever reinventing itself, is the only viable alternative to the sclerosis of the industry, the only real chance for the freedom of cinema, freedom of writing, freedom of thought, for the micro utopia of a community set free from the stupid laws of commerce and the fundamental alienation that results when creativity is tamed by the industry of the spectacle alias 'the grand family of cinema'. But which now, here as elsewhere, triumphs beyond measure. And the same people who approve of it also approve of Cassavetes.

Naturally, therefore, one is led to question the unanimity that surrounds his work, posthumously of course. Do we really know how to read the work? Do we fully understand that the radical alternative he is proposing is primarily subversive? Do we recognise the significance of his example, one which is about constantly questioning the rules and laws of film making? Oh on paper, of course everyone agrees. But I am not just talking about the way the system works, I am also talking about the way the audience works. Cassavetes based his films on disruption, and the spectator is not exempt from that process. But nowadays the audience just sits there and watches his films as passively as they do everything else.

It's the eternal paradox: the innovator finally achieves recognition when he is no longer too hot to handle, when the advances he made, blunted by time, vulgarised through more amiable works, are taken up in different ways, the shock having lost all its edge. His transgressions congeal into rules and are turned into a new norm, in a way that avoids facing up to the dangerous questions he provoked, questions by which he was consumed.

A way of recreating order around him.

Even if he always stood for the opposite: the irresponsible anarchy of true art.

Olivier Assayas
(Writer/director: *Cold Water, Irma Vep, Late August,*
Early September, Les Destinées Sentimentales)

12

Post Scripts

'Love is a stream. It's continuous. It doesn't stop.'
Sarah (Gena Rowlands)

John Cassavetes died February 3, 1989 from cirrhosis of the liver. He was 59 years old.

According to Carney, John was given six months to live in 1983, just as he began to shoot *Love Streams*. He kept it a secret from all but a few, although in retrospect it was obvious that he was ill. His skin was sallow, his body shape was changing. For a few months he did stop drinking. Then he started again.

During publicity for the film, he sometimes sounded uncharacteristically melancholy – although again, the impression is purely retrospective. Robert and Sarah "really are in solitude," he said. "It's something you feel if you live in California. You feel that life is really a dream. Nothing can bother you. Even the hospitals are so enormous and splendiferous that you feel you're in a social club. You're dying and people are coming to visit you in the emergency ward, bringing drinks and beautiful women. Los Angeles is quite an empty place. You see the same people and you grow old before you know it because the sun is the same every day."[1]

John Hough remembers meeting him in the mid-Eighties at a bar: "He was eating an orange, but what was strange was that he ate the peel as well. He told me he'd heard that orange peel was beneficial against cancer. He was planning another film, but said that he might have to come and make it in Europe, he was finding it hard to get financing in Hollywood."

Was Cassavetes an alcoholic? Al Ruban says that "John drank often and a lot, but in the 28 years we worked together I never saw him drunk. He was the sort of guy, in order to have a conversation he would have a cigarette in one hand and a drink in the other."

Elaine Kagan (née Goren), his secretary from 1970 to 1975 and a close friend thereafter, agrees: "Was he an alcoholic? Not to me he wasn't. I never saw him drunk. Never."

But ten years later, working in a similar capacity, Helen Caldwell had a different experience. "When I first met him he was a very heavy drinker," she says. "He would sometimes put away a whole fifth of liquor while we worked, and smoke five packs a day. By the end of the night he'd be telling me stories, drunk, for a couple of hours, and I wouldn't take him home until three or four in the morning."

That was while they were in pre-production on *Love Streams* at the Cannon offices. Caldwell confirms that by 1985 Cassavetes was drinking heavily again, even though he must have known what the consequences would be.

"Lots of people tried to get him to stop. I remember one woman used to hide his bottles. But you know how most people who drink too much have serious underlying issues? I never got that feeling with John. He was a happy drunk. Never got mean or emotional or upset. I think he drank because it was fun, because he laughed a lot and told a lot of stories and it was a lot of fun."

Mike Lally – who had worked on *A Woman Under The Influence* – died in February of 1985. Peter Falk and John went to pay their respects at a funeral home in Hollywood one afternoon. "It was the afternoon, nobody else was there," Falk says. "Mike was laying there in the box, and John turned to me and he said, 'Listen, if Mike reaches up and grabs me – you pull the other way!' As we got up to the box, I tried to look solemn and respectful, you know. But John, he goes right up to him, he says 'Hey, Mike! You look good! I like that tie you got on there,' and he's touching him, loving him. He had that force."[2]

It was during the fiasco of *Big Trouble* that it became obvious to many of his friends that John was seriously and perhaps terminally ill.

Peter Bogdanovich remembers John telling him about his encounter with the studio doctor, checking his health for insurance purposes: "He saw John had this condition and he said, 'Oh no, John! No! Not you, John! No! Oh no!' John's telling me this laughing, because it was so ridiculous how obvious the guy was. I was screaming with laughter, and then I said 'This isn't funny,' and he said, 'No it isn't, is it? But it is funny.' He didn't act like he was dying. Didn't play that martyred thing. Right through to the end it was just like everything was okay. The last four years I saw him a lot, maybe once a week. I'd come over to cheer him up and instead he'd cheer me up."[3]

Big Trouble was a vehicle for Peter Falk and Alan Arkin, who had teamed with great success as *The In-Laws* a few years previously (Arkin as a bourgeois dentist, Falk as a wild CIA operative). Scripted and directed by Andrew Bergman (who had written the earlier film), *Big Trouble* followed the same template: this time Arkin would play an insurance salesman with financial problems who gets looped into a crazy scheme to rip off his company by taking out a double indemnity policy against accidental death on Beverly D'Angelo's terminally ill husband – and then killing him so that it looked like a freak accident. (Any similarities to a certain *film noir* classic may not have been entirely coincidental.) Falk played the husband, who turns out to be not so dead after all when he turns up disguised as D'Angelo's lawyer. As the scheme unravels, it transpires he's a chameleon actor and quick-witted con-man with just enough charm to keep the addled Arkin on team.

A film scholar with a particular interest in screwball comedy, Andrew Bergman had co-written *Blazing Saddles*, and turned director in 1981 with *So Fine*, starring Ryan O'Neal as a college professor who accidentally sparks off a craze for skintight jeans with see-through behinds. *Big Trouble* was to have been his second credit, but halfway through shooting he left the production, and adopted the pseudonym 'Warren Bogle' for the screenplay credit.[4]

Cassavetes was invited to take over, presumably at the behest of Peter Falk (who prefers not to talk about the film). One can only guess that he agreed to do so as a favour to his friend, and perhaps because he suspected it might be his last opportunity to make a movie. It's worth noting, too, that his old agent Guy McElwaine was head of Columbia at the time.

Some critics (notably in *Cahiers du Cinéma*) have made the case that *Big Trouble* merits some consideration in the Cassavetes' oeuvre – and it's his name on the print, after all. They point to Falk's performance as Steve Rickey – the actor as auteur, directing scenes through pretence and role play – and Alan Arkin's regression into mute shock and anarchic hysteria, sounding distant echoes of Mabel, Myrtle and Sarah Lawson. But these arguments smack of rationalisation. It's virtually impossible to say to what extent Cassavetes 'directed' *Big Trouble* because Columbia refused to let him go back and reshoot material he deemed essential to fix it, and instead put together a cut comprising some of Cassavetes' scenes with some Andrew Bergman shot before his departure. It's obvious though that the comedy is much broader than anything he wrote himself, the *noir* parody is crudely conceived, and there's none of the emotional authenticity which slams up against the comedy in *Minnie And Moskowitz* or *Love Streams*.

Aside from Falk, none of Cassavetes' closest collaborators was involved, though Bill Conti, who scored *Gloria*, was brought in to do the soundtrack (with large doses of Mozart) and John Finnegan, a bit-part actor who crops up in a number of the movies (he was the taxi driver who delivered Sarah Lawson's portable zoo), appears in a late scene as a police detective.

It wasn't a happy shoot. Cassavetes' friend and colleague Jeremy Kagan visited the set. "It was very clear it was just a job," he says. "It was a totally different energy from the other films of John's I had visited. The heart wasn't in it."

Alan Arkin took against his new director, perhaps suspicious that Falk would be gifted the picture. He hated Cassavetes' tantrums, his hands-off approach to directing the actors and his propensity for shooting seemingly endless takes. As one witness describes it, "Alan was offended, actually. His attitude was, 'I'm an actor, just tell me what you want and I'll do it.' Sometimes John would be very unreasonable with everyone, just to create an atmosphere. He believed that tension showed up on film. Alan Arkin did not like that technique. One time he saw John bawl somebody out and he came over and said, 'Why do you put up with this jerk?' When John got under the gun, it was like, 'Duck!'"

Not surprisingly, the movie is a mess. Surprisingly, it's also pretty funny. Cassavetes kept his name on it to honour his contract – and to get paid. Was he depressed by the experience? "I don't know if 'depressed' is a good word," Helen Caldwell says. "I think 'disgusted' is a better one. It wasn't pleasant."

✱ ✱ ✱

Although she operated on a freelance basis, Caldwell worked with Cassavetes as closely as anyone in the last seven or eight years of his life, picking up on *Love Streams* from the summer of 1981, and typing virtually every script he wrote until his death. Their friendship began with her storming out of one early session reading him the riot act. "John could be very snippety with people, very impatient," she says. "The first time he got nasty with me I said 'Look buddy, here's the way it's gonna work. I own my own business, I don't have to get in my car and come to your house and take your shit, so if you want me to work with you, you are going to treat me like a professional, like an adult, with respect, or I'm not going to do it.' I packed my stuff up and by the time I got to the door he was cackling that John laughter. He called me the next day and teased me about it."

Caldwell was in her early twenties, a Midwesterner from a conservative upbringing. She didn't know who John Cassavetes was and didn't much care either. "He told me he was a director, and I said 'Yeah, so?' I hadn't heard of any of his movies. I think that's why he took a liking to me. There were so many people around him wanting to get close to him. He was very loyal to the people he liked, but he could not stand ass-kissers. I saw him really trash a lot of people who were dying to become his students – he could make mincemeat out of people in a heartbeat."

207

Cassavetes' working methods were much as he'd settled on with Elaine Goren in the early Seventies. "He didn't want to talk to a machine," Caldwell says. "He would sit and tell me the story and talk about the characters, and I'd take shorthand, and he would watch my reactions. If I didn't think a character would behave in this way or that, we'd sit and bicker for an hour or as long as it took. Sometimes he'd take my suggestion, or sometimes my suggestion wasn't that good, but it would lead him to something better. He would sit and explain his logic to me, and sometimes it went around the block about four times before I could understand it. But it always made sense. I think his films were like that too."

"He would stew on an idea and talk about it. Sometimes we'd take a break from the script, kick a different idea around. For the most part he would have worked it out in his head before he even sat down with me, and then he would just tell me the story. I would go type up the script and bring him the rough draft pages, and usually he would not rewrite until we got through the first draft. He would put out the first draft in a week. Sometimes less. It was a miracle to me. He must have done so much of the homework in his head in order to pump it out in seven days, it was amazing."

In the period she knew him, Caldwell reckons they worked on eight or nine scripts together. Some of these were long-gestating works in progress, most were new plays or screenplays. During these last years Cassavetes seems to have blurred the distinction between film and theatre works – perhaps because he still envisaged previewing them on stage prior to mounting a film production, or because he suspected that even if he could muster the necessary strength to direct another film he would be unable to get insurance cover. Nevertheless, according to Caldwell, no matter what form the script took, they were all movies in John's head.

They included a couple of relatively commercial prospects: the thriller *Dead Silent*, and the aforementioned *Gloria II*. Most were more personal, even esoteric.

Caldwell's favourite was *Son* (also known as *Second Son*), a surreal comic allegory written for Jon Voight about the second coming. At the age of 33, Lewis learns from his Jewish mother (a role earmarked for Carol Kane) that his father is none other than God Almighty, and that God has a mission for him, a new message to spread to the World. Lewis resists, and God punishes him by taking away his girlfriend. When he finally complies, everyone thinks he's crazy. God's message is this: things are going to change. Women are going to start laying eggs, "like the ants do." "It ended with Lewis meeting his father – Peter Falk – and getting his girlfriend back – only she's holding an egg in her arms."

Begin The Beguine was a sequel of sorts to *Husbands*, written for Falk and Gazzara, who would play two men looking for love in the arms of a couple of hookers. Cassavetes even dusted off his unpublished novel of *Husbands* and took another pass at it to get back into the mindset. *Begin The Beguine* (originally known as *Husbands II*) was written as a play, and Seymour Cassel made some attempts to produce a stage version at Lincoln Centre after John's death. Peter Bogdanovich remembers the last time Peter Falk, Ben Gazzara and Cassavetes got together for dinner: "The three of them were so funny, kidding each other constantly. It was a rollicking evening. Because John ignored this gut hanging out over the table, everyone else did. He was trying to get them to do a picture, *Begin The Beguine*."

The last John Cassavetes script to be performed publicly in his lifetime was *A Woman Of Mystery*, a vehicle for Gena Rowlands which was intended for the stage. By this time Cassavetes knew he would never be insurable to direct another movie, even if he could muster the strength within himself.

A Woman Of Mystery concerned a homeless woman on the streets of New York, how she got that way – and will stay that way. She meets a young woman, Georgie (Carol Kane) who seems to recognise her and claims they are mother and daughter, but the bag lady has no name, no memory, no kinship whatsover. Further encounters threaten to draw her out of her isolation – but they *are* a threat. A number of seats had been removed from the auditorium, and during the intervals in what was a three-act piece, the spotlight would pick out these areas to single out actual street people, who would come forward and perform some music, poetry, or a comic monologue.

In the second act the woman's circumstances are transformed: she's well dressed, and in a swank nightclub where she is toasted by a gentleman affecting a French accent. Understandably, she is disturbed by this turnabout.

In the third act, she is back on the streets, and again encounters Georgie, who swears she is her daughter. However, to quote Cassavetes' own programme notes: "normal feelings of affection are too difficult to return to. The woman has been permanently disabled by the long discontinuance of feelings of love."

The critic Jonathan Rosenbaum was lucky enough to witness one of the dozen or so performances at the Court Theater in West Hollywood during its two-week tenure in May 1987: "Its treatment of the homeless couldn't be described as an act of either condescension or abstract piety," he wrote. "Terrifyingly human, tragic and mysterious, it revolved around the heroine's lost identity – literally, her lack of definition – and the difficulty others, including the audience, had making contact with her."[5]

The only one of Cassavetes' scripts to have been made posthumously is *She's Delovely* – retitled *She's So Lovely* when the Irving Berlin estate refused to sanction it. This was a crazy love story Cassavetes had started in the Seventies and fiddled with off-and-on throughout the Eighties. As late as 1987, Cassavetes entertained hopes of directing it himself, with Sean Penn in the lead. Peter Bogdanovich agreed to be on set as a 'stand-by' director for insurance purposes. The project foundered, allegedly because Cassavetes refused point blank to countenance Penn's then-wife Madonna as Maureen.

> *Eddie is a lovelorn naif with a psychiatric history, madly in love with his pregnant wife Maureen but (for reasons barely explained) three days AWOL as the movie begins. Maureen is a piece of work herself: equally in love with Eddie, but only a shade more worldy wise. A drunken binge with the man down the hall sets a disastrous train of events in motion, cul-minating in Eddie having a breakdown and shooting a psychiatric nurse in the stomach. Outrageously, the movie jumps forward ten years to Eddie's recovery and release. Maureen has since remarried and is a mother of three (the eldest is Eddie's child). When Maureen tells her new husband, Joey, that she still loves her Eddie he can't let it lie, and insists Eddie comes over to the house so that they can have it out between the three of them.*

A romantic comedy which plays with dramatic emotional material, the film works some intriguing variations on familiar Cassavetian tropes, notably by allocating the role of love-crazy to the male: a charming but wildly unpredictable improviser, Eddie makes Seymour Moskowitz look like a safe bet. Maureen is the living embodiment of Sarah Lawson's contention that "love is a continuous stream – it doesn't stop," and she doesn't hesi-tate to choose Eddie's irresponsible love over the security and comforts afforded her by the wealthy Joey (choosing 'street life' over 'family life'). Perhaps the most interesting part of the triangle is Joey, with his kamikaze refusal to let sleeping dogs lie, his need to put Maureen's love for him to the test despite her explicit warning that he can't possibly win any such competition.

Eddie is a fantastic and unusual male role – funny, romantic and nuts, he even gets the girl in the end – so it's not too surprising that Sean Penn was desperate to star in it. After Cassavetes' death, Penn suggested Hal

Ashby make it, then he was going to direct it himself, with Gary Oldman in the lead – but he decided to direct his own script *The Indian Runner* instead. Finally in 1997 Nick Cassavetes took up his father's screenplay and made it with Penn, his new wife Robin Wright, and John Travolta as Joey. (Penn, Travolta and Gérard Depardieu are credited as co-producers.)

Penn picked up an acting prize in Cannes, but there was something tokenistic about the award. The film proves how integral John Cassavetes' direction was to his art: it feels much flimsier than anything he made, you never really believe in these people or their love for each other. Nick Cassavetes fails to carry the jarring shifts in tone (from rape to ballroom dancing, for example), and Robin Wright can't make sense of Maureen's switch from drop-out to housewife. With the best will in the world, it's not a film which discovers anything along the way.

But there are good things in it. Harry Dean Stanton and Debi Mazar are fun as Eddie's barroom buddies. Nick Cassavetes is a good director of children, and there is touching, deft interplay between Eddie, Joey, and the daughter that one of them sired and the other reared.

The finest thing in the film is Penn's distraught delivery of a key speech at exactly the halfway point. Eddie has just been put in a straightjacket. Although he doesn't know it, he won't see Maureen for ten years.

Eddie: I think we ought to start up old and we have all the pain, and we're feeble. We look at our friends and they're feeble – they're a hundred. But every day we get younger and have something to look forward to.

Maureen: You start out old and you get younger.

Eddie: You tell yourself there's hope. And then you reach twenty, and nineteen. Twelve. Ten. Every day is really a new day – it's really a miracle. And then you're a baby and you don't know your life is ending. You just suck on your mother's tit and then you die.

✳ ✳ ✳

'Cirrhosis' comes from the Greek word kirrhos, for yellow. As the liver cells die, a fibrous scar tissue grows up around them, and the organ becomes jaundiced from fat accumulation. Gradually, over the years, the jaundice spreads across the body. In Cassavetes' case, the flesh seemed to shrink from his face and his limbs. His arms and legs became twigs; his head a skull. But that wasn't what shocked people when they saw him. For years he'd had a little paunch, a pot belly. It was noticeable to the crew of Paul Mazursky's film *Tempest* as early as 1981. With the cirrhosis, his stomach became increasingly distended. Liver damage affects the albumin content in the blood. The scar tissue blocks the blood supply through the big veins in the abdomen, causing a build-up of fluid. John took to wearing a bathrobe at all times to cover this cancerous ghost pregnancy. Eventually he couldn't reach around his own stomach.

"We'd go have a Chinese or something for lunch, and people would stop me and say 'Is that John Cassavetes?'" Al Ruban remembers. "It made me realise what he must be going through."

The cirrhosis was inflamed by alcohol, but for its root cause you have to look back further, to 1967, when Cassavetes was sent home from filming Brian Hutton's *Sol Madrid* (aka *The Heroin Gang*) in Mexico – one of a number of roles he took to bankroll the completion of *Faces*.[6]

He was hospitalised with hepatitis – probably caused by nothing more sinister than drinking contaminated water. In such cases, patients are advised to steer clear of alcohol for six months until the liver has had time to recover. By ignoring this advice Cassavetes may have caused permanent damage, and almost certainly left himself vulnerable to cirrhosis.

* * *

In these last years John was more irrascible than ever. Some friends he kept close – Peter Falk, Carol Kane, Peter Bogdanovich – others felt he pushed them away. "His attitude was he didn't want people to see him this way, because he couldn't stand for people to feel sorry for him," Helen Caldwell says. "He said to me once, 'I don't mind dying, at least then I won't have to go to lunch with anybody.'"

"I don't think he was embarrassed," Jeremy Kagan says. "I think some of us weren't mature enough to deal with it, and he was sparing us pain. There was a calmness about him when I saw him. He was white haired and grey-faced, gaunt, with this giant belly, but there was a kind of glow and a calm that I wasn't in touch with then. Now I have seen more death in my own life, I think there was a Buddha-like quality to him: not just physically, I think he was dealing with death on that plain of understanding. He wasn't avoiding anything."

* * *

Just as he had with Elaine Kagan on *A Woman Under The Influence*, John pressed Helen Caldwell into acting as script supervisor on *Love Streams*. "There was a scene when he's coming down the stairs smoking a cigarette," she recalls. "We shot the scene once and when we went to do coverage he said 'Helen, which hand did I have the cigarette in?'"

I said "Oh! I don't know – I forgot to check."

He said "Ok, watch this," and if you look in the movie, it always cracks me up, he's coming down the stairs and he puts his cigarette in with his left hand and he pulls it out with his right, puts it back in with his right, pulls it out with his left. It's looks silly, but you know when I look at that I think what a charming man to do that, he didn't scream or yell. He didn't need to do that.'

The job stuck, and Caldwell became a script supervisor on studio movies – after every picture she would come back, call John, and check if he had a script he wanted to write.

"One time I got back from a film and called him and he gave me a cheque for $5,000 and said 'I want to buy your time for the whole month, I want to write a script, I don't want you running off to do another movie.' So he gives me the cheque, I went home that night, and the phone rings, it's John Huston, calling me to work on *The Dead*: so cool! I called up John and said 'John, I haven't cashed your cheque yet. John Huston just called and offered me work on *The Dead*.'

"He said 'You fucking bitch! If you leave and go work with John Huston then I will never speak to you again.'

"I said 'Okay, okay I was just checking.'

"So I go work with John the next day, and he fixes me a coffee and he says, 'Helenski' – he always called me 'Helenski' – he said 'I know you're pissed off, I know you wanted to work with Huston, but look at it this way, it's probably going to be his last film, but this will probably be my last film, so you want to make the last film wtih John Huston or John Cassavetes?' "

A couple of years later, they had a deeper falling out:

"John got very mad at me before he died. I was one of the last people he would permit to see him. He said to me one time, 'You're my only link with the outside world, if it wasn't for you I wouldn't know what was happening out there.' As he got sicker and sicker and started looking worse he didn't want anybody to see him that way.

"I guess it was 1988. Because he got me started in script supervising I would go off and do films, and he didn't want to write his scripts with anyone but me, so he would wait until I got back to write a script. I had left town to work on a film, but this time when I got back immediately I got a call to do another one, which Nick was in, actually, and I really needed the money, so I just took it and didn't call John. When I finished that one I called him, and I guess it was five or six months later, and he was so pissed off at me. He said 'This probably would have been my last movie, but it wasn't important enough to you was it?' He called me a whore for money, and he hung up on me. This was probably about eight months before he died. It just devastated me.

"I called him back about three months later, and said 'John this is Helen.' He did this really funny thing: when he didn't want to talk to people, he would put on this really stupid voice and pretend it wasn't him. It was so blatantly obvious. So he puts on this phoney voice, and I said 'John don't do this, man. It's not worth it. You're going to die but you're not dead yet, we've had a good long friendship.' And he sat and listened to everything I said, but he would not open up, he never said another word to me and I ended up hanging up. He went to his grave angry at me. Broke my heart for a long time."

Most of his goodbyes were more gracious. They were enacted over a period of months, and seem almost to have been directed by John. Out of the blue, friends and collaborators who hadn't seen him for years would get a phone call or a note, perhaps with a dinner invitation attached. Jenny Runacre, John's young co-star in *Husbands* was one such: "He came over with Al Ruban and Gena and I was invited out to dinner with them two months before he died, I think – I didn't know he was dying, but I realised later. I thought what a nice man, a nice normal man you could talk to normally. My God! I never realised it when we were doing the film, because I was too young and scared and overwhelmed. I wish I'd got to know him better. I wish I'd relaxed and treated him more as a human being."

One day Zohra Lampert – Dorothy Victor in *Opening Night* – answered the phone and it was John. "I was startled to hear from him,' she writes. 'We spoke a while, and when he casually mentioned being ill, by way of explaining his relative inactivity, I suppose, I took it up, with shadow casualness: 'Is it serious, John?' 'Oh, darling,' he replied, laughing, without bitterness, in fact with tenderness, and with characteristic mischief, 'it's fatal.' I understood only afterward that he had called to say goodbye."[7]

In January 1989 he called Al Ruban. "I must say it was one of the more traumatic conversations I've ever had in my life," Ruban says. "We'd had this rough-and-tumble relationship, and suddenly for the first time ever, thanking me. For the things I had done that he had never mentioned before, blah, blah blah, and I knew he was going to die. Toughest conversation I ever had."

One thinks of Robert Harmon, alone in his house – John's house – at the end of *Love Streams*. But of course John was never alone. His family was right beside him: Gena, Nick, Xan, Zoe ... a family closer even than his film-making family, and entitled to the private succour of their own most intimate and loving memories.

Cassavetes was a finer artist than any of his alter-egos had been, and a better man. In a way few can manage he was able to bring together his work, his art and his family so that each aspect sustained the rest: the work of his life had been the life of his work. He cast wife, parents, in-laws and friends in his films, and he shot them where they lived (during *Love Streams* the Cassavetes' younger kids slept 13 weeks on set, among the lights and cables).

These were 'home movies' in the most profound way; documentaries of their own production. As a result they have been labelled self-indulgent, but the labelling is complacent, and the films anything but. (How much more self-indulgent it would have been for Cassavetes to capitulate to the mainstream for much greater fame and fortune.) They are demanding films: demanding of the artist and the audience both. Not cerebral. Heartfelt. They say: We are alive . . . how then are we to live? We love. Is this then how we live?

They ask us to watch, to see, and to look into ourselves.

John Cassavetes died February 3, 1989. His will was brief and to the point: "I leave all and everything I own to my beloved wife Gena Rowlands Cassavetes. I leave nothing to anyone else, whomsoever they may be. I owe no one any debt or obligation, other than usual and ordinary bills. No one has done me a special service that I feel obligated to." He left his life-works behind him.

"Philosophy is the study of love. 'Philos' is 'friend' or 'love' – synonymous in Greek – 'ophy' is 'to study.' To have a philosophy is to know how to love, and to know where to put it. People live with anger and hostility and problems – so what they need is a philosophy. What everybody needs is a way to say where and how can I love? Can I be in love so I can live with some degree of peace? I guess every picture we've ever done has been to try to find some kind of philosophy for the characters. I have a one-track mind. It's all I'm interested in, is Love."

John Cassavetes[8]

1 JC interviewed by Richard Combs, *MFB*, v51 n603, April 1984.
2 Peter Falk, 'Out of the Shadows' TV interview by Paul Joyce, Lucida Productions.
3 Peter Bogdanovich, Author's interview (2000).
4 Mr Bergman declined to be interviewed for this book. His subsequent directorial credits include *The Freshman*, *Honeymoon In Vegas*, *It Could Happen To You* and *Striptease*.
5 Jonathan Rosenbaum, 'Love Films,' *Chicago Reader*, September 20, 1991.
6 Due to his illness, the role was recast and his scenes reshot with Rip Torn.
7 Zohra Lampert: letter to the author, (2000).
8 *I'm Almost Not Crazy* documentary, directed by Michael Ventura.

Appendix I

Filmography as Director

There was no firm job demarcation on John Cassavetes' pictures. Everyone mucked in. Crew members came and went. An actor like Seymour Cassel, or a script supervisor like Elaine Goren would be drafted in to help out on camera or on sound as the occasion demanded. On *Husbands*, the continuity girl, Peggy Lashbrook, suddenly found herself in front of the camera in Ben Gazzara's climactic scene. On *The Killing Of A Chinese Bookie* there is no cinematographer credit on the film: Al Ruban, Fred Elmes, Mitchell Breit and Mike Ferris all contributed to its look, as of course did Cassavetes himself, who operated a second camera on many occasions without taking a screen credit. Like most directors, he also oversaw the editing of his films, again without screen credit, although he was often much more hands-on than most directors in this capacity. And because he spent so long editing and re-editing his films, he often outlasted more than one official editor, so that on *A Woman Under The Influence* Peter Tanner worked on it for a while, Tom Cornwell and Robert Heffernan both contributed a good deal, but so too did Elizabeth Bergeron, David Armstrong, and Sheila Viseltear – and Bo Harwood, and any number of friends who would get a call sometimes at 3am, and be dragged out of bed to help finesse a scene. In part this chaotic working practice was inevitable given Cassavetes' minimal budgets; in part it was a reflection of a genuine democratic zeal – he believed anyone could do anything on a film set – and then, paradoxically, it may have worked to secure Cassavetes' complete control of the movie, in as much as he was the only one who really knew what was going on in each and every department.

Talking about Charlie Mingus, Cassavetes told Brian Casc, 'He was always torn between the mathematical beauty of the composition and the freedom of improvisation. We had the same kind of artistic fury that hits you. You're all loose – well, we pretend we're loose and in the end we're dictators.'

With the exception of the studio productions *Too Late Blues*, *A Child Is Waiting*, *Gloria* and *Big Trouble*, the credits that follow can only be taken as a rough guide to who did most of what. Except where it seemed inadequate or misleading to do so, I have followed the lead Cassavetes set in the films' screen credits.

Shadows
(filmed 1957–1959; screened 1959)
Directed by John Cassavetes
Written by John Cassavetes (based on an acting workshop improvisation)

Cast: Ben Carruthers (Ben); Lelia Goldoni (Lelia); Hugh Hurd (Hugh); Anthony Ray (Tony); Dennis Sallas (Dennis); Tom Allen (Tom); David Pokitillow (David); Rupert Crosse (Rupert); Davey Jones (Davey); Pir Marini (Pir the Piano Player); Victoria Vargas (Vickie); Jack Ackerman (Jack, Director of Dance Studio); Jacqueline Walcott (Jacqueline); Joyce Miles, Nancy Deale, Gigi Brooks (girls in restaurant); Lynne Hamilton, Marilyn Clark, Joanne Sages, Jed McGarvey, Greta Thyssen (girls at party); Cliff Carnell (tough guy in restaurant); also featuring: Jay Crecco, Ronald Maccone, Bob Reeh, Joyce Miles

John Cassavetes appears in a silent, unbilled bit to 'rescue' Lelia from unwelcome attention outside a 42nd Street cinema.

Produced by Maurice McEndree and Nikos Papatakis;

Associate Producer Seymour Cassel; Music by Charles Mingus (saxophone solos by Shafi Hadi); Cinematography by Erich Kollmar (16mm black and white); Lighting David Simon; Camera Assistant Al Ruban; Assistant Director Al Giglio; Editing by John Cassavetes, Maurice McEndree and Len Appelson; Production Design by Randy Liles, Bob Reeh; Production Manager Wray Bevins; Production Assistants Maxine Arnold, Anne Draper, Mary Ann Ehle, Ellen Paulos, Leslie Reed, Judy Kaufman.

Running time: 60 minutes (1958 16mm version); 87 minutes (1959, 35mm version).

Too Late Blues (1961)
Directed by John Cassavetes
Written by John Cassavetes and Richard Carr

Cast: Bobby Darin (John 'Ghost' Wakefield); Stella Stevens (Jess Polanski); Everett Chambers (Benny Flowers); Nick Dennis (Nick); Vince Edwards (Tommy); Val Avery (Frielobe); Marilyn Clark (Countess); James Joyce (Reno); Rupert Crosse (Baby Jackson); Cliff Carnell (Charlie, the saxophonist); Richard Chambers (Pete, the trumpeter); Seymour Cassel (Red, the bassist); Dan Stafford (Shelley, the drummer); also featuring J Allen Hopkins (Skipper); Slim Gaillard (party singer); June Wilkinson (girl at bar).

Produced by John Cassavetes for Paramount

Original music by David Raksin with songs by Milt Bernhart, Benny Carter, Shelly Manne, Red Mitchell, Uan Rasey, Jimmy Rowles. Cinematography by Lionel Lindon (35mm black and white); Editing by Frank Bracht; Production Design by Hal Pereira; Art Direction Tambi Larsen; Costume Design by Edith Head; Special Effects John P. Fulton; Dialogue Coach Jud Taylor; Assistant Director Arthur Jacobson; Production Manager William Mull.

Running time: 103 minutes.

A Child Is Waiting (1962)
Directed by John Cassavetes
Written by Abby Mann based on his teleplay

Cast: Burt Lancaster (Dr Matthew Clark); Judy Garland (Jean Hansen); Gena Rowlands (Sophie Widdicombe); Steven Hill (Ted Widdicombe); Paul Stewart (Goodman); Gloria McGehee (Mattie); Lawrence Tierney (Douglas Benham); Bruce Ritchey (Reuben Widdicombe); John Marley (Holland); Mario Gallo (Dr Lombardi); Bill Mumy Elizabeth Wilson (Miss Fogarty); Fred Draper (Dr Sack); also featuring Brian Corcoran; Butch Patrick; Jay Phillips; Noam Pitlik; Michael Stevens. John Cassavetes appears uncredited as Retarded Adult Who Walks Toward Camera

Produced by Stanley Kramer, a Larcas Production for United Artists. Associate producer Philip Langner; Original music by Ernest Gold; Cinematography by Joseph LaShelle (35mm black and white); Editing by Gene Fowler Jr and Robert C Jones; Casting Lynn Stalmaster; Production Design by Rudolph Sternad; Set Decoration Joseph Kish; Costume Design by Joe King and Howard Shoup; Makeup Department George Lane, Al Paul, Robert Schiffer; Production Management Nate H Edwards; Assistant Directors Douglas Green and Lindsley Parsons.

Running time: 102 minutes.

Faces
(filmed 1965; released 1968)
Directed by John Cassavetes
Written by John Cassavetes

Cast: John Marley (Richard Forst); Gena Rowlands (Jeannie Rapp); Lynn Carlin (Maria Forst); Seymour Cassel (Chet); Fred Draper (Freddie); Val Avery (Jim McCarthy); Dorothy Gulliver (Florence); Joanne Moore Jordan (Louise); Darlene Conley (Billy Mae); Gene Darfler (Joe Jackson); Elizabeth Deering (Stella); also featuring James Bridges (Jim Mortensen);

219

John Finnegan (JP); Anne Shirley Anne); Nita White (Nita); Erwin Sirianni (Harry Selfrine); Don Kranz (Edward Kazmier); George Sims (barman); OG Dunn (comedian).

Produced by John Cassavetes and Maurice McEndree;

Original music by Jack Ackerman; song Charlie Smalls ('Never Felt Like This Before'); Cinematography by Al Ruban (16mm black and white); Camera George Sims. Editing by John Cassavetes, Maurice McEndree and Al Ruban;

Production Design by Phedon Papamichael; Sound Don Pike; Production Manager James Joyce.

Running time: 129 minutes.

Husbands (1970)
Directed by John Cassavetes
Written by John Cassavetes

Cast: Ben Gazzara (Harry); Peter Falk (Archie); John Cassavetes (Gus); Jenny Runacre (Mary Tynan); Jenny Lee Wright (Pearl Billingham); Noelle Kao (Julie); John Kullers (Red); Reta Shaw (Annie); Leola Harlow (Leola); Delores Delmar (The Countess); Eleanor Zee (Mrs Hines); Claire Malis (Stuart's wife); Peggy Lashbrook (Diana Mallabee); Eleanor Gould ('Normandy'); Sarah Felcher (Sarah); Gwen Van Dam ('Jeannie'); John Armstrong ('Happy Birthday'); Antoinette Kray ('Jesus Loves Me'); Lorraine McMartin (Annie's mother); Carinthia West (Susanna); Rhonda Parker (Margaret); Joseph Boley (Minister); Judith Lowry (Stuart's grandmother); Joseph Hardy ('Shanghai Lil'); David Rowlands (Stuart Jackson); Alexandra Cassavetes (Xan, uncredited); Nick Cassavetes (Nick uncredited); Edgar Franken (Ed Weintraub); Anne O'Donnell (Nurse); KC Townsend (Barmaid) Gena Wheeler (Nurse); Fred Draper (uncredited).

Produced by Al Ruban and Sam Shaw;

Cinematography by Victor J. Kemper; Camera Operators (NY) Richard Mingalone and Mike Chapman; Camera Operator (London) Jeff Glover. Production Supervisor Fred Caruso; Supervising Editor Peter Tanner; Assistant Editor Tom Cornwell; Post-production Editor Jack Woods and Robert Heffernan (assistant); Art Direction Rene D'Auriac; Costume Design by Louis Brown; Production Coordinator James Joyce. Musical director Jack Ackerman; Sound (NY) Dennis Maitland; Sound (London) Barrie Coplan. Script Continuity (London) Peggy Lashbrook.

Running time: 140 minutes (original Columbia release version); 131 minutes (extant version).

Minnie And Moskowitz (1971)
Directed by John Cassavetes
Written by John Cassavetes

Cast: Gena Rowlands (Minnie Moore); Seymour Cassel (Seymour Moskowitz); Val Avery (Zelman 'Zelmo' Swift); Timothy Carey (Morgan Morgan); Katherine Cassavetes (Sheba Moskowitz); Elizabeth Deering (Girl); Elsie Ames (Florence); Lady Rowlands (Georgia Moore); Holly Near (Irish); Judith Roberts (Wife); Jack Danskin (Dick Henderson); Eleanor Zee (Mrs Grass); also featuring Santos Morales, Kathleen O'Malley, Jimmy Joyce, Chuck Wells, Sean Joyce (Ned); David Rowlands (Minister); John Cassavetes (Jim uncredited).

Produced by Paul Donnelly for Universal;

Associate producer Al Ruban; Cinematography by Alric Edens, Michael Margulies and Arthur J Ornitz; Post-production supervisor Fred Knudtson; Editing Robert Heffernan; Costume Design by Helen Colvig; Assistant Director Kevin Donnelly, Louis A Stroller; Art Department Victor E Petrotta; Sound M.M. Metcalfe; Camera operator Vince DeLaney; Assistants to producer Elaine Goren and James Joyce; Music supervisor Bo Harwood; Script Supervisor Dalonne Jackson.

Running time: 115 minutes.

A Woman Under The Influence
(filmed 1972/73; released 1974)
Directed by John Cassavetes
Written by John Cassavetes

Cast: Peter Falk (Nick Longhetti); Gena Rowlands (Mabel Longhetti); Katherine Cassavetes (Mama Longhetti); Matthew Cassel (Tony Longhetti); Christina Grisanti (Maria Longhetti); Matthew Laborteaux (Angelo Longhetti); Lady Rowlands (Martha Mortensen); Eddie Shaw (Doctor Zepp); Fred Draper (George Mortensen); Nick Cassavetes (Adolph); Elizabeth Deering (Angela); OG Dunn (Garson Cross); John Finnegan (Clancy); Mario Gallo (Harold Jensen); Angelo Grisanti (Vito Grimaldi); Charles Horvath (Eddie the Indian); Sonny Aprile (Aldo); Vince Barbi (Gino); Cliff Carnell (Aldo); Hugh Hurd (Willie Johnson); James Joyce (Bowman); Leon Wagner (Billy Tidrow); Sil Words (James Turner); Tina (Jacki Peters); Elsie Ames (Principal); Joanne Moore Jordan (Muriel); Xan Cassavetes (Adienne Jensen); Dominique Davalos (Dominique Jensen); Pancho Meisenheimer (John Jensen).

Produced by Sam Shaw;

Original music by Bo Harwood; Cinematography by Mitch Breit and Caleb Deschanel; Camera Operators Mike Ferris, David Nowell. Assistant Operators Gary Graver, Tony Palmieri, Fred Elmes, Leslie Otis and Larry Silver; Lighting crew Chris Taylor, Bo Taylor, Merv Dayan; Editing by Tom Cornwell and Robert Heffernan; Production Design by Phedon Papamichael; Sound Bo Harwood; Sound Mix Mike Denecke; Production Secretary and Wardrobe Carole Smith; Script Continity Elaine Goren; Assistant Directors Jack Corrick and Roger Slager.

Running time: 146 minutes.

The Killing Of A Chinese Bookie
(filmed 1975/76; released 1976; recut and rereleased 1978)
Directed by John Cassavetes
Written by John Cassavetes

Cast: Ben Gazzara (Cosmo Vitelli); Timothy Carey (Flo, gangster); Seymour Cassel (Mort Weil, gangster); Robert Phillips (Phil, gangster); Morgan Woodward (John, head gangster); John Kullers (Eddie-Red); Al Ruban (Marty Reitz, gangster); Azizi Johari (Rachel); Virginia Carrington (Betty, the mother); Meade Roberts (Mr Sophistication); Alice Fredlund (Sherry); Donna Marie Gordon (Margo); Haji (Haji); Carol Warren (Carol); Derna Wong Davis (Derna); Kathalina Veniero (Annie); Yvette Morris (Yvette); Jack Ackerman (Musical director); David Rowlands (Lamarr); Trisha Pelham (Waitress); Eddie Ike Shaw (Taxi Driver); Salvatore Aprile (Sonny); Gene Darcy (Commodore); Ben Marino (Bartender); Arlene Allison (Waitress); Vince Barbi (Vince); Val Avery (Blair Benoit); Elizabeth Deering (Lavinia); Soto Joe Hugh (Chinese Bookie); Catherine Wong (The Bookie's Girl); John Finnegan (Taxi Driver); Miles Ciletti (Mickey); Mike Skloot (Scooper); Frank Buchanan (Flo's Friend); Jason Kincaid (Parking Lot Attendant); Frank Thomas (Poker Player); Jack Krupnick (Poker Player).

Produced by Al Ruban;

Associate Producer Phil Burton; Original music by Bo Harwood; Music Conductor/Arranger Anthony Harris; Lighting by Al Ruban and Mitchell Breit; Camera Fred Elmes and Mike Ferris; Assistant Camera Michael Stringer; Lighting Crew Donald Robinson, Chris Taylor, Bruce Knee; Editing by Tom Cornwell and Robert Heffernan; Sound Bo Harwood; Sound Editing Jack Woods; Sound Mixer Buzz Knudson; Production Design by Sam Shaw; Art Direction Phedon Papamichael; Production Manager Art Levinson; Script supervisor Sandy King

Running time: 135 minutes (1976 version); 108 minutes (1978 version).

Opening Night (1977)
Directed by John Cassavetes
Written by John Cassavetes

Cast: Gena Rowlands (Myrtle Gordon); John Cassavetes (Maurice Adams); Ben Gazzara (Manny Victor); Joan Blondell (Sarah Goode); Paul Stewart (David Samuels); Zohra Lampert (Dorothy Victor); Laura Johnson (Nancy Stein); John Tuell (Gus Simmons); Ray Powers (Jimmy); John Finnegan (Prop man); Louise Lewis (Kelly); Fred Draper (Leo); Katherine Cassavetes (Vivian); Lady Rowlands (Melva Drake); Carol Waren (Carla); Briana Carver (Lena); Angelo Grisanti (Charlie Spikes); Meade Roberts (Eddie Stein); Eleanor Zee (Sylvia Stein); David Rowlands (Doorman); Sharon Van Ivan (Shirley); Jimmy Christie (News Stand Operator); James Karen (Bell Boy); Jimmy Joyce (Bartender); Sherry Bain (Bar maid); Sylvia Davis Shaw (Hotel Maid); Peter Lampert (Maitred'); also featuring Peter Bogdanovich as himself and Barbara Perry (uncredited).

Produced by Al Ruban;

Executive Producer Sam Shaw; Associate Producer Michael Lally; Original music by Bo Harwood; Arranged and conducted music by Booker T Jones; Cinematography by Al Ruban; Camera Operators Fred Elmes and Mike Ferris; Editing by Tom Cornwell; Sound Bo Harwood; Production Design by Bryan Ryman; Costume Design by Alexandra Corwin-Hankin; Production Managers Ted Ledding and Foster H Phinney; Assistant Director Lisa Hallas; Sound Assistant Joanne T Harwood; Sound mixer Bill Varney; Sound editor Joe Woo Jr; Stunts Donna Garrett, Victor Paul, Charlie Picerni stunt driver; Assistant Editor Kent Beyda, Nancy Golden, Hal Bowers.

Running time: 144 minutes.

Gloria
(filmed 1979; released 1980)
Directed by John Cassavetes
Written by John Cassavetes

Cast: Gena Rowlands (Gloria Swenson); Julie Carmen (Jeri Dawn); Tony Knesich (1st Man/Gangster); John Adames (Phil Dawn); Gregory Cleghorne (Kid in Elevator); Buck Henry (Jack Dawn); Lupe Garnica (Margarita Vargas); Jessica Castillo (Joan Dawn); Tom Noonan (2nd Man/Gangster); Ronald Maccone (3rd Man/Gangster); George Yudzevich (Heavy Set Man); Gary Klar (Irish cop); William E Rice (TV Newscaster);

Frank Belgiorno (Riverside Drive Man #5) JC Quinn (Riverside Drive Man #4); Alex Stevens (Riverside Drive Man #7); Sonny Landham (Riverside Drive Man #8); Harry Madsen (Riverside Drive Man #6); Shanton Granger (Car Flip Cabbie); John Pavelko (Bank Teller); Ray Baker (Assistant Bank Manager); Ross Charap (Ron/Vault); Irvin Graham (Clerk/Adams Hotel); Michael Proscia (Uncle Joe); TS Rosenbaum (Desk Clerk/Star Hotel); Santos Morales (New York Cemetery Cabbie); Meta Shaw (Hostess); Marilyn Putnam (Waitress); John Finnegan (Frank); Gaetano Lisi (Mister); Richard M Kaye (Penn Station Hood #3); Steve Lefkowitz (Penn Station Hood #5); George Poidomani (Penn Station Hood #4); Lawrence Tierney (Broadway Bartender); Asa Adil Qawee (104th Street Cab Driver); Vincent Pecorella (Boy in Bitch Mother's Apt); Iris Fernandez (Bitch Mother #1); Jade Bari (Bitch Mother #2); David Resnick (Subway Person #2); Thomas J Buckman (Man in Newark Station); Joe Dabenigno (Man in Newark Station); Bill Wiley (Bellman); John M Sefakis (Greek Cashier); Val Avery (Sill); Walter Dukes (Newark Cabbie)'; Janet Ruben (Lincoln Tunnel Cabbie); Ferruccio Hrvatin (Aldo); Edward Wilson (Guillermo D'Antoni); Basilio Franchina (Tony Tanzini); Carl Levy (Milt Cohen); Warren Selvaggi (Pat Donovan); Nathan Seril (The Baron); Vladimir Drazenovic (Tonti); Edward Jacobs (Desk Clerk/Newark Hotel); Brad Johnston (1st Traveler); Jerry Jaffe (Pittsburgh Cabbie); Filomena Spagnuolo (Old lady).

Produced by Sam Shaw for Columbia;

Associate Producer Stephen F Kesten; Original music by Bill Conti; Cinematography by Fred Schuler; Editing by George C Villaseñor; Casting Vic Ramos; Production Design by Rene D'Auriac; Costume Design by Peggy Farrell (Gena Rowlands' clothes by Emmanuel Ungaro); Production Manager Steve Kesten; Title Design Sam Shaw; Paintings by Romare Bearden; 1st Assistant Director Mike Haley; 2nd Assistant Director Tom Fritz; Assistant Editor Lori Bloustein; Camera Operator Lou Barlia; 1st Assistant Cameraman Sandy Brooke; 2nd Assistant Camera Ricki-Ellen Brooke; Script Supervisor Nancy Hopton.

Running time: 121 minutes

Love Streams
(filmed 1983; released 1984)
Directed by John Cassavetes
Written by Ted Allan and John Cassavetes based on Allen's original stage play.

Cast: Gena Rowlands (Sarah Lawson); John Cassavetes (Robert Harmon); Diahnne Abbott (Susan); Seymour Cassel (Jack Lawson); Margaret

Abbott (Margarita); Jakob Shaw (Albie Swanson); Eddy Donno (Stepfather Swanson); Joan Foley (Judge Dunbar); Al Ruban (Milton Kravitz); Tom Badal (Sam the lawyer); also featuring Risa Blewitt (Debbie Lawson); Alexandra Cassavetes (Backup Singer) Dominique Devalos (Backup Singer); Michele Conway (Agnes Swanson); Robert Fieldsteel (Dr Williams); Leslie Hope (Joanie); John Roselius (Ken); David Rowlands (The psychiatrist); Raphael De Niro (Billy); John Roselius (Ken); Jessica St John (Dottie); Tony Brubaker (Frank); John Finnegan (Taxi Driver/Animals); Frank Beetson (Cashier, Bowling Alley); Gregg Berger, Phedon Papamichael, John Qualls, Jim Jones (Taxi Drivers); Christopher O'Neal (Phyllis George Delano); Doe Avedon (Mrs Kiner); Susan Wolf (Jane Meadows Swift);Julie Allan (Charene); Renee Le Flore (Renee); Bronwyn Bober (Jeannie); Victoria Morgan (Laurie); Barbara di Frenza (Mary); Cindy Davidson (Annette); Jamie Horton (Porter, Victoria Station); Francois Duhamel (Porter, Paris).

Produced by Yoram Globus and Menahem Golan for Cannon;

Executive Producer Al Ruban; Production Directors Chris Pearce, Al Ruban; Original music by Bo Harwood; Cinematography by Al Ruban; Camera Operators George Sims; Alan Caso and Stephen St John (Steadicam); Sound Richard Lighstone, Michael Denecke, Bo Harwood; Editing by George C Villase or; Production Design by Phedon Papamichael; Sound Editor Dessie Markovsky; Script Supervisor Helen Caldwell. Songs: 'Kinky Reggae' (Bob Marley); 'I Can't Get Started' (Ira Gershwin and Vernon Duke); 'Deep Night' (Rudy Vallee, Charles Henderson, Hugo Napton); 'Where Are You?' (Jimmy McHugh, Harold Adamson, Mildred Bailey); Love Streams Operetta (Bo Harwood, John Cassavetes); 'True Love', 'I'll Leave It Up To You' (Bo Harwood, Bobbi Permanent); 'You Say You're Only A Little Lonely' (Bo Harwood); 'A Piece Of Pie', 'Love Love With You' (Bo Harwood, John Cassavetes, Anthony Harris).

Running time: 141 minutes

Big Trouble (1985)
Directed by John Cassavetes
Written by Warren Bogle (Andrew Bergman)

Cast: Peter Falk (Steve Rickey); Alan Arkin (Leonard Hoffman); Beverly D'Angelo (Blanche Rickey); Charles Durning (O'Mara); Robert Stack (Winslow); Paul Dooley (Noozel); Valerie Curtin (Arlene Hoffman); Richard Libertini (Doctor Lopez); Steve Alterman (Peter Hoffman); Jerry Pavlon (Michael Hoffman); Paul La Greca (Joshua Hoffman); John

Finnegan (Detective Murphy); Karl Lukas (Police Captain); Maryedith Burrell (Gail); Edith Fields (Doris); Warren Munson (Jack); Rosemarie Stack (Mrs Winslow); Barbara Tarbuck (Helen); Al White (Mr Williams); Teddy Wilson (Porter); Gloria Gifford (Wanda); Herb Armstrong (Night Security Guard); Jaime S nchez (Chief Terrorist); Gaetano Lisi (Gaetano Lopez); Chester Grimes (Flavio Lopez); Irene Olga (L¢pez Lopez' Receptionist); Daphne Eckler (Receptionist); Carol Reinhard (Winslow's Secretary); Conroy Gedeon (Reporter); Leonard P Geer (Whitlow Kepler); Melvin Jones (Terrorist #1); Luis Contreras (Terrorist #2); John M Kochian (Terrorist #3); Domingo Ambriz (Terrorist #4); John Bianchini (Terrorist #5); Nafa Rasho (Terrorist #6); Roger Ito (Terrorist #7); Perry Fluker (Terrorist #8); Lynn Ready (Terrorist #9); Steven Lambert (Terrorist #10); Yukio G Collins (Terrorist #11); Howard Clapp (Executive #1); Jeff Howard (Executive #2); Leland Sun (Chinese Laborer #1); Al Leong (Chinese Laborer #2); Danny Lew (Chinese Laborer #3); Michaelani (Chinese Laborer #4); Dennis Phun (Chinese Laborer #5); Walter Soo Hoo (Chinese Laborer #6); Richard Walter (Hot Dog Eater); Joseph G Medalis (Salesman).

Produced by Mike Lobell and Andrew Bergman for Columbia;

Original music by Bill Conti; Non-original music by Joseph Haydn (from 'Trio No. 15') Wolfgang Amadeus Mozart (from 'Eine kleine Nachtmusik'); Giacomo Puccini (from 'La Bohème'); Cinematography by Bill Butler; Editing by Donn Cambern and Ralph E Winters; Casting Jane Feinberg, Mike Fenton, Judy Taylor; Production Design by Gene Callahan and Peter Landsdown Smith; Set Decoration Lee Poll; Costume Design by Joe I Tompkins; Camera Operator James R Connell; Assistant to Cassavetes Helen Caldwell.

Running time: 93 minutes.

Appendix II

Stage Works

In the Eighties Cassavetes became more interested in producing work for the theatre, principally as a means of road-testing scripts for future film projects (see Chapter 12). Those plays which were professionally staged include *East/West Game* (1980), a satire about a playwright resisting selling out to Hollywood, which starred Nick Cassavetes (see Chapter 10) and *A Woman Of Mystery* (1987) with Gena Rowlands (see Chapter 12).

However Cassavetes' most remarkable stage production was to mount *Three Plays Of Love And Hate* in 1981. *Love Streams* and *The Third Day Comes* were written by Ted Allan; the third play *Knives*, was by Cassavetes himself, a bizarre and atypical black comedy which he had first drafted in 1978 and subsequently re-written.

Knives concerns Larry (played by Peter Falk), a popular Jewish stand-up comedian. It begins with a London agent telling him his sense of humour won't play in Britain, but when he does an audition in London he's a big hit and gets signed for a run of performances, during which he tells a joke about his wife constantly throwing up in the toilet. He gets back to the hotel room and recalls events for his wife, detailing his anxiety at possibly losing the job and his happiness about it eventually going over pretty well.

The action proceeds with a lot of jump-cuts. Next we find ourselves in court, where Larry has been charged with murdering Maureen, his wife. He's guilt-stricken enough to want to present himself as a witness for the prosecution. He answers questions indirectly, but implies that his marriage was very turbulent, since they didn't see eye to eye on a lot of things (he hated parties, for instance), and their physical relationship was not happening. He admits that he had regularly raised his hands to his wife in the past.

Cut to his apartment, where he recalls a party. It had been important to Maureen: she thought it was their last chance. The first guest to arrive had been Larry's 83-year-old father, much to his wife's disgust and chagrin. Later Maureen had started to juggle with a combination of fake stage knives and genuine steak knives. She stabs herself in the heart with a fake knife while dancing with Larry. The guests are shocked because they think it's real and that Larry has stabbed her. The police are called. Larry shouts at everyone to go home, after which there's a confrontation between husband and wife. She stabs him in the shoulder with a real knife and then in the stomach with a fake knife. There's a scuffle, and Maureen is wounded, but she's still alive at this point. Later in prison, Larry is visited by his father, a failed comedian, who feels that his son has always criticised his own lack of success.

Larry is taken to the electric chair by a priest, even though he protests that he wants a female rabbi instead. The light flashes, Larry is electrocuted, his body raises up to the sky and scatters into small versions of Larry. We focus on one of these individuals, who claims that he believes in God and feels no guilt. Cut to a hospital, where Larry is visited by two doctors. They ask him whether he remembers the electric chair, his wife Maureen or his sister-in-law DeeDee. Larry insists they're all fictions that he made up.

Another hospital scene, with Larry and DeeDee. Larry asks her who she is and she says she's his wife. She tells him that he vomited his brains out on stage in London, and he's been in hospital for six months since then. He continues to insist it's all a fiction he's written, even though DeeDee reminds him that Maureen is actually his voluptuous sister-in-law. He's very puzzled that DeeDee appears to be his spouse.

The final scene: a big stadium with a spotlight on Larry. He says it was all his idea, a family show he wanted to do, gathering all his relatives together in the cause of personal expression rather than commericalism. He reckons that ideas are there to be criticised, and starts telling jokes about wives. Spotlight in turn on Maureen, DeeDee, his dad (who says the problem is whether we can still see things even when we close our eyes). Lights then on all four of the characters, who look around at each other. Darkness again, spotlight on Larry, who questions whether life is an illusion or disillusion, or a baseball match in which some people get bored while others get excited. Spotlight on Maureen, who starts singing the old standard 'Dancing In The Dark' – she asks if she can find her true soulmate, or whether indeed she's actually with him but hasn't realised he's her ideal. Spotlight back to father, who sings an unaccompanied 'Dancing In The Dark'. Curtain.

(This synopsis translated from a Japanese account by Tomoko Johnston Yabe).

＊ ＊ ＊

Bo Harwood produced the plays. He remembers: 'John called me and said he wanted to do these three plays, he had some money to spend for the first time in his life. I flew down and lived with John and Gena for about six months. First thing we did, we went and checked out theatres. We found this little theatre, a rehearsal room really, down on a little side street in Santa Monica near the male hooker district. We liked the space. We brought in some workers and tore some walls down. My friend James Eric came in and designed the theatre, an amazing L-shaped stage with an alley that split the L, which worked for each of the three different plays (every day we had a different play running), and swivel chairs and tiered seating for 80 to 90 people, and we had hidden speakers everywhere.

"It was a small theatre but three huge productions: three three-act plays. Nobody was getting paid, and we had anything from 20-50 actors around a table in the backroom reading and rewriting the different plays, maybe 200 people working on it all told, and this went on every day for months: John spent a lot more of his money than he had meant to. Then we were about to open, when we heard that a cable TV company wanted to show the plays".

"Cable TV was just starting out, then, and they were desperate for product, and John was approached and offered, as I remember it, $2 million per play to videotape them, $6million in total. Meanwhile we were charging $4.50 a ticket, $2.50 matinees".

"John had a big meeting with everyone, he said 'Look, what am I going to do? Give $100,000 to Peter Falk? $10,000 to Diahnne Abbott? How do we do it? You know what, we're creating something here. The money will change it. We started off with a premise, let's just stick with it.' And he turned them down".

"The plays were a huge success: they were amazing, and we could only run for five weeks because he and Gena were doing *Tempest*, so he knew it would have to close in five weeks. At least two of the plays were invited to New York, but John said 'Look, did we have a good time? Did we create an event here? Let's walk away.' And that's exactly what he did, left this incredible theatre we'd made in the hands of these assholes who owned it. And it was enough to say 'this is beautiful'. John knew money changed things. It sounds idealistic, but I feel blessed, because I got to live it, I got to be there and experience it".

Appendix III

Acting Out – John Cassavetes
As Film Actor

1951
Fourteen Hours (directed by Henry Hathaway) uncredited bit part

1953
Taxi (Gregory Ratoff) uncredited bit part

1955
The Night Holds Terror (Andrew Stone) as Robert Batsford, psychotic ringleader of a criminal gang who improvises a risky kidnapping plan.

'John Cassavetes, always effective in pathological roles, is especially subtle and compelling'. Blake Lucas, *Film Noir*, Alain Silver and Elizabeth Ward eds, Secker and Warburg, London (1980).

1956
Crime In The Streets (Don Siegel) as Frankie Dean, charismatic tenement punk. Mark Rydell and Sal Mineo are his stooges, James Whitmore the social worker who tries to avert disaster.

"A rain-slicked wharf, a foghorn sounds, and the rumble starts. With just a single back-alley set and a five-and-ten cent script, Siegel's early B gang picture can make 'the street' more real than all the stylisations of later efforts like *The Wanderers*. There's a street-corner girl who dances with her mouth, and there's Cassavetes as Frankie, the leader who can't bear to be touched, dripping all the bug-eyed surliness of his grown-up movies and hiding all the dirty little secrets that each family contains. [. . .] If it's a shade heavy on the psychodrama, at least the confrontations have spine". Chris Peachment, *Time Out Film Guide*.

Brian Case: "I'll never forget scenes of you hooked over this high balcony in New York looking down over your patch, and you looked to me like a wolf. Projecting this wolfish intensity".

Cassavetes: "That I could do! Wolfish intensity was in my repertoire! I had these crazy eyebrows which have kind of simmered down as I got older".

Edge Of The City (Martin Ritt) as Axel North (aka Nordman), an army deserter who gets a job as a stevedore on the New York docks under the bad graces of foreman Jack Warden, but is befriended by colleague Sidney Poitier. Ritt's first picture was based on Robert Allan Aurthur's teleplay *A Man Is Ten Feet Tall*, which also co-starred Poitier and Cassavetes.

"Its crazy mixed-up hero (portrayed in the Method manner, but with an almost total lack of Method distinction, by John Cassavetes) blames his mixed-upness on every blessed thing he can lay his hands on. He was persecuted to the point of desertion by his army sergeant. He accidentally killed his brother. (It happens every day.) He was (inevitably) a stranger to his father. And he spends a large proportion of his time as a docker, an innocent abroad, putting through inarticulate phone calls to his equally inarticulate Poor Old Ma". Douglas McVay, *Films and Filming*, December 1964.

In his introduction to the published screenplay to *Faces* Cassavetes writes: "In 1965 [. . .] I looked back at my accomplishments and I could find only two that I considered worthwhile, *Shadows* and *Edge Of The City*. All the rest of my time had been spent playing games – painful and stupid, falsely satisfying and economically rewarding".

Val Avery has a small supporting role as one of the longshoremen.

The Purple Plain (Robert Parrish) a small uncredited role in a British-made WWII movie based on an Eric Ambler story and set in Burma. Gregory Peck stars.

1957

Affair In Havana (Laslo Benedick) as a songwriter in love with a crippled man's wife. Co-starring Raymond Burr, Sara Shane and Celia Cruz. Filmed in Cuba.

Cassavetes: "I don't care what anyone says about me as a director, but it always hurts [as an actor] even if you know you're in a lousy show and you know you're lousy: when somebody says 'Oh I saw the late show, and you were in *Affair In Havana*, oh, you were terrible!'." (AADA seminar)

1958

Saddle The Wind (Robert Parrish) as Tony Sinclair, Robert Taylor's kid brother in an MGM Western. (Cassavetes was third billed behind Taylor and Julie London, but still had his name above the title.) Rod Serling's script is essentially a juvenile delinquent 'problem picture' transposed to the West. Tony is a 'gun-happy loco kid' brought up by his brother from the age of four. Cassavetes plays him with loud precocity, smirking and rebellious, but with a neurotic self-loathing underneath, kissing London with a violence that repels her, and shooting at his own reflection in a muddy pool.

"Tony never got born", Taylor muses. "I think somebody found him wedged into a gun cylinder and shot him out into the world by pulling the trigger".

Virgin Island (Pat Jackson) as Evan, an enterprising young writer who buys an island for the girl he intends to marry (Virginia Maskell). This light, British-made love story was shot in the Virgin Islands. A pseudonymous Ring Lardner Jr contributed to the screenplay. Sidney Poitier co-stars.

1960
Middle Of Nowhere (released in the US as *The Webster Boy* in 1962, Don Chaffey) as Vance Miller. Seymour Cassel has a supporting role, and Ted Allan wrote the script with Leo Marks. See Chapters 3 and 11.

1964
The Killers (Don Siegel) as Johnny North. See Chapter 4.

1967
Devil's Angels (Daniel Haller) as Cody, the aging leader of the biker gang 'Skulls'. 'Inspired casting,' Jim Morton writes in *Lost Highways* (Creation Books, 2000, edited by Jack Sargeant and Stephanie Watson). "The aging gangster [from *Crime In The Streets*] now a pathetic loser with nowhere left to go".

Cassavetes: "Dan Haller is a very sweet guy. He came to me and said 'Look, this thing is really an exploitive movie, but I'd really like to try and accomplish something within that framework'. And so I figured that I'd learn to ride a motorcycle, be with some people out on location and just open up a little more. Within its given area Dan did a very good job with it". (to David Austen, *Films And Filming*, September 1968) See Chapter 5

The Dirty Dozen (Robert Aldrich). As Victor Franco. See Chapter 5

1968
Roma Come Chicago aka *Bandits In Rome*, aka *Murder On Via Veneto* aka *The Violent Four* (Alberto De Martino), top-billed as Corda. Low budget Italian gangster movie from peplum hack De Martino.

Gli Intoccabili aka *Machine Gun McCain* (Giuliano Montaldo) as Hank McCain, a gangster in the Bogart mould.

Cassavetes: "Peter and I played the leads, it was in Rome, and Gena came in and she said 'I'll do the picture if you give me a villa, no salary'. She's so smart! So we had a lovely villa. Peter and I killed ourselves trying to make the picture good for ourselves, Gena just walked in, did her job, did three wonderful scenes, and then the picture came out and all the critics were 'Oh God, if there'd only been more of Gena!'" (Brian Case interview transcript)

Rosemary's Baby (Roman Polanski) As Guy Woodhouse. See Chapter 5 Al Ruban: "John didn't care too much for the way Polanski worked, but when he signed on as an actor he was 100% actor, he didn't try to direct, he lived up to his contract. You know Polanski likes to play the parts for everybody; he gives line-readings. For some actors, particularly like John, you can talk to them, but don't play it out for them. They had a falling out, and I don't believe there are any close-ups of John in that picture".

1969
If It's Tuesday, This Must Be Belgium (Mel Stuart) cameo role as a card player, along with Ben Gazzara.

1970
Husbands as Gus

1971
Minnie And Moskowitz uncredited, as Jim

1975
Capone (Steve Carver) a supporting role as Frankie Yale to Gazzara's Capone. (Sylvester Stallone, Dick Miller and Royal Dano have small roles and Roger Corman produced.)

1976
Mikey And Nicky (Elaine May) as Nicky, a fringe gangster convinced he's been marked for assassination. He calls his best and oldest friend, Nicky (Peter Falk) and they deviate around the city all night, one step ahead of a professional killer (Ned Beatty). Filmed in 1973, this bleak, very Cassavetian study in male fear, friendship, rivalry and betrayal wasn't released in the US for three years (and took ten years to reach Europe). See Chapter 8.

Ned Beatty: "It was intended as a black comedy: lower middle class hoods who can't do anything right. Elaine May insisted on shooting everything at night, even the interiors. When you're working at 4am, that does something to your head. She edited it at night too! It was a long shoot, and John directed a lot of the second unit stuff. Two or three weeks after we wrapped, Elaine was holed up in a hotel in Hollywood with the rushes – I don't think she can have watched any during the shoot because she shot and printed so much of it! – I had reason to go over there and she didn't recognise me. Blank for minutes! Then it clicked, and she said 'Ned, great news! Great news! I've watched all your footage and none of it is funny!'" (Author's interview)

Peter Falk: "If you get a fresh thought while you're acting then you're acting well. When we're on the bus I'm taking him to his death. Elaine said to me concentrate on one thing about John, and I thought about his pores. He had high cheekbones, when he laughed it was a devilish thing. And I thought you could see the skeleton there. Then I thought I'm no longer on the bus, I'm in a hearse". (Falk to James Lipton, 'In the Actors Studio', Bravo TV)

1976
Two Minute Warning (Larry Peerce) as SWAT leader Buttons, second billed to Charlton Heston. Gena Rowlands has a supporting role in this cynical thriller about a gunman who threatens to shoot into the crowd at a football stadium. "The paranoid, edgy movie (best represented by Cassavetes' SWAT sergeant) finally erupts when the crowd turns and devours itself in a climax of panic". – Chris Peachment, *Time Out Film Guide*.

1977
Heroes (Jeremy Kagan) uncredited cameo.

Opening Night as Maurice Adams

1978
The Fury (Brian de Palma) as Childress, an evil government agent experimenting with psychic teens for military purposes. He even carries a paralysed arm in a black sling. In the film's spectacular climax, Childress is telepathically levitated by a wrathful Amy Irving and explodes like a Catherine Wheel – a sequence shot in ghoulish slow motion from multiple camera angles. "In so far as the film lives at all, it's in its shock effects, which are adaquately cruel if too thin on the ground – although the heartwarming sight of Cassavetes getting his just desserts compensates for a lot". – Tony Rayns, *Time Out Film Guide*.

Brass Target (John Hough) as Major Joe De Luca. See Chapter 10

1981
Incubus (John Hough) as Dr Sam Cordell, investigating a series of attacks on women in a small town in Canada in this explicit, badly reviewed horror movie.

John Hough: "John didn't want to do the first screenplay at all, so he locked himself up in a hotel room and rewrote the entire screenplay. He didn't come out of his room for four or five days. Didn't even open the door, except to me. From dawn to dusk, all through the night. I remember the producer coming up to ask what John thought he was doing, and John told him 'You think I've locked myself up for five days for no reason? I did it because this is how I want the picture to go!' They had major stand-up rows. I backed up John, of course. The producer wasn't happy, he wanted what he'd already paid for. I would say apart from the stuff that was shot afterwards, it was 80 percent John's screenplay. So it was a big disappointment to us when the film wasn't a success, because while we were making it we thought we were doing something really interesting and exciting. The special effects were put in afterwards and it didn't turn out how I visualised it. But we could only blame ourselves when it failed. Because John rewrote the screenplay and I backed him up. I thought he did a hell of a job. We both believed in it".

It's a film about sex?

"No, it's about possession. Someone who is possessed by the incubus spirit. There are sexual connotations and innuendos in it, but you never saw any rapes in what we made".

1981

Whose Life Is It Anyway? (John Badham) as Dr Michael Emerson, tending to Richard Dreyfuss as a paralysed man who wants to die.

"The movie is so bland that every time Cassavetes makes an entrance (which he knows how to do), you wake up. He carries the kind of authority that makes you want him as your doctor. when he gets tense, he smiles very faintly. And he takes everything very personally; pointing to a dead patient: 'This makes me sick. It ought to make you sick. Look there. There's the enemy. The enemy has won'. Trust him, he's a doctor". (Gavin Smith, 'Actor's Fury', *Film Comment*, May/June 1989)

1982

Tempest (Paul Mazursky) as Phillip Demetrius, a modern day Prospero, in Mazursky's update of Shakespeare's 'The Tempest'. His marriage falling apart, he flees to a Greek island with his daughter, Miranda (Molly Ringwald) and his lover (Susan Sarandon). Finally he calls down a mighty storm: proof of his magical powers, or a symbol for a nervous breakdown? An old friend of the Cassavetes, Mazursky cast Gena Rowlands as Phillip's estranged wife, Antonia. He also tried to cast Elia Kazan as Phillip's father – an inspired notion which sadly didn't come to pass. Paul Stewart from *A Child is Waiting* and *Opening Night* played the role.

In his autobiography *Show Me The Magic*, Mazursky writes that Cassavetes was a genius at "making situations in the script real for himself by carrying the situations over to 'real life'." He talks about an incident late in the film, in which Phillip is supposed to sacrifice a goat in front of Antonia: 'Gena came to me and said she would not appear in the goat sacrifice scene. She explained that John had told her he was going to sacrifice a real, live goat. "He's disgusting," she said.

"I confronted John in front of Gena. He looked at me and smiled his most devilish smile. 'Oh no. I'm going to slice that goat's neck'. And he showed us how he'd do it".

"For two weeks this charade went on. Finally, I began to believe that John might actually think he would kill the goat". The night before the scene was to be shot, Mazursky invited John and Gena to dinner, both to calm her fears, and his own: "I told them I was worried sick about tomorrow's work. 'Please, John. Tell Gena you're kidding'."

He laughed. "I'm not kidding. I'm going to kill that little squiggly, eensie weesie, baaing goat." Gena excused herself and went to the ladies room.' She didn't come back. Eventually John called the hotel and spoke to her, and for the umpteenth time assured her he really meant to carry out the sacrifice.

"The next morning I got to the set at Cinecitta early and tried to decide what to do . . . when I saw John and Gena, arms around each other's waists, strolling ever so happily to the set. They smiled at me as if nothing had ever been the matter. Not a word was said about last night's aborted dinner. He had put her on long enough to scare her (and me) but now it was time for these professionals to go to work".

"Not only did John never admit to his game, but neither did Gena. It was as if it had never happened. Gena was perfect in the scene. So was John. He had shown me something about digging for the truth in acting, about not settling for some comfortable semblance. I don't think John was just playing a game. I think he wanted to carry out the brutality of what he was about to do as 'Phillip'; I think he wanted to go past that comfortable zone that actors can get into. Gena knew what John was doing, but she too wanted to take the situation into a more dangerous place so that the work would be richer, subtler, more real, less expected". (Simon and Schuster, NY, 1999)

1983

Marvin And Tige (Eric Weston) as Marvin Stewart. Marvin has fallen on hard times, but he intercedes to stop 11-year-old back street kid Gibran Brown from killing himself and takes him under his wing. "Good performances from Cassavetes and Brown are undermined by poor development. It may give you a cry, but not one that is earned". *Variety*, December 14, 1983.

1984

Love Streams as Robert Harmon.

Gavin Smith: "At his most moving, Cassavetes was never funnier. The spectacle of his hard-boiled cynicism being worn down by sister Gena Rowlands' emotional guerilla warfare is one to relish. To wit: after Gena hangs up on her estranged husband and daughter, she shuts herself in the bathroom:

Cassavetes: 'You alright?'

Rowlands: 'I'm washing my face'.

Cassavetes: 'Oh, well, love is dead, love is a fantasy little girls have'.

It's the oh-so-casual way he says it.

Cassavetes always knew how to make bad dialogue sound good and good dialogue sound great – like it was the most natural thing in the world to say. He knew that words don't matter – it's their spin. And there was always something spinning inside him". (*Film Comment*, May-June 1989)

Cassavetes can be glimpsed by sharp-eyed viewers in both *Shadows* and *A Child Is Waiting*.

Television

Cassavetes made hundreds of TV appearances throughout his career, most famously as *Johnny Staccato* in the series of that name. Some of his notable live TV roles in the Fifties are discussed in Chapter 2. In the Sixties and Seventies, he made numerous guest appearances in such shows as *Rawhide*, *Alfred Hitchcock Presents*, *Burke's Law*, and *The Virginian*. In 1972 he appeared in a lead role opposite Peter Falk in an episode of *Columbo*, 'Étude In Black'.

In 1979 he was in the TV movie *Flesh And Blood*, directed by Jud Taylor.

Cassavetes also directed five episodes of *Johnny Staccato*. These were:

'Murder For Credit', broadcast September 17, 1959, co-starring Charles McGraw, Martin Landau and Jimmy Joyce.

'Evil', October 29, 1959, written by Richard Carr.

'Solomon', December 3, 1959, co-starring Cloris Leachman and Elisha Cook.

'Piece Of Paradise', December 10, 1959.

'Night Of Jeapardy', January 21, 1960, co-starring Jimmy Joyce and Mario Gallo; written by Richard Carr and Everett Chambers.

In 1962 he directed two 30 minute dramas:

A Pair Of Boots, starring Lloyd Bridges and Beau Bridges, Seymour Cassel, Royal Dano, Gene Darfler, John Marley, Maurice McEndree and Lawrence Tierney; scripted by Mort R Lewis and coproduced by Aaron Spelling and Everett Chambers.

    My Daddy Can Lick Your Daddy, starring Lloyd Bridges, Fred Draper, Lelia Goldoni and Gary Lockwood; scripted by Robert Towne and produced by Aaron Spelling.

In addition, he is credited as director of a feature-length episode of the short-lived CBS TV series *Shaft* (1973), a spin-off from the blaxploitation movie hit with Richard Roundtree reprising his role as a New York private detective, now working in tandem with the cops. As far as can be determined Cassavetes took on this job in the summer of 1972 as a personal favour and in order to raise money for *A Woman Under The Influence*. The series only ran for seven episodes.

Appendix IV

Supporting Characters

Ted Allan
Writer: scripted *Middle Of Nowhere* and collaborated on *Love Streams* with Cassavetes, based on his play.
Other notable credits: *Lies My Father Told Me*.

Val Avery
Actor: Faces; Minnie And Moskowitz; The Killing Of A Chinese Bookie; Gloria.
Other credits: *Edge Of The City* (bit); *King Creole; Hud; The Laughing Policeman; Heroes; The Wanderers*.

Joan Blondell
Actress: *Opening Night*.
Other credits: *Public Enemy; Golddiggers Of 1933; Footlight Parade; Dames; Stage Struck; Stand-In; A Tree Grows In Brooklyn; Nightmare Alley; Will Success Spoil Rock Hunter; The Cincinatti Kid; Grease*.

Peter Bogdanovich
Director. Bogdanovich knew Cassavetes from the late Sixties to his death; he has a cameo in *Opening Night*; shot a second unit scene in *Opening Night* and in *Love Streams*.
Other credits: *Targets; The Last Picture Show; What's Up Doc?; Saint Jack, They All Laughed; Mask*.

Helen Caldwell
Cassavetes' script secretary 1981-1988, also personal assistant *Big Trouble*.
Script Supervisor: *Love Streams*.
Screenwriter: *Unhook The Stars* (co-written with Nick Cassavetes).

Lynn Carlin
Actress: *Faces*.
Other credits: *Taking Off; Wild Rovers; Battle Beyond The Stars*.

241

Ben Carruthers
Actor: *Shadows.*
Other credits: *The Dirty Dozen.*

Nick Cassavetes
John's son and eldest child appears alonside sister Xan at the end of *Husbands*, and alongside Xan and little sister Zoe at the end of *Minnie And Moskowitz*. A promising basketball player, he turned to acting after a knee injury forced him out of the sport, attended the American Academy of Dramatic Arts, and has since made a name for himself as a writer and director. He directed his mother in *Unhook The Stars* (1996), and then Sean Penn in his father's script *She's So Lovely* (1997).
Other credits: *Face/Off* (actor).

Seymour Cassel
Actor: *Shadows* (cameo); *Too Late Blues*; *Faces*; *Minnie And Moskowitz*; *The Killing Of A Chinese Bookie*; *Love Streams.*
Helped on the crew of *Shadows* and worked with the children in *A Child Is Waiting*. His wife Elizabeth Deering appears in *Minnie And Moskowitz* and *A Woman Under The Influence*. Their son Matthew also appears in *A Woman Under The Influence*.
Other credits: *The Killers* (cameo); *The Last Tycoon*; *Convoy*; *Tin Men*; *Dick Tracy*; *In The Soup*; *Indecent Proposal*; *Rushmore*; *The Crew*; *Animal Factory.*

Fred Draper
A friend from the American Academy of Dramatic Arts, Draper appeared in *A Child Is Waiting, Faces* (as Freddie), *Husbands* (cameo) and *A Woman Under The Influence* (as Mabel's father). Latterly he taught acting. He died in 1999.

Frederick Elmes
Cameraman: part of Caleb Deschanel's original camera crew on *A Woman Under The Influence*, he returned for *The Killing Of A Chinese Bookie* and *Opening Night*.
Other credits: *Eraserhead*; *Blue Velvet*; *Rivers' Edge*; *Wild At Heart*; *Night On Earth.*

Peter Falk
Twice nominated for best supporting actor before he met Cassavetes, Falk became friendly with him in the late Sixties when they discussed Elaine May's *Mikey And Nicky*. Subsequently they co-starred in *Machine Gun*

McCain (1968), prior to *Husbands, A Woman Under The Influence* (which he co-financed) and *Big Trouble*. Falk also starred in the play *Knives* (one of the *Three Plays Of Love And Hate*).

Other credits: *Wind Across The Everglades; Murder Inc; Pocketful Of Miracles; The Great Race; The In-Laws; All The Marbles* (aka *California Dolls*); *Happy New Year; Wings Of Desire; Tune In Tomorrow; Columbo* (TV)

Mike Ferris

Cameraman: *A Woman Under The Influence; The Killing Of A Chinese Bookie; Opening Night; She's So Lovely*.

Other credits: *The Other Side Of The Wind* (Welles); *Scarface* (De Palma); *Colors; Die Hard; The Game* and over 200 others.

Ben Gazzara

Actor: *Husbands; The Killing Of A Chinese Bookie; Opening Night*. He co-starred with Gena Rowlands on stage and in the TV movie *An Early Frost*.

Other credits: *The Strange One; Anatomy Of A Murder; Capone; Saint Jack; They All Laughed; Tales Of Ordinary Madness; Buffalo 66; The Big Lebowski, Happiness*. In 1990 he wrote and directed *Beyond The Ocean*.

Lelia Goldoni

Actress: *Shadows*.

Other credits: *The Italian Job; Alice Doesn't Live Here Anymore; The Day Of The Locust; Invasion Of The Bodysnatchers* (Kaufman)

Bo Harwood

Music: *Minnie And Moskowitz, A Woman Under The Influence, The Killing Of A Chinese Bookie, Opening Night, Love Streams*.

Also produced *Three Plays of Love And Hate* and did the music for *A Woman of Mystery*.

Other credits: (sound) *My Bloody Valentine; Kings And Desperate Men* (audio consultant); *My So-Called Life* (TV).

John Hough

Director: *Brass Target, Incubus*.

Other credits: *Dirty Mary, Crazy Larry; Escape To Witch Mountain; The Watcher In The Woods*.

Hugh Hurd

Actor: *Shadows, A Woman Under The Influence, Gloria* (cameo as a cab driver).

Elaine Kagan (née Goren)
Secretary to Cassavetes 1969-1974; script supervisor *A Woman Under The Influence*.
Other credits: Kagan has acted in *ER* and *Chicago Hope*. She appears as the young Henry Hill's mom in *Goodfellas*. She is also a novelist: *Somebody's Baby; Blue Heaven; The Girls; No Goodbyes*.

Jeremy Paul Kagan
Married Elaine Goren. An AFI graduate in direction, he got to know Cassavetes during *A Woman Under The Influence*, and visited the sets of *Killing Of A Chinese Bookie* and *Big Trouble*.
Other credits: *Katherine* (TV); *The Big Fix; Heroes; The Chosen; The Journey of Natty Gann*.

Stanley Kramer
Producer: *A Child Is Waiting*.
Other credits: *The Men* (p); *Death of a Salesman* (p); *High Noon* (p); *The Defiant Ones* (p&d); *On The Beach* (p&d); *Inherit The Wind* (p&d); *Judgement At Nuremburg* (p&d); *It's A Mad, Mad, Mad, Mad World* (p&d); *Guess Who's Coming To Dinner* (p&d).

Zohra Lampert
Actress: *Opening Night*.
Other credits: *Splendor In The Grass; A Fine Madness; Teachers*.

John Marley
Actor: *A Child Is Waiting; Faces*.
Other credits: *America America; Cat Ballou; Love Story; The Godfather*.

Harry Mastrogeorge
A friend from the American Academy of Dramatic Arts, where he served on the staff for many years, prior to teaching in LA and directing plays, TV and features.

Paul Mazursky
A contemporary from the New York acting scene in the Fifties (*Fear And Desire; Blackboard Jungle*), Mazursky directed Cassavetes in *Tempest*.
Other credits: *Bob & Carol & Ted & Alice; Harry And Tonto; An Unmarried Woman; Down And Out In Beverly Hills; Enemies, A Love Story*.

Jonas Mekas
Avant-garde film critic and film-maker. Praised the first version of *Shadows* in his magazine *Film Culture*, then disparaged the second version as a sellout. Director of super-8 'diary' films.

Other credits: (as director) *The Secret Passions Of Salvador Dali; Guns Of The Trees; As I Was Moving Forward Occasionally I Saw Brief Glimpses Of Beauty.*

Gena Rowlands
Starred in her husband John Cassavetes' *A Child Is Waiting, Faces, Minnie And Moskowitz, A Woman Under The Influence, Opening Night, Gloria* and *Love Streams.*
Other credits: *The High Cost Of Loving; Lonely Are The Brave; Tony Rome; Two Minute Warning; The Brink's Job; Light Of Day; Another Woman; Once Around; Night On Earth; Crazy In Love; The Neon Bible; Something To Talk About; Paulie.*

Al Ruban
Ruban worked on the crew of *Shadows*, was cinematographer and editor on *Faces*, produced *Husbands, Minnie And Moskowitz, The Killing Of A Chinese Bookie* (also camera); *Opening Night* (also camera) and *Love Streams* (also camera).
Ruban appears as an actor in *Chinese Bookie* and *Love Streams* (Sarah's lawyer).
Other credits: *Texasville* (co-producer); *Happy New Year* (exec p); *The Beautiful, The Bloody And The Bare* (p); *The Sexploiters* (dir); *Coogan's Bluff* (actor); *Madigan* (actor); *The Big Fix* (actor); *Swamp Thing* (actor); *Mr North* (actor).

Jenny Runacre
Actress: *Husbands.*
Other credits: *Goodbye Mr Chips; The Mackintosh Man; Passenger; Joseph Andrews; The Duellists; Jubilee; The Witches; Restoration.*

Sam Shaw
Producer: *Husbands, A Woman Under The Influence, Gloria.*
Executive producer: *Opening Night.*
Production design: *The Killing Of A Chinese Bookie.*
Shaw was a professional photographer who became a mentor to Cassavetes in the mid-Fifties. He photographed Cassavetes at home and at work throughout his life. Shaw died in 1999.
His son Larry also took photographs on some of the films; his brother Eddie apears as Dr Zepp in *A Woman Under The Influence*; and grandson Jakob appears as the boy in *Love Streams.*

Paul Stewart
Actor: *A Child Is Waiting; Opening Night.*
Other credits: *Citizen Kane; Champion; The Window; The Bad And The Beautiful; The Cobweb; King Creole; In Cold Blood; The Day Of The Locust.*

Peter Tanner
Editor: *Husbands* and (early on) *A Woman Under The Influence.*
Other credits: *Kind Hearts And Coronets; The Cruel Sea; The Blue Lamp; The House That Dripped Blood; Hamburger Hill.*

INDEX